PRAISE FOR *UNION HEARTLAND*

"From the conditions of Civil War prisons in the Midwest, to the Midwest's critical agricultural role to keep the soldiers and the Union fed, to the trials and travails of midwestern Union soldiers' wives, *Union Heartland* is fascinating, heavily researched, and thoughtfully presented."   —James A. Cox, *Midwest Book Review*

"This compilation is recommended both as an example of the value of regional studies in their own right and how they can enhance our understanding of the Civil War, the central event in American history, by providing new contexts and perspectives."
                            —James E. Potter, *Nebraska History*

"Undoubtedly, the Midwest deserves attention for its contributions during the [Civil War], which included crops, soldiers, supplies, and political upheaval. By treating the Midwest as its own entity as opposed to studying the North and Midwest as one monolithic region, these essays provide new insight into the wartime experiences of midwesterners."   —Megan Birk, *Kansas History*

"*Union Heartland* deserves our attention, not only for the many lessons it teaches on its particular subjects but even more so for its demonstration that all the North was not New England or the mid-Atlantic, as so much literature has it. It is time to find the war where it was lived day-to-day in specific places. This book points the way."
          —Randall M. Miller, *Register of the Kentucky Historical Society*

"[Aley and Anderson] have advanced our understanding of the significant role the Old Northwest (what became known as the Midwest) played in the Civil War. Their introduction is a model of scholarship, reviewing the historiography and providing guideposts for the essays included in this collection."
—Kenneth J. Heineman, *Journal of the Illinois State Historical Society*

"These well-written essays appropriately emphasize regional features of this sectional period and deepen understanding of the midwestern home front during the Civil War. A step forward in explaining the distinctiveness of the midwestern experience, this welcome and valuable collection augurs further scholarship that will enhance thinking about and knowledge of the historical Midwest."
—Kenneth H. Wheeler, *Journal of American History*

"This collection will be of interest to scholars of the Civil War, as well as to those interested in the Northern home front or nineteenth-century rural history. The authors have demonstrated the vitality of this region and its variety of experiences."
—Jeff Bremer, *Civil War Book Review*

"Aley and Anderson present a compelling collection of essays that introduces the Midwest as the 'heartland' of the Union and further expands the historiographic discussion of the Northern home front during the war. *Union Heartland*'s emphasis on place signifies a shift in the way historians examine the Civil War, and more attention should be paid to the rich history of this region in the future."
—Lindsey Peterson, *Humanities and Social Science Online*

"[*Union Heartland*] provides nuanced views of life on the midwestern home front and offers new frameworks for scholars to examine the Northern people and their wartime experiences."
—John Michael Foster Jr., *The Historian*

Union Heartland

Union Heartland

THE MIDWESTERN HOME FRONT DURING THE CIVIL WAR

Edited by Ginette Aley and J. L. Anderson
With a Foreword by William C. Davis

Southern Illinois University Press
Carbondale

Southern Illinois University Press
www.siupress.com

26 25 24 23   4 3 2 1

Cover illustration: Foreground, detail from an advertisement
showing a woman operating a hay rake because her "brother
has gone to the war," Prairie Farmer, 10 June 1865. Background, farm in Indiana, circa 1860s, from the Robert N.
Dennis Collection of Stereoscopic Views, Miriam and Ira D.
Wallach Division of Art, Prints, and Photographs, The New
York Public Library, Astor, Lenox, and Tilden Foundations.

Frontispiece: Farm in Indiana, circa 1860s, from the Robert
N. Dennis Collection of Stereoscopic Views, Miriam and
Ira D. Wallach Division of Art, Prints, and Photographs,
The New York Public Library, Astor, Lenox, and Tilden
Foundations.

The Library of Congress has catalogued the 2013 hardcover
and e-book editions as follows:
ISBN 978-0-8093-3264-9 (cloth)
ISBN 978-0-8093-3265-6 (ebook)

Library of Congress Cataloging-in-Publication Data
Names: Aley, Ginette, 1963- author, editor of compilation.
   | Anderson, J. L. (Joseph Leslie), 1966- editor. | Davis,
   William C., 1946- writer of foreword.
Title: Union heartland : the midwestern home front during
   the Civil War / edited by Ginette Aley and J. L. Anderson
   ; with a foreword by William C. Davis.
Identifiers: LCCN 2022041932 |
ISBN 9780809338993 (paperback)
Subjects: LCSH: Middle West—History—Civil War,
   1861-1865—Social aspects. | United States—History—
   Civil War, 1861-1865—Social aspects.
Classification: LCC E470.8 .U55 2023 |
DDC 973.7/1—dc23/eng/20220923
LC record available at https://lccn.loc.gov/2022041932

Printed on recycled paper ♻

SIU
Southern Illinois University System

For our parents,
Evelyn L. Anderson and Ronald D. Anderson,
and the memory of Robert B. Turner and Micheline Corbeil Turner

CONTENTS

———

Gallery of illustrations follows page 96

CIVIL WAR HISTORY PLOWS A NEW FIELD

———:———

William C. Davis

There was a time when "American Civil War history" meant in the minds of all but academics nothing except campaigns and battles, generals and regiments. Much has happened in the past half century to change that perception. Historians, and later the popular writers working in the field, turned their eyes backward from the battle line and began to look more and more at the host of issues that sent those armies to the field and the dynamics of the home fronts that sustained the armies and were impacted by them. Even the generals and the soldiers and the battles are looked at increasingly through a different lens, as what some call the "new military history" approaches the subject from a professional standpoint often lacking in the old days.

Most gratifying, however, has been the advance in study and understanding of the home front in all its aspects, from the daily lives of women to the politics of support and opposition that occupied the rival governments. More than ever before, scholars today have a grasp on how women helped to keep Northern and Southern agriculture functioning, feeding their sons and husbands who were away in the armies. The role of wives and sweethearts in sustaining the morale of their men at the front has finally come into the light as well. Black Americans, North and South, have stood at the top of home-front studies for generations, yet still there is much more being done and yet to be done. Meanwhile, real work on subjects like war's effects upon communities and families, education at home, loyalty and disloyalty, industry and agriculture is starting to burgeon.

And regional studies are taking shape at last. Naturally, the South as the Confederacy has been a dominant topic virtually since the war was over and even before if one looks at what was being published in the Confederacy during the conflict. Northern studies, perhaps because they lack the romance of the "lost cause" mythology, have been slower to appear and still are not adequately represented in the literature. State studies abound, mostly concerned with two concurrent stories—the political and social events at home and the activities of the local boys in the field. Other topical slices have been taken from the pie in recent years, such as ethnic and religious studies on American Indians in the war or the Irish, the Germans, the Methodists, Jews, Freemasons, and more. The dish, it seems, offers endless varieties of approach to the diner.

Yet, some regions have received rather little attention, most logically because they were far afield from the war fronts. The Far West yet remains to be thoroughly explored as a topic for Civil War study and not surprisingly. After all, no engagements of any size greater than a skirmish by Eastern standards occurred in California or the Northwest, and even most of those involved only small detachments of Union soldiers policing native populations. For the Southwest, the story is barely better told, though at least there were one minor Confederate campaign and a handful of actual engagements. Many of those involved Hispanic soldiers on both sides, and it may well be that through growing Hispanic studies, the full story of the war in that region will finally emerge. One book on Utah and the Mormon experience in the war has appeared, but, otherwise, Rocky Mountain Civil War history remains largely an unplowed field.

Then there is the Midwest. Here the dynamics are different. Hundreds of thousands of soldiers from the Midwest participated in the war all the way from Kansas to Virginia. So the war can definitely be told at least from the perspective of the region's contributions to the fronts. No major battles were fought in the Midwest, but Indiana and Ohio saw Confederate raiders, and every midwestern state hosted prison camps for Confederates prisoners of war. One of the boldest—and most exaggerated and impractical—of all Confederate plots centered on northern Illinois, and Confederate partisans even planned actions on Lake Erie.

The Civil War was a midwestern war, too, and at last that region's part in the drama is being explored, not least in the intriguing and suggestive chapters in the present volume. In examining women's roles, the nature of families and the war's impact on them, and the stresses between wives and the parents of husbands away in the war, the distaff side of the midwestern experience is explored in innovative ways. If the Midwest is known internationally for one thing, it is the crops that spring from its soil, yet the fundamental importance of agriculture is only now starting to attract in-depth study based on the latest scholarship. Similarly, education, including higher education, has been an afterthought in studies, but here midwestern university students and their responses to the war are detailed.

The ever-present problem of what constitutes disloyalty in wartime was especially trenchant in 1861–65, and for the North, the hotbed of disloyalty was in the Midwest, where opposition to the war and the Republican regime led to something approaching treasonous scheming. Certainly, it produced epic court rulings like *ex parte Milligan*. Here, the Republican response to opposition in one leading state illustrates the challenges faced by a democracy in civil war. And an often-connected issue was the thousands of Confederate prisoners held in or near midwestern cities, the danger they posed to the locality, and the target they offered for Confederate overt and clandestine attempts to free the inmates. The treatment those prisoners received at local hands also posed a dilemma for midwesterners, as they had to balance their patriotic dislike for their enemies with the fact that those enemies were fellow Americans and often personal relations.

Much more remains to be done, of course, and it will be done, much of it by the authors contributing to the present volume. If the story of the Midwest in the Civil War is not wholly new, still it is coming into a new era, largely thanks to these contributors. *Union Heartland: The Midwestern Home Front during the Civil War* is not an end but a beginning and a fine one at that. Like the waving grain of the prairies, midwestern studies promises no end of sustenance for minds hungry for more understanding of America's greatest trial.

ACKNOWLEDGMENTS

We, the editors, are grateful to the many people who made this book possible. In particular, Sylvia Frank Rodrigue, our editor at Southern Illinois University Press, has provided excellent guidance, congeniality, and a much-welcomed nurturing and collaborative spirit. William C. ("Jack") Davis suggested that SIUP would be a good home for this project and he was more than correct. J. Matthew Gallman and an anonymous reader for the press made numerous valuable suggestions. We appreciate their efforts. Mount Royal University provided a subvention to defray some production costs of this book. Dr. Robin Fisher of Mount Royal facilitated the grant. We are grateful to him and Mount Royal University for their support. Marvin Bergman, editor of the *Annals of Iowa*, consented to republish the essay titled "The Vacant Chair on the Farm: Soldier Husbands, Farm Wives and the Iowa Home Front" from volume 66, numbers 3 & 4, Summer/Fall, 2007 issue. The following librarians and archivists were instrumental in assisting us in obtaining the remarkable range of images for this volume: Mary Bennett and Becki Plunkett of the State Historical Society of Iowa (Iowa City and Des Moines, respectively), Mary Stuart and Kirk Hess (Farm, Field, and Fireside Agricultural Newspaper Collection) of the University of Illinois Library, Karen Jania of the Bentley Historical Library, and Ron Davidson of the Sandusky Library. Nikki Taylor, who authored an essay on the important African-American perspective for this collection, unfortunately had to withdraw, but we thank her for her efforts. Joe extends his thanks to his parents for their support over the years, but especially for encouraging a childhood interest in history. Ginette would like to extend a special thank you to her son Jonathan whose engagement with the project included coming up with a prospective title that remained in our top three until the final one was selected. More than anything, we feel privileged to have worked with the finest group of contributors; we are grateful for their shared interest in the subject. Their level of commitment and professionalism is demonstrated by the high quality of their essays.

Union Heartland

THE GREAT NATIONAL STRUGGLE
IN THE HEART OF THE UNION

AN INTRODUCTION

Ginette Aley and J. L. Anderson

In the momentous spring of 1861, Galena, Illinois, was "throbbing with patriotism," according to Julia Dent Grant, wife of future U.S. General Ulysses S. Grant. The rhetoric of secession and war followed by the attack on Fort Sumter sparked a fury of activity across the heartland that was typified by events in Galena. Almost instantly, the daily transacting of business ceased. Julia later recalled that men held meetings, called for volunteers, and began to muster and drill while boys imitated the men and played at soldiering. Women young and old also held meetings and determined to act upon their patriotism and support the "great national struggle" at hand. For Julia and other Galena women, this entailed a range of activities, including hulling strawberries for jam and whatnot as well as participating in sewing and knitting meetings that were formed to produce clothing for their soldiers. The women obtained a description of the U.S. infantry uniform, subscribed funds and purchased the material, hired tailors to cut out the garment pieces, and then sewed the uniforms themselves in their own parlors. Within days, the enlistees were outfitted and ready to depart. Hasty preparations were also made to ensure that the loss of many men from households and communities could be to some degree absorbed by women and noncombatants at home—at least for a time.[1]

The engagement of the midwestern home front in war-related activities and support, while immediate and ubiquitous, did not simply appear out of nowhere. Indeed, much of the intensifying political and ideological turmoil of the 1850s had played out within the region and fired its people with a powerful sense of being actors in this important drama. Consider the circumstances and consequences of the following: the 1850 federal Fugitive Slave Law and subsequent highly visible efforts to recapture former bondsmen and women who had escaped, many even settling north of the Ohio River; the so-called underground railroad stations and supporters throughout the region, despite persistent anti–African American sentiment; publication of Ohioan Harriet Beecher Stowe's widely influential and best-selling *Uncle Tom's Cabin*; the controversial Kansas-Nebraska Act of 1854, which fairly quickly caused the Kansas territory to degenerate into the aptly named Bleeding Kansas because of rampant fighting, involving free-state midwesterners, over the slavery issue; the zealous, murderous abolitionist John Brown, who gained notoriety and hero status attacking proslavery advocates in Kansas but was known in Ohio and Iowa; and the emergence of the Republican Party and Illinoisan Abraham Lincoln.[2]

Neither the issues nor the personalities of the impending national crisis were abstract or remote to midwesterners. They experienced these events and lived their passions. Ulysses S. Grant encountered this when as a clerk in his father's Galena leather-goods store, he visited customers in southwest Wisconsin, southeast Minnesota, and northeast Iowa during late 1860 and early 1861: "[W]herever I stopped at night, some of the people would come to the public-house where I was, and sit till a late hour discussing the probabilities of the future." Although "trying" in the implications of war (especially for those like him who had served previously in other military campaigns), Grant identified the period as one of "great excitement" among the citizenry of what was then referred to as the Northwestern United States, a forerunner to the early-twentieth-century regional labels Middle West and Midwest.[3]

Yet, this great excitement among midwesterners that Grant observed is often lost or muted within a larger, relatively undifferentiated master narrative historians have constructed about the Northern or Union perspective. Was there really only one relatively cohesive North, any more than there was one cohesive South? Everything we have learned about the American Civil War thus far tells us otherwise. The starting point for this study, then, is the premise that multiple Norths existed that were marked by regional differences and distinctiveness on several levels, and each, like the Midwest, asserted its own counternarrative of the larger Northern narrative of the Civil War. The contributors to the current volume aspire to not only offer fresh considerations and insight of the era but also contribute toward the construction of a usable regional past that remains neglected.[4]

Historically, the Midwest comprised a mixed population of northerners and southerners in a way that people from the states of the northeast and south could not claim. This is particularly apparent in some of the early-nineteenth-century drives for statehood in the Old Northwest in the very public clash of interests between proslavery and antislavery forces—despite the Northwest Ordinance's Article VI prohibition of slavery. These distinctions and influences continued to matter in an emerging regional identity. Exemplifying this, northeast Ohio was dominated by Yankees, but the southern sections comprised in large measure Virginians and their descendants. In 1850, southerners outnumbered northerners in Illinois and Indiana. In Iowa, southerners made up almost 17 percent of the population in 1850, although that percentage declined to approximately 5 percent by 1860. Settlers in the Midwest were from every state in the Union, and many of them had previously resided in at least one other midwestern state. The regional Midwest of the Civil War era includes Indiana, Illinois, Iowa, Michigan, Ohio, Minnesota, Wisconsin, and, perhaps prematurely, Kansas.[5]

Another important regional distinction was its pronounced rural environment. While a majority of the North was rural, this was especially true of the Midwest. New England and the Mid-Atlantic states shared a comparable rural-urban ratio in 1860, with the former 63 percent rural and the latter 65 percent. The Midwest, by contrast, was 88 percent rural. Indeed, it was agriculture and agricultural production that most profoundly shaped the Midwest and its regional identity. The cash grain-and-livestock frontier expanded into the Old Northwest just as the cotton frontier expanded into the southwestern states. The superintendent of the U.S. Census wrote in 1864, "There is, perhaps, no one fact which gives a clearer idea of the great growth of the west . . . than the amount of grain which is shipped each year from Chicago." Chicago was, he observed, "the greatest grain market in the world." The geographically large states of the Old Northwest along with the "new" northwestern states of Iowa and Minnesota became significant producers of farm products, erasing the leading status of New York and Pennsylvania in wheat production and eroding the lead of several older states in other categories. Six of the top-ten wheat states in 1860 were in the Midwest. Illinois led the way with 23.8 million bushels, followed by Indiana at 16.8, Wisconsin at 15.6, and Ohio at 15.1. Virginia, Pennsylvania, and New York occupied the fifth, sixth, and seventh positions, while Iowa followed with 8.4 million bushels and Michigan at 8.3. Kentucky rounded out the top ten.[6]

One of the more remarkable aspects of this growth is the rapid emergence of Iowa and Wisconsin, both newcomers, admitted to the Union in 1846 and 1848, respectively, and followed soon after by Minnesota in 1858 and Kansas in 1861. The regional Midwest, then, was distinct from much of the rest of the north in terms of its pervasive rural character, the rising significance of its agricultural production, and the relatively recent admission of several of the states that constituted it. Ironically, these same traits that differentiated the region from the rest of the North gave midwesterners something in common with their southern counterparts.

Midwestern origins and settlement patterns shaped how people of the region responded to the war and contributed to regional distinctiveness. Numerous historians have skillfully explained the ways in which north met south in the antebellum Middle West. Out of this came the influence of now also being a westerner. In his 1953 book, *Planting Corn Belt Culture: The Impress of the Upland Southerner and Yankee in the Old Northwest*, Richard Lyle Power claims that these different and sometimes opposing groups created a new society that blended elements of both cultures. This theme has been echoed many times with many permutations, from John Mack Faragher's study of the settlement along Sugar Creek, Illinois, to more recent works by Susan Sessions Rugh and Susan E. Gray. All three of these authors describe the varying degrees of cultural blending and clash in the region and further refine the definition of the Midwest. Nicole Etcheson, a contributor to the current volume, examines the persistence of these regional identities in shaping midwestern politics and culture up to 1861 and beyond, most recently in *A Generation at War: The Civil War Era in a Northern Community*. In the end, being a westerner would serve as a unifying factor on some level. "The process of defining the Midwest," Etcheson writes, "began when Northern and Southern migrants began to identify themselves more as Westerners than as Southerners and Northerners." The firing on Fort Sumter, however, would cause a resurgence of divisions.[7]

There is yet another important rationale for the regional focus for the current volume that is best illustrated by returning to the Grants' Galena experience. The initial wave of patriotic fervor and excitement of early 1861 soon gave way to a complex new reality marked by uncertainty, disruption, and anxiety as well as divisions. Swept up in the immediacy and passions of the national crisis, midwesterners learned that outfitting and equipping sons, brothers, courting lovers, husbands, and fathers along with other male kin and neighbors would be easier than enduring the long, dark days ahead. At the community level, it was as if they had sent off a part of themselves. Randall Miller observes that these regiments "were extensions of the community, closely watched and worried over." And while, as Ulysses Grant and others remembered, for a brief time "all were Union men, determined to avenge the insult to the national flag," existing divisions persisted and resurfaced in ways that reveal the home front as a complicated and dynamic place. Julia Grant, in one example, describes how all of Galena turned out to escort its first company of men to the depot with high spirits and pride and did so again for the second company. Yet, this second send-off (for the 19th Illinois Infantry) was an uneasy one on account of the underlying community and family politics it exposed. The company captain was apparently an "enthusiastically loyal" Democrat postmaster whose wife was not "in sympathy with him." "I was standing with my children in the station house," Julia relates, ". . . and, turning, saw Captain [Bushrod B.] Howard stride in and stop within a few feet of his wife and two little boys and her mother. . . . Folding his arms, he gazed sorrowfully at her. She returned his look but did not move." Not even her mother's prodding could move her to his arms to say good-bye. This incident was doubly lamented because shortly thereafter, the town was in deep mourning for Captain Howard and about a dozen of the Galena men who had been killed, and even more were crippled and wounded, in a horrific accident when the train carrying them into military service plunged off a bridge in Indiana, forty-six miles east of Vincennes.[8]

Tragic train wreck notwithstanding, the community's send-off of its soldiers signals the opening chapter of the typical Civil War narrative. Until recently, at this point of the story, the historian's focus would shift from the home front to follow the soldiers to the battlefields, where the story might also incorporate parallel narratives of women who served as nurses and as war-relief workers. The Northern home front, like the North in general, has long been depicted in simple terms as essentially one broad, monolithic place from which soldiers departed and, if lucky, returned. The North was also depicted as the symbolic hearth for soldiers and for women war workers who preserved their connections to it through a tremendous amount of letter writing. It has also been portrayed as a place of polarized views in the form of political dissent and draft riots. But a substantive overview of the home-front experience was elusive. This changed with the work of scholars, such as Philip Shaw Paludan, author of *A People's Contest: The Union and Civil War, 1861–1865* (1988), and J. Matthew Gallman, author of *The North Fights the Civil War: The Home Front* (1994), who ably demonstrated that the Northern home front was a remarkably busy, dynamic, sometimes divided, and vitally important place. It was also a place of struggle and hardship for the largely agrarian women and families, who, along with other community members, were forced to cope with the consequences of the absence of so many men.

As prolific Civil War scholar William C. Davis's foreword in the current volume indicates, newer attention to the home front has succeeded in uncovering new details, perspectives, and topics. It has also caused us to realize that our understanding of the Civil War era remains incomplete without this fuller appreciation of the home front, home-front issues, and especially the interrelatedness of a society at war. Moreover, these topics surely compel us to seek more insight about a country once at war with itself. "Study of the war and society has become paramount," insist James McPherson and William J. Cooper Jr. A successful method at bringing these two areas together has been through collections of essays that bring to light a variety of compelling and revealing experiences, as exemplified by *The War Was You and Me: Civilians in the American Civil War*, edited by Joan E. Cashin, and two edited collections by Paul A. Cimbala and Randall M. Miller, *Uncommon Time: The Civil War and the Northern Home Front* and *Union Soldiers and the Northern Home Front: Wartime Experiences, Postwar Adjustments.*[9]

While Northern home-front overviews, such as Paludan's and Gallman's, pushed the historiography toward a coherent narrative, one could not fail to notice that the implied unity of experience could not really be sustained by virtue of the North's great diversity—of people, places, and conditions. If there was not one North, as we assert, then what characterized the midwestern experience? A host of additional questions flow from this initial question. In what ways would the Galena, Illinois, of Ulysses and Julia Grant be typical or atypical of the home front? Was the home-front experience of the well-settled East more similar or different than that of the more recently settled and overwhelmingly agrarian Midwest? In what ways did these differences matter? Did these differences manifest themselves more severely on one or more groups of people than others? Can we look not only at the lives of specific segments of the population (e.g., college students, farmers, politicians, gawkers at prisoners-of-war, families) but also these segments' regional locales and derive a sharper understanding of where and why these home-front differences existed? The editors and contributors of the present volume assert that these kinds of questions do matter and, more important, reflect the recent shifts in the historiography as the remainder of this overview will show.

The variety of the Northern home front is evident in just a cursory look at some of the approaches scholars used to capture the wide range of civilian experiences. Overall, however, Paludan's contention in 1998 that "studies of northern society have been very few indeed"—echoed by Miller in 2002—remains more true than not in relation to the rest of Civil War historiography. Urban studies include Theodore J. Kara-manski's *Rally 'Round the Flag: Chicago and the Civil War* and Gallman's *Mastering Wartime: A Social History of Philadelphia during the Civil War.* Yet, when one considers that the United States was still more than 75 percent rural, the absence of this particular perspective is curious. One must revisit Paul Wallace Gates's *Agriculture and the Civil War* from 1965 for a monograph on the topic. Examples of the state-level approach include the excellent essay collection of editors William Blair and William Pencak, *Making and Remaking Pennsylvania's Civil War,* as well as editor Christine Dee's primary-source–focused *Ohio's War: The Civil War in Documents.* Older studies on dissent include Frank L. Klement, *Clement L. Vallandigham and the Limits of Dissent* and "Middle Western Copperheadism and the Genesis of the Granger Movement," in the *Mississippi Valley Historical Review;* Stanley L. Jones, "Agrarian Radicalism in Illinois' Constitutional Convention of 1862," *Journal of the Illinois State Historical Society;* and Herbert H. Wubben, *Civil War Iowa and the Copperhead Movement.* A revealing study of how the intersection of wartime economics, politics, and ideology would ultimately affect Northern civilian labor and livelihoods is Heather Cox Richardson, *The Greatest Nation of the Earth: Republican Economic Policies during the Civil War.*[10]

As so many of the published and archival letters of soldiers and families articulate, God and faith were close at hand in mid-nineteenth-century America. Home-front studies rooted in a religious group's response to the war, including those that deal with the pacifist's dilemma, are particularly illuminating of different (and on some level dissenting) perspectives, such as in Jacquelyn Nelson, *Indiana Quakers Confront the Civil War;* Phillip E. Webber, *Zoar in the Civil War;* and Peter Hoehnle, a *Communal Societies* article concerning Iowa's Amana Society, "With Malice toward None: The Inspirationist Response to the Civil War, 1860–1865." A first-class overview of the topic, Union and Confederate, is *Religion and the American Civil War*, a collection of essays edited by Randall Miller and Harry Stout. The recent *A Visitation of God: Northern Civilians Interpret the Civil War* by Sean Scott is impressive in its probing of spirituality on the home front and in demonstrating how strongly religion influenced civilians' responses to the war.

Important inroads have been made with regards to race and gender home-front issues on the Northern home front. More study is needed, and the areas of ethnicity and class are still wanting. Jon Gjerde's impressive *The Minds of the West: Ethnocultural Evolution in the Rural Middle West, 1830–1917*, reminds one that the Middle West constituted a "setting of great ethnic diversity" as a result of the migration of large numbers of foreign-born into the region during the antebellum years. Although the current chapter largely focuses on the resurgent tensions in those advocating Northern and Southern interests among the westerners, clearly the "foreign minds" asserted an important influence as well, especially in rural areas. This topic warrants more study in the context of the Civil War home front. Russell L. Johnson links class, industrial development, and military service in his case study of Dubuque, Iowa, in *Warriors into Workers: The Civil War and the Formation of Urban-Industrial Society in a Northern City*. As will also be seen with regards to women, some of the insight gained about the Civil War experience of a segment of the population is achieved through an essential "soldiering" of the topic, that is, examining a group's direct contribution to the war effort, especially as it relates to the battlefield. For example, Laurence M. Hauptman in *Between Two Fires: American Indians in the Civil War* examines the long-overdue history of the approximately twenty thousand American Indians who served on both sides of the conflict. We know, for example, that nearly all of the 150 men of Company K of the First Michigan Sharpshooters were of Odawa and Ojibwa descent. The Civil War narrative as it pertains to Native Americans is further complicated in the Midwest with the 1862 Sioux Uprising in Minnesota. The subject of Native American soldiering now brings up the question: What characterized their families' and communities' home-front experiences? The greater American Indian presence in the Midwest and the period's tense relations there suggest another justification for a distinctively regional home-front interpretation.[11]

Perhaps one of the best starting places to understand the landscape of prejudice that surrounded African Americans in the North at the time of the war is V. Jacque Voegeli's *Free but Not Equal: The Midwest and the Negro during the Civil War*. Voegeli traces the political conflicts over race and emancipation in the region and their effects upon the black population, demonstrating how even from the beginning "the Middle West wove the doctrine of racial discrimination into its legal and social fabric." This important work, like Gates's study of agriculture, dates to the 1960s and would become even more useful with a fresh update. Robert Dykstra offered a statewide examination of racial politics in Iowa in *Bright Radical Star: Black Freedom and White Supremacy on the Hawkeye Frontier*, demonstrating how one of the most racist-oriented states in the region became a beacon for egalitarianism. A more recent study of how African Americans adapted to change along the border between slavery and freedom is Darrel E. Bigham's *On Jordan's Banks: Emancipation and Its Aftermath in the Ohio River Valley*. A model study documenting rural African American life and struggles in the Midwest, including negotiating the Civil War era, is Stephen A. Vincent's *Southern Seed, Northern Soil: African-American Farm Communities in the Midwest, 1765–1900*. Some of the most promising and exciting recent research deals with the theme of wartime and postwar migration as seen, for example, in Jack S. Blocker's *A Little More Freedom: African Americans Enter the Urban Midwest, 1860–1930* and Leslie A. Schwalm's *Emancipation's Diaspora: Race and Reconstruction in the Upper Midwest*. Northern African American women endured a Civil War of their own, but as observed elsewhere in this chapter, their identification with the North does not necessarily accurately reflect their midwestern experiences. Rooting and interpreting African American women's Civil War experiences in the region will allow us to really "see" them in the context of their lives and to bring together these internal stories. Two important resources from which to glean and build upon are *We Are Your Sisters: Black Women in the Nineteenth Century*, edited by Dorothy Sterling, and Ella Forbes's *African American Women during the Civil War*.[12]

We know considerably more about how white women of the North and, to some extent, the Midwest fared during the war although the research has tended to follow certain patterns. Drew Gilpin Faust notes in a 1998 publication that the historical literature on white Northern women has directed "considerable attention to women's political activism and to wartime extensions or embodiments of the much-studied antebellum reform impulse" and that a "regional imbalance" between Union and Confederate women has existed in which "the study of northern women [is] comparatively neglected." This is perhaps less true today, but there is much left unsaid in many areas. Major studies on Northern women often examine their wartime roles in terms of political possibilities, patriotism, relief workers, and nurses and have resulted in a number of insightful studies, including Elizabeth D. Leonard, *Yankee Women: Gender Battles in the Civil War*; Jeanie Attie, *Patriotic Toil: Northern Women and the American Civil War*; Judith Ann Giesberg, *Civil War Sisterhood: The U.S. Sanitary Commission and Women's Politics in Transition* and *Army at Home: Women and the Civil War on the Northern Home Front*; Nina Silber, *Daughters of the Union: Northern Women Fight the Civil War*; and Jane E. Schulz, *Women at the Front: Hospital Workers in Civil War America*.[13]

The all-encompassing label of Northern, however, continues to be problematic as do implications of a singular "female home front." A notable exception to the latter, and one that could serve as a model, is Giesberg's *Army at Home*, which shifts the focus to marginal, rural and working-class Eastern women. The largely rural Midwest presented its own peculiar set of circumstances for women on the home front. While farming was not unique to the Midwest, it was more pervasive here than anywhere else in the North, and this factor alone significantly influenced the patterns of lives. For these women, coping and surviving the absence of so many men were their most immediate concerns, as their numerous letters and accounts clearly illustrate. Broader studies of Northern women have at times mischaracterized or misunderstood the dynamics of the rural Midwest. An example of this is in the portrayal of home-front women as suffering during the war *because* of having been "dependent" upon their now-absent male relations, instead of realizing that mid-nineteenth-century farm husbands and wives tended to view themselves as partners, both of whose contributions to the farm were absolutely necessary. With one-half of the partnership gone, the farm (along with these women's survival and their futures) was instantly in jeopardy; yet, farmwives did not falter, as shown in J. L Anderson's contribution in the current volume, "The Vacant Chair on the Farm: Soldier Husbands, Farm Wives, and the Iowa Home Front, 1861–65." Gender and family dynamics in the Civil War Midwest are especially discernible in the growing number of published correspondences, such as *Love and Valor: Intimate Civil War Letters between Captain Jacob and*

Emeline Ritner, edited by Charles F. Larimer, and Andrea Foroughi, *Go If You Think It Your Duty: A Minnesota Couple's Civil War Letters*.[14]

In 2001, Andrew R. L. Cayton and Susan E. Gray brought out the important and influential collection *American Midwest: Essays on Regional History*, which has all but become the cornerstone for considering how to organize the stories of the Midwest. Cayton and Gray urge students of the region to resist adhering to one master narrative at the expense of numerous counter- or alternative narratives. And they, too, argue that the Civil War was "the central event of Midwestern history." The current volume builds upon the *American Midwest* as well as accepts Cimbala and Miller's invitation from their own collection for scholars to "assay other northern home fronts." While no collection can ever encompass all of the myriad home-front issues, what follows indicates the diversity of subject matter and approaches that characterize new home-front history. It also unabashedly speaks from the Midwest.

The essays that follow reflect new treatments of old topics as well as new topics. Given its importance as a topic to the region and the Union effort, agriculture figures prominently in the collection.

Prisons have been studied from numerous perspectives, most often from that of the prisoners, but Michael P. Gray focuses on Sandusky, Ohio, the site of Johnson's Island. He turns attention to the people who consumed the war experience without confronting the reality of the battlefield. To the people of Sandusky and the surrounding area, the "captivating captives" on Johnson's Island were celebrities, freaks, and enemies. Accounts of observers who boarded excursion boats as well as those of prisoners tell a similar tale of exploitation. Excursionists taunted the prisoners with patriotic songs, and the captives retaliated by flying Confederate flags and other banners. The prisoners' response to the crowds of gawkers reinforced the observers' negative views of the enemy, dehumanizing both parties in the process.

Julie A. Mujic provides a fascinating look at how college men interpreted their wartime experiences. Many young men at the University of Michigan enlisted in the military, but many more stayed, and university enrollment in Ann Arbor surged during the war. Campus men inevitably compared themselves to soldiers and, perhaps surprising, justified their absence from the battle front rather than shrinking from it. In the first months of the war, they recognized the distance between the relative comforts of campus and the privation of camp and battlefield. As the war continued, however, they equated their educational experience with military service. Soldiers battled rebels, but the students battled each other through their club and literary society activities. They eventually justified their presence on campus in terms of preparation for national service in the political arena in the postwar period. Mujic's essay raises the provoking question of how college men competed for political office with one-armed or one-legged opponents whose limbs were buried at field hospitals at Ringgold Gap and scores of other places.

The United States was a predominantly rural place during the war, and agriculture was one of the defining characteristics of the Midwest. By 1860, the states of the Old Northwest ranked among the leading states in terms of corn, cereal grain, and livestock production. R. Douglas Hurt chronicles the stunning contributions and agricultural power of midwestern farmers to the war effort. These farmers experienced the Civil War as a period of high prices and increased costs and as a catalyst for changes in farm practices and increased production. The war strengthened the position of midwestern farmers in the local, regional, and national economy.

Women's experiences on the home front continue to attract scholarly interest due to the wealth of potential insight they represent. Nicole Etcheson pursues the perspective of relations between women and their in-laws and how the exigencies of war brought about changes in family interactions. This is one of the most overlooked issues of the wartime experience yet perhaps one of the most significant issues that women confronted during the war, given that the departure of male relatives caused many midwestern women to temporarily combine households. Etcheson highlights the importance of kinship as well as the often-contentious nature of family relations by demonstrating how women resisted and accepted the authority of male in-laws. For many midwestern women, the war was not a liberating experience.

Ginette Aley's essay analyzes the major ways in which the challenges and hardships confronting rural midwestern women differentiated their wartime experiences from other Northern home-front women. Many of these inescapable realities sprang from the region's overwhelmingly rural and agrarian way of life and the frontier-like environment in many areas. Laborers were already in high demand, and when the call for enlistments came and men began departing in 1861, an especially heavy burden descended upon the shoulders of farm women and their families. Aley finds that this reality more than any other shaped their wartime experiences and largely explains why, for example, many midwestern women gave little thought to organized war-relief work. Indeed, she argues, their letters and other accounts reveal that beyond meeting the new needs of the day, their consuming goal was to preserve family unions just as the President Abraham Lincoln was actively seeking to preserve the federal union.

Farm families experienced tremendous dislocation as a result of war-time separation, a subject J. L. Anderson addresses in an Iowa context. Spouses collaborated to maintain the family farm, even as they relied on in-laws, neighbors, and trusted friends for advice and labor. With husbands gone, most women found that they were unable to perform all of the physical work needed to maintain the farm, but they were the managers who mattered, a fact to which their husbands regularly attested when they wrote home that wives best knew the particulars of any situation that might arise and urged them to do their best.

Brett Barker offers a fresh perspective on one of the oldest topics in home-front studies: political dissent. This examination of the threats and violence directed toward Democratic editors and their papers in southeast Ohio demonstrates the extent to which Republican operatives attempted to silence the opposition press. Democratic gains in the 1862 election and the rise of Clement L. Vallandigham inspired Republicans to fight back on the home front. Barker emphasizes that the threats, boycotts, and violence chilled Democratic opposition not only in advance of the 1863 elections but also the critical election of 1864. Barker argues that military and civil authorities had active collaborators in silencing dissent, challenging and complicating our understanding of civil liberties during wartime.

If, as William David Barillas, author of *The Midwestern Pastoral: Place and Landscape in Literature of the American Heartland*, writes, the Midwest "is the nation's middlescape, its 'heartland,' a regional label that associates geographical centrality with a defining role in national identity," then the midwestern voices that follow may have more to say on the subject of the Civil War than you might have thought.[15]

Notes

1. Julia Dent Grant, *The Personal Memoirs of Julia Dent Grant (Mrs. Ulysses S. Grant)*, ed. John Y. Simon (New York: G. P. Putnam's Sons, 1975), 89; Ulysses S. Grant, *Personal Memoirs of U. S. Grant* (New York: Charles L. Webster, 1885–86), 1:217, 230–31. Although written in the flowery and sometimes overstated style of the era, for a comparable midwestern experience of the war's outbreak, see S. H. M. Byers, *Iowa in War Times* (Des Moines, IA: W. D. Condit, 1888), chap. 3.

2. The turmoil of the 1850s is covered in James M. McPherson, *Battle Cry of Freedom: The Civil War Era* (New York: Oxford University Press, 1988), chaps. 3–6. But see also Michael F. Holt, *The Political Crisis of the 1850s* (New York: Wiley, 1978); Nicole Etcheson, *Bleeding Kansas: Contested Liberty in the Civil War Era* (Lawrence: University Press of Kansas, 2004); Orville Vernon Burton, *The Age of Lincoln* (New York: Hill and Wang, 2007); Leland L. Sage, *A History of Iowa* (Ames: Iowa State University Press, 1987), 138–40, 142–43; Byers, *Iowa in War Times*, chap. I.

3. U. S. Grant, *Personal Memoirs*, 1:215–16, 222, 225, 227. On the emergence of the Midwest regional label, see James R. Shortridge, *The Middle West: Its Meaning in American Culture* (Lawrence: University Press of Kansas, 1989), chap. 2.

4. William David Barillas, *The Midwestern Pastoral: Place and Landscape in Literature of the American Heartland* (Athens: Ohio University Press, 2006), 23.

5. A number of strong studies discuss the Old Northwest's struggles over the slavery issue, but see John Craig Hammond, *Slavery, Freedom, and Expansion* (Charlottesville: University of Virginia Press, 2007); Peter S. Onuf, *Statehood and Union: A History of the Northwest Ordinance* (Bloomington: Indiana University Press, 1987); U.S. Department of Commerce, Bureau of the Census, *Historical Statistics of the United States: Colonial Times to 1970, Part I* (Washington, DC: GPO, 1975), 23–37. No studies have been done on the Midwest during the Civil War, so we based our regional definition for the era upon the common interpretation as found in James H. Madison, *Heartland: Comparative Histories of the Midwestern States* (Bloomington: Indiana University Press, 1988), 2. We dropped the Dakotas, Nebraska, and Missouri from the usual twelve-state definition because the Dakotas and Nebraska did not attain statehood until after the war, and Missouri was a border state.

6. Ibid.; U.S. Bureau of the Census, *Agriculture of the United States, 1860* (Washington, DC: U.S. Bureau of the Census, 1864), xlii, xxix–xxxi.

7. Nicole Etcheson, *The Emerging Midwest: Upland Southerners and the Political Culture of the Old Northwest, 1787–1861* (Bloomington: Indiana University Press, 1996), xii.

8. Randall M. Miller, introduction, in Paul A. Cimbala and Randall M. Miller, eds., *Union Soldiers and the Northern Home Front: Wartime Experiences, Postwar Adjustments* (New York: Fordham University Press, 2002), xii; U. S. Grant, *Personal Memoirs*, 230; J. D. Grant, *Personal Memoirs*, 90, 114 n2. The "frightful" train accident involving several companies and resulting in 24 deaths and 105 seriously wounded (more would die later) is detailed in "19th Illinois Infantry," Histories of Illinois Civil War Regiments and Units, *Illinois Genealogy*, http://www.illinoisgenealogy.org/civil_war/19th_illinois_infantry. htm (accessed August 3, 2012). For a comparable older study that pieces together primary accounts about a community's response to prepare and send off its own men, see Ethel Alice Hurn, *Wisconsin Women in the War between the States* (Democrat, 1911), chap. I. For the general topic of Northern soldiering, see Reid Mitchell, *The Vacant Chair: The Northern Soldier Leaves Home* (New York: Oxford University Press, 1993), esp. chap. 2.

9. James M. McPherson and William J. Cooper Jr., eds., *Writing the Civil War: The Quest to Understand* (Columbia: University of South Carolina Press, 1998), 3.

10. Phillip Shaw Paludan, "What Did the Winners Win? The Social and Economic History of the North during the Civil War," in ibid., 175; Miller, introduction, xiv.

11. Jon Gjerde, *The Minds of the West: Ethnocultural Evolution in the Rural Middle West, 1830–1917* (Chapel Hill: University of North Carolina Press, 1997), 2 (but see also his introductory chapter). An insightful thesis is Jami Ann Keegan, "Scandal of

Patriotism: The Forgotten Contributions of Michigan's Native Americans, Women, and African-Americans during the Civil War" (master's thesis, Eastern Michigan University, 2000).

12. V. Jacque Voegeli, *Free but Not Equal: The Midwest and the Negro during the Civil War* (Chicago: University of Chicago Press, 1967), 1. See also Michael P. Johnson, "Out of Egypt: The Migration of Former Slaves to the Midwest during the 1860s in Comparative Perspective," in Darlene Clark Hine and Jacqueline McLeod, eds., *Crossing Boundaries: Comparative History of Black People in Diaspora* (Bloomington: Indiana University Press, 1999), 223–45, and Nikki Marie Taylor, *Frontiers of Freedom: Cincinnati's Black Community, 1802–1868* (Athens: Ohio University Press, 2005).

13. Drew Gilpin Faust, "'Ours as Well as That of the Men': Women and Gender in the Civil War," in McPherson and Cooper, *Writing the Civil War*, 234, 239.

14. Two studies that illustrate this partnership between agrarian husbands and wives (and that also include the role of extended family) are Emily Foster, ed., *American Grit: A Woman's Letters from the Ohio Frontier* (Lexington: University Press of Kentucky, 2002), and the postwar, Iowa-based (despite its title) volume, Daniel Tyler, ed., *Love in an Envelope: A Courtship in the American West* (Albuquerque: University of New Mexico Press, 2008). See also Nancy Grey Osterud, *Bonds of Community: The Lives of Farm Women in Nineteenth-Century New York* (Ithaca, NY: Cornell University Press, 1991), especially part 3. For more analysis of the historiography of Northern women, see Ginette Aley's essay in the current volume.

15. Andrew R. L. Cayton and Susan E. Gray, eds., *The American Midwest: Essays on Regional History* (Bloomington: Indiana University Press, 2001), 15. See also Ginette Aley, "'Dwelling within the Place Worth Seeking': The Midwest, Regional Identity, and Internal Histories," in Timothy R. Mahoney and Wendy J. Katz, eds., *Regionalism and the Humanities* (Lincoln: University of Nebraska Press, 2008), 95–109; Cimbala and Miller, *Union Soldiers*, xvi; Barillas, *Midwestern Pastoral*, 4.

CAPTIVATING CAPTIVES

—————

AN EXCURSION TO JOHNSON'S
ISLAND CIVIL WAR PRISON

Michael P. Gray

In the vast historiography of the Civil War, scholars have especially concentrated on the battlefield, from strategy and tactics to the leaders that put their plans into motion. Eventually, there was a filtering down to the common soldier, and while historians continue to evolve beyond battlegrounds with much fresh social and cultural input—this natural progression from a "behind the lines" perspective can be further developed by studying "behind the stockade walls" of Civil War prisons. Some audiences may be more interested in the romantic image of the honorable soldier stepping onto fields of glory rather than examining those who were captured; however, those imprisoned should not be discounted, nor should their scholarly investigation. More often, when scholars delve into the camps, they tend to gravitate toward stockades with high mortality rates. This is largely due to the notoriety of Andersonville and the many comparisons made to that Georgia pen. Consequently, other confines are overshadowed. Moreover, a recent pattern in Civil War prison scholarship follows this trend, focusing on the administrative policy of prisons with a tendency to emphasize mortality among captives. This occasionally leads to generalizations that neglect other significant dynamics in and out of the stockade walls. Civil War prison studies constitutes a largely untapped subject that merits going far beyond death figures and, indeed, compels a deeper examination into prison yards and their host communities with regional, economic, social, and cultural approaches.[1]

Within Civil War prison scholarship, one theme that is particularly overlooked has to do with the impact of camps beyond their specific locale.[2] This chapter seeks to correct this deficiency and lay some groundwork for more investigation into an intriguing and, hopefully, growing aspect of not only Civil War prisons but also "the viewing" of Civil War soldiers generally. It might also better explain the importance of how contemporaries scrutinized captured soldiers under the lens of societal norms and to what extent people might undertake to see them in the broader context of the nineteenth century. Little scholarly investigation of the "looking," "viewing," or even "gawking" of prisoners has been undertaken nor of the reaction inmates might give in response to being considered spectacles.[3] How various prison populations might be treated differently by the enemy, along with how civilians entered into the framework of the prisoners' captivity, might seem astonishing when compared to present-day standards. Moreover, soldiers' shame in being labeled as "prisoners of war" resulted in a shared benefit that meshed victory on the military front at having taken the enemy with a celebratory sensation on the home front in the surrounding publicity as found in their advertising and promotion; meanwhile, prisoner humiliation only grew worse.

An excellent example of this occurred in the Midwest (at the time referred to often as the Middle West) at a prison that had minimal deaths and one that has received little attention by academic historians. Contemporaries, however, certainly recognized its significance, and they left behind a record of an unusual fascination that subsequent generations ignored. The decision to select Johnson's Island in Ohio as a prison camp led to consequences that reverberated throughout the entire Northern home front. Like other prisons, Johnson's Island has a complex history with many layers, yet it, nonetheless, possesses a distinctive place among prisons because of its unique prison population: Union leaders had decided it would be used to confine Southern officers. In reality, its population was even more diverse. Again like other camps, this Ohio prison brought about dramatic economic benefits for the host community, Sandusky, that eventually trickled to other locales in the Midwest and Great Lakes region. But it was the Southern gentry that first caught the eyes of many midwesterners' imaginations as they could hardly contain themselves in anticipation of seeing their new, rare, exceptional, if not exotic, island guests.

In early fall 1861, William West was working at his store in Sandusky, Ohio, when a courier entered with a message that an important military man who recently checked in at West's boardinghouse wanted to see him. The anxious Sanduskian went off immediately to West House and found the newly appointed commissary general of Union prisons colonel William Hoffman, who had recently arrived from Cleveland, waiting. West removed his hat as Hoffman told him that he was recommended to him in far-off New York. As West listened attentively, Hoffman explained that the secretary of war requested a new prison depot to be built for one thousand captives, and it was the colonel's task to find the proper place.[4] The journey for the longtime soldier had taken him to Cleveland, Detroit, and Toledo with strict instructions "to use all the economy in his power, as the government was on a strain for its existence."[5] Hoffman admitted to West that he thought the army would find a more suitable location elsewhere, particularly Detroit, since it had a very competitive lumber market. Plus, Hoffman's mother and brother resided in Detroit, and it might make for more pleasant travel rather than the smaller port at Sandusky, which had about eight thousand residents.[6]

Regardless, Colonel Hoffman handed West design plans for the buildings and suggested he find a carpenter to work out the figures for barracks that might accommodate 270 men, mess rooms included. West realized the opportunity this might bring Sandusky and also the urgency in acting fast. He hurried to R. B. Hubbard and Co. and told Hubbard the situation, along with the economic benefits it might bring, so they proposed a low bid at $8 per thousand feet of lumber. West also chose local carpenter Samuel Catherman to help calculate expenses for five, two-story barracks. The practical West, thinking that he could not match his more sophisticated competitors, took an additional 25 percent off the total price from the lumberman. In the meantime, the prison commissary boarded the side-wheeler *Island Queen* and steamed to the Put-in-Bay islands. He seemed unimpressed with North Bass as it was too close to Canada and too far from the mainland for travel; Middle Bass had similar problems, while South Bass was still twenty-four miles from port, and families living there were unwilling to rent their valuable vineyard acreage. Twelve miles south, Kelley's Island had even more families, and although some were willing to rent, Hoffman was unwilling to negotiate, due in part to the brandy and wine enterprises he thought might tempt the future guard force. Before Hoffman left Sandusky, West took him to Johnson's Island in Sandusky Bay. He made a final "pitch" as this location was much closer, afforded three hundred acres with just one owner, L. B. Johnson, who would lease the entire island for $500 annually.

After looking over the semi-forested site, Hoffman bid farewell and made his way to Toledo, Detroit, then to back to Washington, D.C., and finally New York City. West thought it "was the last that I expected to see or hear from Col. Hoffman."[7]

To West's surprise, he received a telegraph from Hoffman: "I have located the prison depot at your place." On October 22, the prison commissary wrote quartermaster general Montgomery C. Meigs that it was "decidedly the best location" as it offered everything the other locales could not, including a forty-acre clearing where the stockade could be built as well as accessibility year round and no objections from residents. Indeed, it gave the military "the entire control" of Johnson's Island "so that no person would be permitted to land on it except by permission."[8] From that point, the history of Sandusky, the state of Ohio, the Midwest, and this portion of the country's North Coast would change decidedly. From that point as well, Northerners living there would be intrigued with their Southern visitors, particularly after it was determined it would best serve as an exclusive officer prison—the largest of its kind distinctive not only in the Midwest but the entire Northern home front. Such a decision was reached after officials were reminded that captured officers were kept separate from the "rank and file" so they would not have leadership in conspiring to escape. Also mindful were newspaper reporters, who closely watched over the developing situation on Mr. Johnson's island.

When Colonel Hoffman returned to Sandusky on November 12, 1861, West signed the army contract. Bonds were set at $40,000 to have the project completed by January 31, 1862. Favorable warm weather brought the project quickly to fruition as West and his lumber partner Philander Gregg used 1,500,000 feet of lumber to build forty structures total, including the designated barracks, within the contracted time frame. The total price was estimated at $26,266 and came with a twelve-foot-high stockade wall costing $900 to ensure privacy from inside and out.[9] On December 14, 1861, the Sandusky *Register* reported, "The Secession city is growing, like magic these pleasant days. Gregg & West seem to have changed the old motto about making hay, & c. They make houses while the sun shines. It already begins to loom up the present quite a town like appearance."[10] Outside communities were also watching intently. Toledo, although coming up short in the selection process, recognized the "Prison Houses on Lake Erie. Johnson's Island in Sandusky Bay is to be put in commission as a second Fort Lafayette."[11] Hoffman needed someone to run the post so West suggested the mayor, who was also one of his boarders, William Pierson. West later wrote that the new commandant "was a clever fellow. He made lots of money out of the job, which lasted him as long as he lived." Pierson would be among many making "lots of money" due to the construction of a new prison on Mr. Johnson's island.[12]

Local hardware supplier H. A. Gale won the bid for furnishing stoves for the prison. The contract called for 170 units of the boxed variety, plus 20 Peckhams' furnaces and boilers for cooking. It amounted to more than $1,500 and did not include expensive piping, which also had to be bought by the government. Bake ovens were required; Edward Cassidy furnished them for the islanders at $225 apiece. Spencer and Townsend supplied forks, knives, spoons, kettles, cups, and lanterns, totaling $680, for the soon-to-arrive captives and guards; A. W. Hendry, who owned a meat shop in the city, provided prisoners beef at $4.24 for every one hundred pounds. Pool and Miner brought in coal oil for illumination, and Johnson, already benefiting in rental space, delivered lime for disinfecting latrines. Other locals sold straw, medicine, liquor, chamber pots, more food, and additional supplies—the work of the quartermaster and commissary would be immense.[13]

Meanwhile, Sanduskians seemed to be growing impatient. The local press wrote in late January that it was "All quiet. No Rebels yet" and made mention that the only thing delivered onto the island were "8-inch Columbiads" to watch over the Southerners. The newly formed Hoffman battalion would serve as guards and learn how to man these guns, in addition to holding their own weapons as they took their periodical shifts on sentry posts. In early February, the *Sandusky Register* reported that "Secesh Gentry" would soon be transferred from Camp Chase in Columbus and exclaimed, "LET THEM COME." A Cleveland newspaper correspondent assigned to Columbus noticed Camp Chase "is divided near the middle so that the 'First Families of Virginia' are kept separate from the 'hunters of Kentucky.' . . . Among the prisoners are all grades, from cattle up to the cultivated." The "cultivated" in Columbus would soon be preparing for life on Lake Erie.[14]

With mounting anticipation as spring approached, the *Register* reminded the construction crew of passage times the sloop *Harlequin* was making "For Secesh City." Some local laborers had been staying overnight on the island, taking bedding, food, and other supplies so the finishing touches might be made on time. Within the week, the paper exclaimed, "Don't get excited about the coming of the prisoners. If they did not come yesterday they are still back to come some other day.

Be prepared to receive them at all times. . . . [D]on't believe every rumor of their coming lest disappointment come to you."[15] Meanwhile, Commissary Hoffman needed a larger vessel in order to transfer prisoners from railroad to ship. He negotiated with captain George H. Bristol and his steamer *Little Eastern*, anchored in Detroit, to shuttle prisoners back and forth from Sandusky and the island. In time, the *Little Eastern* proved too little, and consequently, quartermaster E. W. H. Read and assistant quartermaster L. M. Brooks negotiated for Bristol's newest steamer, *Princess*, at $40 a day. A dock was required, so the quartermaster's department rented one from Thornton and Fitzhugh for $80 yearly.[16]

On April 10, the *Register* highlighted that "200 Rebel Officers" were being sent from Camp Chase; the next day the paper warned, "Fisherman, yachtsmen and others need now be careful not to land on Johnson's Island, especially near the lower end and near the fence. The guards carry loaded pieces. . . . The island is under Uncle Sam's jurisdiction and he will have it well watched." Subsequently, as the prisoners along with fifty guards finally arrived, the *Ohio State Journal* poked fun: "The immense anxiety of the Sandusky folks, lest the beautiful 'summer residences' on the island would mould from disuse will now be relieved." The Sandusky *Register* not only responded to the Columbus paper but also made a revealing comment: "Kind—Well, send 'em on. The Hoffman Battalion is ready to try a hand on anything you choose to rid of. They . . . can make them toe the mark, if they have toes like other men."[17] The next week, the *Register* observed, "More Rebel Colonists—A special train on the S. M. & N. Railroad brought from Camp Chase yesterday 191 Rebel prisoners." Prisoners would travel on two rail lines on their way to Johnson's Island: the Sandusky, Mansfield, and Newark and the Sandusky, Dayton, and Cincinnati Railroads.[18] After prisoners were ferried across the lake, they got to see their new confines. Captain Robert Bingham, 44th North Carolina, wrote what he thought when he first entered into the stockade: "This place is a great improvement. . . . The enclosure is about 16 acres & one can go all about during the day. The view of the lake is pleasant—& the air pure—& the fare mostly good. . . . I will do very well." He also noticed that some women were allowed on the island, probably family to the Union officer guards, and, moreover, they "most certainly like to look at naked rebels. The fence leaves a walk on the lake shore—& there it is made with bars & spaces alternating. The pumps are there & men are nearly always washing themselves." These ladies had a habit of "nearly always walking there & very near of said naked men—12 to 15 steps at most. Today some saw a man washing & passed by & one little one, about 15 was so anxious that she looked back over her shoulder [un]til she fell into the ditch leading fr[om] the pump."[19]

As more and more officer prisoners were being concentrated in Sandusky Bay, a larger if not more intimidating guard was required. The *Cleveland Herald* reported, "The U.S. Steamer Michigan arrived here from Erie. . . . She will stop at Johnson's Island . . . so that the rebels there can see what sort of craft Uncle Sam has on his fresh water ponds to keep wicked boys in order."[20] Commander Pierson also flexed his military power as his post increased. His headquarters announced on Monday morning, April 21, 1862, "It may prevent misunderstanding and disappointment, especially with persons residing at a distance, to announce that no persons will be allowed to land on Johnson's Island without written consent of the Commanding Officer." Pierson's dictate concludes, "Also, that no one will be permitted to visit prisoners, except the nearest relatives, in case of severe sickness." On the chance that anyone missed his military mandate, the *Register* warned "KEEP AWAY FROM JOHNSON'S ISLAND. . . . It has been decided that the rebels over there are to be 'let alone.'"[21] Yet, the paper also enticed its readers four days later with, "REINFORCEMENTS—The enemy on Johnson's Island received a reinforcement of 200 from Camp Chase. . . . [T]he Southern gentry are becoming quite the rage now. . . . The knowing ones have long predicted that our bay and lake islands would one day become a favorite resort for the pleasure seekers of our sister states of the south. . . . [S]ome . . . thought Uncle Sam had made a great mistake in erecting such commodious accommodations on Johnson's Island. . . . [T]he thing is likely to be well patronized. . . . Those who came yesterday had baggage which indicated they were to stay the season, and we are informed that the party which proceed them had some nine tons of luggage." And three days later, "Another party of 250 rebel gentry from Dixie came yesterday . . . over to Uncle Sam's hotels on Johnson's Island."[22] Eventually, the notion of being "let alone" and not seeing these "hotels," along with the men that occupied them, proved far too compelling for many from near and far, whether prisoners were wearing clothes or not.

Seeing Southern prisoners of war was particularly appealing to Northerners on the home front. When the captives were spotted en route to prison, onlookers followed, fascinated by the fact that these Confederate soldiers were in their proverbial backyard. This had been the circumstance at other prison-camp communities as well. At Chicago's Camp Douglas prison, for example, although its fence was fairly low, nonetheless, an entrepreneur built a wooden tower on Cottage Grove to view inmates and charged patrons ten cents a person to do so.[23] A newspaperman there noted how Sundays were especially crowded in this tower. Perhaps "Yankee ingenuity" was taken to a new level, literally, in Elmira, New York, where similar structures appeared with "a constant stream of people." First was the Nichols Upper Observatory, constructed for onlookers to peer over the twelve-foot-high stockade wall. Nichols's price was set at fifteen cents, although he might at least justify his higher New York price by having spy glasses on hand so one might see the "vermin" on Confederates. Then a newspaper advertisement announced a new structure built by W. and W. Mears "at considerable expense" with a twenty-foot level with the same admission promoted in Chicago. Prisoners at these enlisted men's pens reacted as one might expect—dismay, derisive circus acts, and obscene gestures.[24] At Johnson's Island, local entrepreneurs could not build upon the island since it prohibited visitors. But the allure that these captives were not only Southerners but also a select group of the highest social order made for even more suspense and curiosity.

To this day, excursion boats have been a popular pastime during Lake Erie summers, particularly among the Put-in-Bay islands in the Western basin, plying their way through its emerald waters, dropping off or picking up picnic-goers, vacationers, wine tasters, or others seeking sport and entertainment. Cedar Point Amusement Park sits in the background of Johnson's Island, with its famed roller coasters dominating the sky, the area known more for its entertaining rides rather than its Civil War history. Astonishingly, a new dimension of Lake Erie tourism took place during the Civil War after the prison was established. It was made quite clear as articles and advertisements began to appear in papers along North Coast ports. On June 5, 1862, the Cleveland *Leader* reported, "There will be an excursion to Johnson's Island on June 26 for the benefit of the west side Bethel Church." When word reached Sandusky, the *Register* gladly welcomed their lakeshore neighbors: "COMING TO SANDUSKY. . . . [A]n excursion has been got up for the benefit of the Bethel cause, on board the 'May Queen;' Johnson's Island and Sandusky being the places to come to. . . . Jack Leland's band is expected to accompany the excursionists. Just let the Clevelanders come right along . . . and see the rebel quarters if not the rebels themselves." The paper as well as local businesses undoubtedly wondered if *May Queen* would come to port: "Whether the excursionists will stop in the city or not we do not know—all events they anticipate a view from the bay of the rebel quarters on the island."[25] The *Herald* promised the *May Queen*'s captain "will 'come right along' with a gay party of Clevelanders and 'slow' past Johnson's Island, so as to afford a good view of the rebel quarters." The editor of the paper also included admission for the trip, a ticket for a "gentleman" costing $1.00, "Ladies" 50 cents.[26]

By the end of June, regular weekly excursions were running locally, as the *Island Queen* not only helped in transporting prisoners but also in carrying civilians to see the prisoners. The *Register* noted, "[R]eturning about 6 o'clock, Capt Orr . . . then passed over the bay to give all hands another look at Seceshville. The soldiers cheered and the ladies waved their kerchiefs the band played and the traitors 'cabined, cribbed, confined,' looked on and listened. . . . At all events they had the benefit of Yankee Doodle and The Star Spangled Banner—whether they appreciated them or not. . . . If rebels hate both may all evil wait upon them, until they return to their 'first love' . . . 'keep step to the music of the union.'"[27] Meanwhile, the Cleveland excursion onboard the *May Queen* was described in their local *Herald* as "delightful" since "[t]he party had a fine view of Johnson's Island and the secesh prisoners." This was made better due to the helmsmanship of the *May Queen*'s captain, who carefully controlled his boat, "not only slowing past their quarters, but kindly backing in up and holding on near shore. The prison yards and barracks are delightfully located on the bank overlooking the bay and lake. . . . There are 1119 prisoners on the island—all rebel officers, bound 'to die in the last ditch.'" Local establishments would be delighted as well, as their business undoubtedly picked up, verified by the press: "The 'Queen' stopped some 2 hours at Sandusky giving all an opportunity to enjoy a ramble over the pleasant city."[28]

One might think when the heavily armed *Michigan* set anchor off Johnson's Island and was poised near the stockade wall, an end would come to excursionist activity. On the contrary, however, it appeared to only rally more patriotic support. On June 30, the Sandusky *Register* reported that the warship "came into the bay on Sat morning and cast anchor off rebel quarters on Johnson's Island. The 'Island Queen' with her load of excursionists passes by her apparently to the delight of both parties. Handkerchiefs were waved on the Queen with great vigor and the flag dipped, caps doffed and handkerchiefs waved on the Michigan. . . . [O]n the return the Michigan was at anchor there and a similar showing of patriotism and gallantry was repeated."[29]

On July 4, 1862, the *Register* took note of the excursionists' celebratory Independence Day spirit topped off by their nationalistic and loyal musical mood—all carefully orchestrated by their passing exhibitions. The *Register* could only hope festivities on the Fourth would extend to Southern inmates "over the bay, today . . . with the reading of the Declaration of Independence and the playing or singing of the Star Spangled Banner from sun rise to sun set . . . without a moment's intermission." The paper rhetorically asked, "Won't they hear national music when the excursionists pass by their quarters? We should not though wonder if they did."[30]

By August, prison excursion parties were coming from Detroit. Like Cleveland, Detroit, too, lost out in having a prison built closer to home, but the Michiganders did not seem to mind having to pay for travel to get their peeks. The going rate for passengers to see these "captivating captives" was fifty cents per person. The steamship *Planet*, captained by J. P. Ward, advertised in the *Detroit Advertiser* and *Tribune*. The *Register* took quick "notice that a grand pleasure excursion comes off today from that city to the prison quarters on Johnson's Island. . . . Whether they will be disappointed when they get only an outside view of rebeldom over the bay, or whether they already know just what is to be seen," the local press seemed unsure. Toledoans had an even closer trip, and although some may have felt previously slighted by the prison commissary, nonetheless, they would not miss out on the opportunity of taking part in the latest stop in the Western Basin island tour, happily granted by their neighborly hosts to the southeast. On the last day of August, the *City of Cleveland* left its dock in Toledo, first stopped at Kelley's Island, and then steamed on to what seemed to be the in-vogue place on Lake Erie during the summer of 1862. The *Register*, as well as Sandusky merchants, could only "hope they will not stop at Rebeldom but come over and see the most pleasant city in the state. Just let them come."[31]

As some Confederate officers were being exchanged and sent home at the end of summer 1862, Toledo excursionists on the *City of Cleveland* hoped to see a new attraction—"The Rebel gentry who have had a summer over the Bay, have departed for the South and now only guerillas remain. Perhaps the excursionists will be as pleased with the sight of them as their predecessors who did not feel pleased to associate with them."[32] As the excursion season was winding down for the year, more and more visitors wanted to venture out before the novelty wore cold and the bay froze. The scene in Sandusky Bay seemed to be unprecedented near the end of summer 1862. Vessels were stopping by the stockade as excursionists crowded the decks, singing along with hired bands to the tunes of "John Brown's Body Lies A-Mouldering in the Grave," "Yankee Doodle Went to Town," and the "O! Say can you see" of the *Star-Spangled Banner*. As the curious gazed upon "Rebeldom," choruses echoed into the prison yard, and Union guards sometimes joining in concert and saluting the onlookers. Excursionists would cheer in response with their eyes focused inside the wooden walls, enhanced by magnification devices to grant a clearer picture as one jostled for position, so that a full view was achieved in return for their fare. Captains had to be careful not to hit each other in the congested waters. The editor of the *Register* seemed awestruck at the "Fleet of Vessels—At one time Saturday afternoon some 11 vessels were visible in the Bay from the back of our office—of these, 4 were laying at anchor off Johnson's Island, 3 more well over to this shore, one down towards the cove, 2 others coming over the northern channel and beating down the Bay."[33] By war's end, excursion parties came from as close as Fremont, Ohio, and as far off as Buffalo, New York.[34] Excursionists, along with prisoners, of course, heard music from the Johnson's Island, Hoffman, Yader, and Leland bands. One article in a newspaper observed, "The *Queen* and *Portsmouth* were literally jammed," the *Morning Star* had an "excursion party of 800 from Detroit," and the "Fremont Excursion" was "loaded" and "came down the Bay yesterday . . . to the islands—touched here and left a few passengers, gave Johnson's Island a view and steamed out into the lake."[35] Vessels that eventually made their way into Sandusky Bay and Put-in-Bay islands include the *May Queen*, *Roeria*, *John C. Reynolds*, *Island Queen*, *Portsmouth*, *City of Cleveland*, *Traveller*, and the *Gov. Cushing*.[36] Also, Detroit's *Philo Parsons* promoted a "new Upper Cabin" when it took out advertisements in the *Register*, as did the smaller but more local "Staunch Steamer" *Island Queen*. The latter two carefully detailed "leave" and "return" times in the newspaper for in and around the islands as well as time schedules for the local rail links to get them inland and home.[37] There would be no leave times nor getting home for many Southerners, as the prisoner-exchange system soon collapsed, and Johnson's Island began filling up with inmates once more. Consequently, it gave ample time for the "captive spectacles" to reflect upon their Lake Erie audience.

Lieutenant Horace Carpenter of the Ninth Louisiana Battalion remembered how "steamers, loaded with excursionists, would occasionally run close in, prompted by curiosity, and taunt us with their shouts and jeers." The Louisianan, with humor, continued, "Their favorite pastime was, or seemed to be, the singing of patriotic songs, which was admissible, and I could find no reasonable cause of complaint as to the sopranos and contraltos, but when basso-profondos and baritones musically expressed their intention to 'rally around the flag,' I thought of thousands of Northern men already engaged in that occupation far to the front, who, if not so vocalistic, were at least equally patriotic."[38] Virginian Joseph Mason Kern of the Hampshire Guards was impressed by the scenery when he entered on the island in early June: "The surroundings are quite picturesque Boats are constantly passing." When he realized what some of these boats were engaged in, he was rather pithy: "The Excursion boat 'Island Queen' of Sandusky passed the prison today—coming close into shore to see the 'Rebels.'"[39]

Captain W. A. Wash of Vaughn's Tennessee Brigade gave a more detailed account of excursion traffic. The native Kentuckian wrote on June 25, 1863, it "was a calm, pleasant day; scarcely a wave rippled. . . . The day was in every wise suitable for the excursion party that went out that morning in the 'Island Queen,' a nice little craft fitted up specially for excursions. The Queen, with loyal pennons floating on the breeze, and a jolly crew and cargo, came alongside Mr. Johnson's Island to get a peep at the 'Rebel Home.'" As they moved in closer, "the ladies waved their white 'kerchiefs as if to tantalize us, for they well knew we would like to have been in their stead, with our sweethearts from Dixie by our side. Our only consolation was the thought that all things work together for the best, and that our day would come bye and bye." An August entry notes "the Island Queen, which makes regular excursion trips, passed close round the island with a cargo of heaven's last and best creation, and they seemed to be astonished that the rebels looked so well and perfectly contented. I dare say they imagine not of the restless, latent fire that is burning in the bosoms of these true but unfortunate sons of the South. Perchance in a future day their brothers and sweethearts will have the occasion to tell them that the fellows who seemed so tame and harmless on Johnson's Island made them smell frost in the shape of gunpowder and lead pills." As different boats were employed in similar practices, Wash tried to make sense of this Northern and Middle West fascination and how people were so "attracted by a curiosity to see how 'Southern chivalry' looked and lived up North. Several excursion boats went out. . . . The steamers came as close as to our prison fence as possible, some three hundred yards, with the stars and stripes flying, the bands playing, and the ladies waving their handerkerchiefs, but we guessed that it was not a token of love for us. In our prison all passed off quietly and soberly that day." Finally, the captain made mention that "a puffing steamer hove in sight, and passing through the opening in the blockade near the lighthouse, directed its course directly toward the island, and came within a few hundred yards of the shore, which is less than 30 yards from our prison wall. It was a gay excursion party, and all of them saluted the Southern boys, who were out watching them, but whether in esteem or derision must be for a longer head to say."[40]

If the shame of being stigmatized as prisoners of war was not enough, Confederates were further humiliated as being curiosities, leading to re-taliatory acts by the "captivating captives." It also became more apparent to whom they would direct their frustration. The semi-literate captain William Henry Asbury Speer of the 28th North Carolina Volunteers noted, on June 30, 1862, "We have been visited to day by a steamboat excu[r]sion from Sanduskey loded with men & women, [who] wave their hankerchiefs in derision of us, our men our waveing from their windows various looking flags Some have the black flagg waving at the Yankees these excursions come off ever few days, but we have got to treating them with Silent contempt."[41] Special indignity came to the Tar Heel soldier on a day he should have been celebrating: "This is my birth day. . . . [W]e have the pleasuer of the excursion boats coming over here with the women and men to look at us, but to day caps all, the niggars are out to day in two boats with their bands of music celebrating the day Augst 1 as the birth day of colonization & of corse they must come by & See the Secesh, O! how the black Bucks wentches laugh at us." Another North Carolinian, Major James Mayo, underscored his protest in mid-August 1863 at the height of the summer excursion season: "Another pleasure excursion on the 'Island Queen' having secured the services of the Hoff-man band. Rather interesting with the ladies waving their handkerchiefs as in exultation, in return we waved a black one, both to indicate that they are negro worshipers and to let them know to what extremity this struggle will be fought if they persist in their vain effort to conquer a people 'born to be free and to rule.'"[42] Meanwhile, Speer's diary entry written near summer's end expresses how far and extensive excursionists might travel in attempts to "conquer" enemy spirits in prison: "[T]o day two large Steam boats from Buffalow loded with men & women all to see the bluddy Secesh on Johnson's Island." Speer concluded his passage with sentiments probably shared by most of his fellow comrades: "[O]ur sperits to day our high on exchange."[43]

The prisoner-of-war experience at Johnson's Island was a special phenomenon cast upon the middle western home front due to the prison's large officer population, not found at other Northern compounds. Union war leaders paid close attention to its care and protection, as did Confederate espionage agents setting out to free the confined Confederate intelligentsia. Civilians were not supposed to enter into the military picture, and not allowed in, they instead passed leisurely by as prisoners' days grew longer and more uncertain. Feelings of exploitation mixed with indignity may have curtailed Southern pride, but these men were held to a higher standard compared to other prisoners of war; undoubtedly humiliated, they would not act out like those at the enlisted men's camps in Elmira, New York, and Chicago. There, prisoners would respond with obscene gestures or role-playing as animals in a circus. The captives being perceived as oddities rather than prisoners demonstrates these civilians' indifference toward the Southerners' plight, but these Great Lakes excursion-boat episodes seem unrivaled in comparison to other confines and most likely magnified due to the class of men held captive. The "Southern gentry" would vindicate themselves by the symbolic displaying of flags for excursionists to see. Confederate flags, white flags, red flags, and black flags were hung out windows or waved. Black flags were especially emblematic as a gesture that could be interpreted in many ways. For prisoners Speer and Mayo, the flags were a symbol of racial disdain for African Americans and a symbol of disdain for Northerners, the latter of whom, Speer and Mayo believed, were in close alignment with the former. Such demonstrations did not sit well with Northerners and the hardening of war. Captain Orr's excursionists on the *Island Queen* saw that Southerners "waved white signals and one ore two ostentatiously paraded black ones."[44] The *Cleveland Herald* reported what excursionists on the *May Queen* saw: "Some of the rebels waved from the windows as good stars and bars as they could extemporize and a few apologies for flags as black as their cause and their hearts."[45] Excursionists down the road from Fremont seemed especially upset. The *Fremont Journal* described, "As the Island Queen, loaded with excursionists from this place on Tuesday last, passed the Rebel headquarters, J. I., our troops cheered the music, but the rebels from one window displayed and waved a black flag, and from another window a blood red flag was flaunted out. We have seen the black flag hung out down South, but never anticipated seeing it in Ohio. Why do our officers in charge of the rebels allow such things? Were we on guard, we'd instantly shoot down the rebel who dared to offer such an insult."[46] The *Plymouth Advertiser* also queried as to why "[t]he rebel flag is permitted to float on Johnson's Island, over the prisoners' quarters, and that loyal soldiers who chafe at the disgrace, are not permitted to take it down?" The paper asked for help: "Do not our neighbors of the Sandusky *Register* know anything of the matter?"[47]

The *Register* seemed somewhat diplomatic: "[W]e cannot well refuse to answer as far as we have information. Besides, these questions are provoking discussion and remarks all about us. No formal flag floats over the prisoner's quarters, but extemporized rebel flags have been permitted to hang out from windows of prisoners quarters as well as extemporized black flags. How the officers regard them, we know not, but presume they pay no attention. . . . [W]e have no control over the prisoners. . . . [W]e presume those in authority will do as they think best. If the prisoners over there had charge of a lot of Yankees in Dixie, they would hardly permit display of the stars and stripes by them." Years after the war had ended, an excursionist remembered, "We were devoted to picnics in those days, the islands in the lake being the objective point. While passing the pen some of our lovers of music would indulge in patriotic songs—"John Brown's Body," etc., being a favorite one. Our island guests exhibited their appreciation of the compliment by hanging out a pair of black pantaloons."[48]

In the end, perhaps, the excursionists were justified in attempting to get their glimpse into prison life on Johnson's Island. After all, it afforded a sight that could not been seen in any other stockade, Union or Confederate. Johnson's Island had one of the most diverse prison-camp populations during the Civil War. Its walled-in community housed prisoners from generals to privates, guerillas to political prisoners, African American servants that followed masters into captivity to a Native American, and even a woman—who dressed as a man in order to gain acceptance into the army. Subsequently, the "man" gave birth "to a 'bouncing boy'" within the prison walls and consequently had her cover blown. The local press could not help but tease: "This is the first instance of a father giving birth we have heard of; nor we have read of it 'in the books,'" then followed up by wondering if the U.S. government was going to pay for the child's rations.[49] Even prisoners realized the significance of their captivity, as many of Johnson Island diarists kept autograph sections in their works or had separate albums signed by the highest ranking prisoners to the lowest, both militarily and socially. Indeed, for the curious outsider looking inside, the high expectations of seeing such captivating captives might make the excursion admission ticket seem worth the price.

Notes

1. Even libraries, repositories, and presses add to a pattern developed by lumping prison titles with those of medical and hospital studies. A popular culture analysis notices movies, such as *Gone with the Wind, Sommersby,* and *Andersonville,* focusing on pens with high death rates. When a well-known Civil War artist was approached with the question why he had not taken his craft to a prison or guard scene, his response was, "It would never sell."

2. See Ovid L. Futch, "Advancing Andersonville: Ovid L. Futch as Prison Camp Micro-Monograph Pioneer," in *History of Andersonville Prison,* rev. ed. (Gainesville: University Press of Florida, 2011) for a recent assessment of Civil War prison historiography with special emphasis on the micromonograph.

3. Two Civil War prison books deal briefly with the viewing of captives. See George Levy, *To Die in Chicago: Confederate Prisoners at Camp Douglas, 1862–65* (Gretna, LA: Pelican, 1999), 301–3, and Michael P. Gray, *The Business of Captivity: Elmira and Its Civil War Prison* (Kent, OH: Kent State University Press, 2001), 23–26.

4. *Sandusky (OH) Register,* August 20, 1891; U.S. Government, War Dept., *The War of the Rebellion: A Compilation of the Official Records of the Union and Confederate Armies,* 128 vols. (Washington, DC: GPO, 1880–1901), ser. II, 348:56–57. Hereafter cited as *OR*.

5. *Sandusky (OH) Register,* August 20, 1891.

6. Ibid.; "Civil War Days in Sandusky," Johnson's Island file, Sandusky Public Library, Sandusky, Ohio.

7. *OR,* 54–55; *Sandusky (OH) Register,* August 20, 1891.

8. *Sandusky (OH) Register,* August 20, 1891; *OR,* 55–58.

9. Ibid.

10. *Sandusky (OH) Register,* December 14, 1861.

11. *Toledo (OH) Blade,* October 31, 1861. Fort Lafayette in New York harbor was one of the earliest Union prisons.

12. *Sandusky (OH) Register,* August 20, 1891; *OR,* 56–57.

13. *Sandusky (OH) Register,* November 25 and December 4, 1861; Johnson's Island Prison Fund, Ohio History Center, Columbus, Ohio. L. B. Johnson was paid $19.75 for his lime, and Pool and Miner paid $184.80 for oil. "Letters Received to Quartermaster Reid," entry 11, record group 249, National Archives, Washington, DC.

14. *Sandusky (OH) Register,* January 23 and February 3, 1862.

15. Ibid., December 4, 1861, March 15 and 18, 1862.

16. After a lengthy selection process, Brooks found the *Princess* to be "better adapted for the business of the Post." "Water Transportation 1834–1900," record group 92, Office of the Quartermaster General, National Archives, Washington, D.C. Bristol also earned $59 for transporting mail to the post. The *Island Queen* would also assist in ferrying prisoners to the island. *Sandusky (OH) Register,* September 12, 1862, March 31, 1863.

17. *Sandusky (OH) Register,* April 10 and 11, 1862; *Columbus Ohio State Journal,* April 9, 1862.

18. *Sandusky (OH) Register,* April 18, 1862. One railroad bill for prisoner travel amounted to $145.82, paid to the Sandusky, Dayton, and Cincinnati Railroad in late 1862. "Johnson's Island Prison Fund, Nov.–Jan.," Johnson's Island File, Ohio History Center, Columbus.

19. Robert Bingham, diary, July 22, 1863, Southern Historical Collection, University of North Carolina, Chapel Hill.

20. *Cleveland (OH) Herald*, June 27, 1862; *Sandusky (OH) Register*, June 28, 1862.

21. *Sandusky (OH) Register*, April 21, 1862.

22. Ibid., April 25 and 28, 1862.

23. Levy, *To Die in Chicago*, 31, 301.

24. Gray, *Business of Captivity*, 23–26.

25. *Cleveland (OH) Leader*, June 5, 1862; *Sandusky (OH) Register*, June 22 and 24, 1862. Captain Viger helmed the *May Queen*.

26. *Cleveland (OH) Herald*, June 25, 1862.

27. *Sandusky (OH) Register*, June 30, 1862.

28. *Cleveland (OH) Herald*, June 27, 1862; *Sandusky (OH) Register*, June 28, 1862.

29. *Sandusky (OH) Register*, June 30, 1862.

30. Ibid., July 4, 1862.

31. Ibid., August 1 and 22, 1862.

32. Ibid., September 3, 1862.

33. Ibid., September 15, 1862.

34. Ibid., August 4, 1863; William Henry Asbury Speer, diary, December 31, 1864, in "A Confederate Soldier's View of Johnson's Island Prison," *Ohio History* 79, no. 2 (1970): 109. Local citizen Marie M. Stowell wrote to her sister at the end of December and seemed unimpressed by the islanders: "Have been over to Johnson's Island once to see the rebs but could only see them from a distance. To my unpractised eyes they looked very much like any other body of men would shut up in an enclosure." Marie M. Stowell to Alida, December 31, 1864, TS, Johnson's Island File, Sandusky (Ohio) Public Library.

35. *Sandusky (OH) Register*, August 27, 1863, September 2, 1863, August 4, 1863; James Mayo, "Recollections, Reminiscences, Memories and Dreams: A Diary Written by Major James M. Mayo 1863–1864," August 22, 1863, TS, Special Collections, Robert W. Woodruff Library, Emory University.

36. *Sandusky (OH) Register*, September 30, 1862, November 10, 1864, August 17, 1863, August 14, 1863; *Cleveland (OH) Herald*, July 16, 1862.

37. *Sandusky (OH) Register*, September 15, 1862, August 22, 1862.

38. Horace Carpenter, "Plain Living at Johnson's Island," *Century* 41, no. 5 (1891): 710.

39. Joseph Mason Kern, diary, June 21, 1863, Southern Historical Collection, University of North Carolina, Chapel Hill.

40. W. A. Wash, *Camp Field and Prison Life; Containing Sketches of Service in the South and Experience, Incidents and Observations Connected with Almost Two Years' Imprisonment at Johnson's Island, Ohio, Where 3000 Confederate Officers Were Confined* (St. Louis, MO: Southwestern Book, 1870), 100, 142–43, 239–40, 158.

41. Speer, diary, June 30 and July 6, 1862.

42. Mayo, "Recollections, Reminiscences."

43. Speer, diary, August 2, 1862.

44. *Sandusky (OH) Register*, June 30, 1862.

45. *Cleveland (OH) Herald*, June 27, 1862.

46. *Fremont (OH) Journal* in *Sandusky (OH) Register*, June 28, 1862; *Sandusky (OH) Register*, August 5, 1862.

47. *Plymouth (OH) Advertiser* in *Sandusky (OH) Register*, August 15, 1862.

48. *Sandusky (OH) Register*, August 15, 1862, March 9, 1891.

49. Ibid., December 12, 1864.

"OURS IS THE HARDER LOT"

STUDENT PATRIOTISM AT THE UNIVERSITY
OF MICHIGAN DURING THE CIVIL WAR

Julie A. Mujic

According to the *Peninsular Courier*, a local newspaper of Ann Arbor, Michigan, students on the University of Michigan campus reacted excitedly in February 1862 to the news of General Ulysses S. Grant's capture of Fort Donelson. All but one student, that is. When confronted by an appointed committee of his peers who demanded an explanation, the law student defended his lack of spirited celebration. The newspaper reported that he "was constitutionally incapable of boo-booing at every telegraph report. As to his sentiments, he had a right to them and he meant to keep them." This answer was highly unsatisfactory to the other Michigan law students, who promptly hired a notary public to come to campus. The notary administered an oath of allegiance to the young men as a way for them to confirm their loyalty to the Union. All of the law students took the oath, including the one whose actions initiated the spectacle.[1]

If the patriotism of these University of Michigan college students was so intense and they felt the need to exhibit it in such an explicit manner, the natural question to ask is why these young, obviously military-age men did not enlist in the Union army and go forth onto the field of battle. Many of them surely did; in fact, more than half the graduating class of 1861 either immediately or eventually served in that capacity. Nonetheless, the university's enrollment grew in the midst of war. In 1860, the University of Michigan boasted more than 670 students.

By the 1865–66 school year, over 1,200 young men registered for classes at Michigan, thus surpassing Harvard as the nation's largest university. While the war may have dismantled many schools across the country, the University of Michigan moved forward in a remarkable manner. This chapter considers how University of Michigan students during the war expressed their understanding of patriotism, the home front, and their role in the hostilities. By examining the shift from ambivalence about enlisting to a notion of patriotism that embraced education as the equivalent of military service, it is evident that most students at the University of Michigan found ways to justify the expressions of nationalism available to them on campus. This study explores the change that occurred in student perspectives on patriotism by the middle of the war and then analyzes the ways in which students utilized university resources to "practice" for what they believed would be their eventual positions on the national stage.[2]

Certainly, university students were a small, distinctive subset of the nation's white, male population. These young students often related to the war in ways different from others in American society. Moreover, far from the throes of battle, college students had a unique opportunity to explore their own maturation process while learning about the world outside of their parents' homes. When a young man arrived at school, often barely eighteen years of age, he learned to take pride in his associations with groups outside of his immediate family. He joined a fraternity, a literary society, or the campus choir. He made friends with others in his same course of study or with his fellow student-residents at a local boardinghouse. For those who came to a university during the American Civil War, circumstances forced them to ponder the pros and cons of staying in school versus enlisting to serve their country. For those who left, it was often a decision weighed down by the knowledge of what they might sacrifice, the money they had worked so hard to raise for tuition, the future that had been so carefully planned, or, like many others, the loved ones they would leave behind. Some left in a passion and never looked back. Others returned later, hopeful that they could pick up the pieces and still achieve their intellectual goals.

As the war progressed, many University of Michigan students made very conscious decisions to pursue their studies rather than enlist in the military. These were not easy choices. A small but vocal segment of young men on campus eventually identified themselves as Copperheads and remained in school because of their ideological opposition to the government. Even those who considered themselves loyal to their new Republican president initially felt ambivalent regarding military duty. However, by the middle of the war, the self-doubt of this latter group disappeared, and they became inclined to rationalize their continued enrollment by arguing that their education at a university of such rising prominence would serve as preparation for their future leadership in the nation. They recognized that there would be a period of postwar reconstruction and intended to use their schooling to build the foundation for their roles in that next era. University of Michigan students engaged their fraternities or literary societies as vehicles through which to practice debating decisions of the national government, including passing judgment on military matters. Even if these men did not intend to become national politicians, they believed that the best citizens in any profession were active, well-educated, political participants. They valued education as the primary tool for shaping the general population into a loyal citizenry and viewed their own intellectual development as the first step in being able to teach the masses.

Rather than portraying patriotism as purely the province of the soldier, many young men at the University of Michigan defined it in alternate ways that mirrored their own home-front experience. Their devotion to their country became, over the course of the years, indistinguishable from pride in their university. In some cases, students went so far as to compare the growth in size and prestige of the University of Michigan to the fate or progress of their nation at war; they believed that their patriotic duty included being a part of the university's success. The students sometimes implied that this version of duty was a contribution equal to that of the soldier. Historian Melinda Lawson argues that Abraham Lincoln believed "the blood sacrifice of the soldiers defined the highest type of patriotism." Surely, Michigan college students heard his rhetoric and understood how their president characterized national duty. However, Lawson further notes, "[T]he notion that loyalty to country entailed sacrifice did not always come easily to Americans." Despite widespread encouragement to join the ranks and serve their country, University of Michigan students managed to assure themselves that their collegiate educations also distinguished them as patriots.

Understandably, these young men sought to justify their decision to remain in school. All men of military age during the Civil War era were motivated to go to war or stay at home by a variety of reasons. Copperheads often continued in school as a way to express their opposition to the war and, in so doing, sometimes drew hostile criticism from pro-Union students and the community at large. Others who resolutely supported Lincoln and his party believed that their interests were best served by comparing themselves favorably to those fighting in the war. Through this choice of rhetoric, these aspiring leaders pursued the ideological course that they felt best positioned them to be significant contributors in the postwar period. The students quickly recognized that soldiers had the opportunity to earn glory and prove their manhood on the battlefield, so they adjusted the way that they depicted their own learning experiences in the classroom to incorporate the patriotic and manly qualities they believed Americans valued in soldiers. These promising scholars had an opportunity to be a part of something thriving; they took pride in their personal potential and the success of their university as a way to offset any criticism that might come their way for not enlisting in the army.[3]

The University of Michigan was one of six institutions of higher education in the state of Michigan before the Civil War. It was by far the most distinguished and it attracted students from nearly every state in the country. The territorial government initially founded the university in Detroit in 1817, but following several reorganizations, the institution moved to Ann Arbor in 1837. Its location in the northern part of the Midwest isolated this university from the physical destruction of the Civil War. The state did not, however, escape the region's notorious political and ideological conflicts between those loyal to the government and the raucous opposition of local Copperheads. Michigan residents, and by extension the students at its state university, were not immune to the turmoil that occurred in surrounding states like Ohio and Indiana, although the pro-Southern posture that held sway in much of lower Ohio, Indiana, and Illinois did not permeate Michigan's boundaries. Instead, prominent New York transplants largely shaped the culture of the town and the university. One Empire State native, Dr. Henry P. Tappan, served as president of the University of Michigan from 1852 until 1863. He oversaw important developments at the school during the prewar era, including a significant increase in enrollment and the opening of a law school. On the eve of war, most students embraced the faculty's political ideologies and enjoyed a promising economic and social relationship with the five thousand residents of Ann Arbor. Faculty encouraged, even expected, antislavery attitudes but did not promote an abolitionist agenda. In fact, students and townspeople drove traveling abolitionist speakers from the village prior to the war. The majority of

Michigan's students supported Lincoln in the election of 1860 and, as the nation succumbed to civil war, reflected the community's eastern influences regarding increasing hostility toward the South.[4]

After the fall of Fort Sumter, Tappan called on the students to organize themselves into military companies, hired someone to train them, set aside university property for practice, and made it clear that he expected them to drill daily. Tappan and another student favorite, history professor Andrew D. White, persuaded most of the students who were preparing to graduate that spring to wait until after commencement to enlist. For those not graduating, the war raised difficult choices. White recalled that in the fall of 1861, two students struggled with the decision of whether to enlist or continue with school. They had saved money for years to pay for college and hesitated to walk away from their dreams. White later recounted, "They could resist their patriotic convictions no longer." The students woke him up early one morning to say good-bye and departed for the army. These two men could not separate their understanding of patriotism from military duty in a time of war. For others, even this initial period of excitement in 1861 did not make enough of an impression. In November 1861, John Bennitt, a medical student, wrote home to his wife that army service did not appeal to him: "I am not very anxious to go into the Army, unless you can go along. Still I will if duty calls. . . . I shall however remain here as long as I can, for the opportunities here are too good to be lost."[5]

Many of the young students were not willing or able to make the decision alone. It is not surprising that the influence of home and parents still held significant sway in something as important as the decision to go to war and the abandonment of the pursuit of an education. Students anticipated that their parents would have strong views on the subject and often did not feel it appropriate to make the choice without consulting them. Immediately following the outbreak of hostilities, Stanton B. Thomas, a sophomore from Schoolcraft, Michigan, wrote home to his mother and inquired, "How does father feel about war? The citizens here had a meeting yesterday and appointed a committee to take the names of volunteers. The students have got up a large company. Don't know but I shall join it?" Presumably, the reply was not favorable, because Thomas graduated with his bachelor of science degree in 1864. Some were more determined in their requests. Joseph V. Quarles, a freshman from Kenosha, Wisconsin, implored his mother in November 1862, "Wm English writes that Col. Lane wants me to take the position of

Adjutant. . . . How I wish you would let me accept it! Although I am much pleased with this institution it would please me more to stake my life in my country's cause—The present time seems one inappropriate to be devoted to one's self when the common interests of mankind are at stake and when the future of our country depends upon the exertions of the American Youth."[6] Many young men who were strongly in favor of leaving school to enlist still requested a parental blessing before making such a decision.

After the war began in earnest, the students were aware that other civilians and soldiers might question their choice to remain at the University of Michigan. Self-consciously, the fraternities published their annual magazine, the *Palladium*, in December 1861 with the following editorial: "Amid the din of a nation at war . . . it is not without some misgivings that the PALLADIUM ventures to present its humble attractions to the world. We are deeply impressed with the fact that we belong to the class of 'nobodies,' who stay at home; and with all-becoming modesty, we publish our names, merely to satisfy agonizing friends and parents that we have not all 'gone to the wars.'" A later *Palladium* editorial, written by Lincoln T. Farr of Michigan and Edward D. W. Kinne of New York, submitted, "Many whose names the Palladium of '62 proudly published to the College world as among the ardent devotees at our 'shrine of Learning' will now be found in the ranks of the army. A less warlike, perchance less patriotic and ambitious class, still remain at the University." These early years reveal that there was a sense of embarrassment running through campus, enough that students felt the necessity to articulate it through a written medium that would be saved for posterity. These thoughts were likely representative of the student body, as egregious distortions would have incurred the disapproval of others enrolled. In this way, the *Palladium* editors succeeded in reflecting the perspectives of their fellow students and giving readers some idea of the state of affairs at the Ann Arbor campus.[7]

In addition to the internal struggle they felt pressed to explain to others, students at the University of Michigan also had to address the way they were preparing for war on campus. "To our friends who may be surprised at the absence of all military organizations, suffice it to say, that we are possessing our souls in patience until the arrival of a new military professor," explained the students in the December 1861 *Palladium*. The board of regents had passed a resolution earlier in 1861 to pursue the creation of a military department, and while waiting for that situation to flesh out, the students felt that the pause in their drilling companies was a "necessary delay" given the circumstances. Their defensiveness of the situation is palpable, as they wrote in their annual publication that they hoped their explanation "will account for all apparent deficiencies in that respect at present." The students hoped to have a professor with more military experience rather than the "mere drill-master" President Tappan provided upon the outbreak of war. The three student companies formed after the fall of Fort Sumter "served their purpose admirably, and supplied an immediate want, that of drill." Such experience "enabled those who went from us at that time to take the positions which belong to those whom a long, arduous course of discipline had fitted to lead, rather than to follow." Nevertheless, outsiders must have been questioning the quiet coming from campus, as the fervor with which University of Michigan students drilled in the earliest days of war seemed to have diminished. The students attempted to reassure the public that their intentions were to continue to train for war, but they deemed mediocre drilling not worthy of their time. They instead chose to do nothing until the state provided funding for suitable military professors. Thus, even as early as the first winter of war, the students who remained on campus blended the war into their paradigm of education. They were no longer driven by a passion for war but felt that only methodical, professional instruction should shape their wartime preparation.[8]

Students also struggled with how to participate in the Union effort from within the confines of Ann Arbor. An author in the Literary Adelphi literary-society journal, the *Hesperian*, lamented in his 1862 article "The Soldier," "Half a million and more are in the field and we are left behind. The great struggle for liberty and the Constitution is being fought; and we are quietly looking on expecting & hoping to enjoy the triumph without helping to gain the victory." An Alpha Nu member remarked in a welcome message at the start of a new term that the young men returned to school in the fall "fresh from the scenes and pleasures of home aloof from the cares of political anxiety, & far from the dangers of the 'tented field.'" Medical student Francis Thomas, a Quaker from Maryland, referred to the war in a letter as "the great game on the chessboard of the union," which "those of us who stand off out of danger" could only follow through newspapers. These young men recognized that their involvement in the nation's challenge would be from a distance.[9]

Many University of Michigan students thus demonstrated their patriotism through their sense of duty on the home front. As one Alpha

Nu member asserted, the students understood that "to be hopeful is our duty." The editor of the *Hesperian* wrote in 1862 that although they could not directly witness the war and feel the emotions that accompany victory or defeat, "does it follow from this, that we can take no part in the conflict? that we have no duties to perform? No! certainly not. Every American of today has a duty to perform. The present should be a time of labor, of activity, of industry, of economy & of self-sacrifice." In his view, the home front was responsible for providing for the needs of the soldiers in the fields and of the families who were left behind with potentially decreased resources. He implored his fellow classmates to assist, both financially and emotionally, those neighbors whose sons, fathers, brothers, and husbands were off fighting. These actions would fulfill their "duty" and "bring honor to the American cause."[10]

One of the ways in which Michigan students felt they were supplying assistance to their nation was through the promotion of education. They consistently asserted that education could aid the country in its current plight and decrease the chances of future national crises. This line of thinking provided both a justification for the students' personal choices regarding enlistment and a way to help them to define their contribution to the nation's cause. In an 1863 article in the Alpha Nu literary-society magazine, *Sibyl*, student William B. Hendryx of Ann Arbor defines patriotism as "that feeling of attachment, which we all possess for the land that gave us birth. It is a nation's bulwark and without it no government can exist. Within the hearts of the people, lies the strength of the nation." He gave an example from Roman times of a soldier who was willing to put the fate of Rome above his own life, ultimately arguing that "the great aim of the American education" should be to instill this devotion in the citizenry. In the fall of 1865, when discussing questions of Reconstruction, Alpha Nu members reasoned that the ignorance of Southerners was one of the most influential factors in causing the war and strongly suggested that the national government focus on educating the Southern populace "for our <u>own</u> safty . . . for <u>their own</u> good. . . . Education is the cornerstone of a republican government when the poor whites and blacks are able to read and understand loyal papers, <u>then</u> they will be <u>loyal</u> citizens." The students even declared that placing an army in the former Confederacy to enforce Reconstruction would be uncalled for "if the masses are <u>properly educated</u>."[11] As part of their own growing belief that education defined their respective contributions to the war, these young men insisted on it as crucial for the rest of the American populace.

The students pursued this spread of education within their own home front in Ann Arbor by inviting speakers to address the public on important topics of the day. Faculty, students, and residents attended the presentations, which were often held in a local church. For example, in 1863, the Students' Lecture Association hosted, among others, Major General Cassius M. Clay, who spoke on the Emancipation Proclamation. The following year, Edmund Kirke, author of *My Southern Friends*, came to Ann Arbor and gave a talk, "The Southern Whites." Author Anna E. Dickinson spoke in 1864 on that year's presidential election, and Benjamin F. Taylor, a journalist for Chicago's *Evening Journal*, came to talk about his observations at Missionary Ridge. The students took their task very seriously and, in fact, stationed themselves around the room, armed with clubs, to allow the controversial abolitionist Wendell Phillips to get through his entire oration in 1862. Even if the young men could not travel south to begin educating the masses immediately, they adhered to their convictions by offering intellectual programs for the university community.[12]

As the University of Michigan students gradually formulated ways to associate themselves with the attributes assigned to soldiers, they began to mix the praise they offered of those who left to become soldiers with reassurances that the school and the men who stayed were also flourishing. In the fall of 1861, Illinois native Theodore Hurd and Reinzi Baker of Michigan, serving as editors of the *Palladium*, offset their inner struggle about remaining at home by linking their personal sense of nationalism with the success of the university: "Our corps of professors is full, classes well nigh swell to their accustomed numbers, and society halls are crowded. But that this is to be imputed to our prosperity, and not to our lack of patriotism, let our 'Army List' show." After less than one year of war, the students differentiated between their contribution on the home front and that of their fellow student-soldiers in the field, stating that those still in Ann Arbor "watch their careers with jealous eyes. . . . Ours is the harder lot, to stay behind, and envy their noble, patriotic self-sacrifice, and their destined honorable reward, whether the soldier's death, or the conqueror's wreath." The students who stayed behind initially expressed frustration at their position as outsiders to the country's martial endeavors but began to articulate their own claim for recognition by invoking the achievements of their college.[13]

Early in the war, the students were more overt in their acknowledgment of the space that separated them from their soldier brethren.

Many of the young men who returned to the university in the fall of 1861 would have known those who chose to forfeit their education to join the army. They were classmates, fraternity brothers, and friends. By the later years, it was not as often that fellow students left school for the battlefield. Instead, most who chose to enlist never began at the university in the first place. Thus, the group of young men who toiled over their books instead of marching with their weapons seemed to have felt further removed from outside judgment than those students who matriculated in late 1861.

The shifting ideology on the part of the students, which made the university the main beneficiary of their affection and honor, was reinforced in June 1863 when the board of regents fired President Tappan after a protracted power struggle. That fall, amid the uproar caused by the unexpected change at the school's helm, the students merely offered a passing comment about the war in their annual fraternity publication. Even then, their brief acknowledgment of the national situation was immersed in rhetoric about the college's greatness. The *Palladium*'s editors likened the "mighty upheavals" of the formerly calm "University sea" to a "clap of thunder from a clear sky" and attributed the frenzy of the prior year in equal parts to Tappan's removal and the "great commotion and turmoil in the great body politic of the nation." The young men of Alpha Nu wrote an emotional editorial in their society journal about the board's action, reflecting the general perspective of the student body. Interestingly, the irate students chose distinctly martial language to express their displeasure. This choice of prose indicates that the students had adapted to living in a world surrounded by references to war and by 1863 found it suitable to appropriate that vocabulary in order to explain their own daily lives. The Alpha Nu piece warned returning students that the "realm of [their] miniature world has been invaded." As change threatened to alter the sense of security offered by the university, the students reacted by defending the institution and its honor, which they associated with Tappan. Their numerous petitions to the board of regents, demanding a reversal of the decision and Tappan's reinstatement, were met with hostility and condescension. The personal war undertaken in Ann Arbor between the students and the board ended in disappointment, as the board told the students to "attend to our books like good boys."[14]

As their idea of patriotism grew more intertwined with the prestige of the university, there was great concern among the students that they properly represent the institution. They felt that their role as students contributed an essential element to what made the school "the third institution of learning in our land" by the middle of the war. The editor of the Alpha Nu semi-weekly journal, the *Sibyl*, noted that the class of 1863 graduated "to join in the good work of those who have preceded them, to do as we trust no dishonor but win laurels for their Alma Mater." As these young men pursued their education, they were protective of their individual reputations and proud to link their names as a group to the University of Michigan. They were quick to defend their school's unique characteristics and were vigilant in monitoring the actions of classmates. In 1863, about thirty-five students went to Windsor, Canada, to see Clement L. Vallandigham, the notorious Copperhead leader from Ohio. William M. Hayes, a Pennsylvania native and a junior in the Law Department, identified the group as being part of the "democratic-copperhead school" and wrote home about the reaction the incident received from the rest of the student body: "[T]he democratic papers throughout this and other western states have published that the students of the University of Michigan visited [Vallandigham] and to counteract this impression the opposition held a meeting yesterday forenoon. It was attended by several hundred of the students and strong resolutions were passed condemning these actions."[15]

This Copperhead presence on campus cannot be overlooked. It was a significant threat to the unity of the students in the development of their wartime ideology of education as patriotism. At points during the war, actions such as this student-led pilgrimage to see a noted Copperhead leader endangered their joint promotion and defense of their enrollment at the university and its growing prestige. Gideon Winan Allen, an outspoken Copperhead student in the Law Department, wrote to his girlfriend, Annie, about the matter. In describing the students' visit to Vallandigham, which he did not attend, Allen insisted that it was "conducted in a modest unostentatious way" and that "it was nobody's business but their own." A student named Henry, in a letter to his mother regarding the same event, wrote regretfully, "[N]othing on earth but poverty hindered my going [to see Vallandigham]." When "<u>loyal</u> students" called a meeting at the university in response, Allen invited his fellow student Democrats to hold their own gathering in order to articulate their position to the public. The faculty tried to suppress the rising tensions by forbidding student political meetings on campus, but that only forced the determined students into a hall in Ann Arbor, where they had a rousing few hours of speeches, music, and resolutions. The zealous Copperheads, which Allen counted at around three hundred, then formed a procession and marched through the town and the campus chanting and cheering for the Union and Vallandigham.[16]

Conditions became so tense during the height of Copperhead activism in the Midwest that at one point, Allen believed that some students with opposing political views would eventually challenge him to a duel. In his letters, he recorded numerous heated confrontations between himself and other students and town residents. Nonetheless, Unionist student reaction to the Copperhead outcry on campus was not always purely emotional. The young men who took offense to what they perceived as disloyalty mostly did so using the same outlets of academic life in which they analyzed the war overall. In a journal of the Literary Adelphi society in January 1864, one student wrote an essay criticizing foreign intervention in the Civil War. As a part of his discussion, he asserted, "we shall never again see the nation as it was. The nation, as a whole is passing through a revolution. Revolutions never go backwards." He called those who demanded "the Union as it was" "short sighted conservatives utterly unread in the progress of human events." Slavery and freedom, the two cornerstones of the republic, were incompatible and were "as explosive as gunpowder and fire." "Thank God such a Union is gone, gone forever," exclaimed this ardent literary-society member, "though we cannot have the old one we will have a better." Students who criticized the Copperheads often cited the latter group's inability to understand the country's circumstances as unalterably moving in the direction of revolutionary change. Historian Jennifer L. Weber aptly asserts that it "remains unclear to this day how [Copperheads] expected the nation to return to the *status quo ante bellum*."[17]

Despite these frictions, it seems that students, whether Copperhead or loyal, agreed clearly on their distaste for conscription. As the Union army determined that drafting soldiers became necessary by 1862, the draft began to decide the fate of some students. For the remainder of the war, conscription was a threat that the students contemplated with mixed reactions. Hayes struggled with his reaction to the draft due to his sincere support for the purposes of the war. He wrote home in late 1863 about his dilemma, "Of course it would not be pleasant or convenient for me to go home to enter the army at the present time." Hayes asked his parents for their input should he be drafted, explaining that he could not oppose the draft because he "insist[s] on a prosecution of the war until . . . every slave is free." He did not trust himself to make the decision because he could not seem to reconcile his ideologies about the purpose of the war with the sacrifice that military service would require of his current academic pursuits. Hayes did not serve his country, by choice or by fate, and returned to Pennsylvania after graduation in 1864 to become a lawyer.[18]

In April 1863, John Hinchman, a freshman from Detroit, wrote to his mother about the students who had recently formed a battalion "for the purpose of learning the drill, in case we should all be drafted." He estimated that five hundred students participated in the one-hour practices, four nights per week. President Tappan remarked that this renewed endeavor by the students "caused no diversion from study, but [took] the place of recreation and questionable indulgences." It is telling that these students prepared to be drafted but did not go enlist of their own free will. However, by May, Hinchman reported to his mother, "Most of the fellows here have made up their minds to go into the army if they are drafted." Again, the point is *if* they were drafted but not otherwise. A resident of Ann Arbor wrote to a friend in July 1864, "[T]imes are here about as usual only that students are not quite so thick—all are excited about a draft and about every one is sure that he will have to go." Members of the student literary society Alpha Nu even proposed a debate in 1863 regarding whether university students should be exempt from the draft, but they never took a vote on the issue. They continued to prepare for the possibility of military service; in May 1863, the Literary Adelphi added three more books related to the conduct of war to its library.[19]

Especially by the middle part of the war when conscription threatened to remove unwilling students from classrooms and place them on the front lines, correspondence between the young men and their loved ones reveals a desire to remain apart from the conflict. Sometimes this was due to political ideology. Henry, the young man who expressed such deep disappointment at not being able to journey with his classmates to see Vallandigham, wrote to reassure his mother, "I don't worry about [the draft], as I have about come to the conclusion that God Almighty never intended that I should fight for the 'poor nigger.'" Allen, the Copperhead law student, received letters during this period from his girlfriend, Annie, about her fear that he would be called in the upcoming draft. "Suppose you should be one of the fated," she wondered, "I will not think of it." In addition to her pleas that his serving in the war would be too hard on her, Annie also tells him she does not believe him to be "strong enough for camp life." Later that year, her mother even expressed panic to Allen about the issue: "Do <u>anything, everything</u> to prevent it [being drafted] except that which is dishonorable. . . . <u>I could not</u> give up <u>my darling boy!</u> . . . No, it <u>cannot, must not</u> be."[20]

Allen took a hard stance toward the draft. After his name was collected during the conscription-enrollment process, he wrote to Annie in June 1863, "If I am drafted you may be sure of one thing, there will be a battle soon after. Perhaps, though, I'll just make a speech denouncing the administration and the war. . . . I'll be arrested, have a mock trial, make myself notorious, be sent South, refuse to take the oath of allegiance to the Confederacy, and be sent back, <u>a la</u> Vallandigham." Allen did not support the draft nor sympathize with its intentions. He was content with his political views and not hesitant to express them. "This much I think I may venture to say," he concluded with vigor, "at all events, that this war is an abomination in sight of God and honest men; and that our government is in the hands of either fools or traitors." Although a devout Republican, Annie agreed with his revulsion with the draft. Her concern continued through the summer and fall as various conscription acts pulled more young men from the North. Allen assured her that he would buy an exemption from serving, mainly because his feelings were too strong against the war. The draft "is not among my troubles," he promised Annie in September 1863, "and I hope you will think of it no more." Though faced with the prospect of conscription several times during the war, Allen did not receive a summons to serve during the conflict.[21]

Not all students were as pensive on the subject. University of Michigan law student Charles B. Howell from Pontiac wrote to his brother, "I suppose the draft which commences to-day will 'gobble' me up, and then I shall perhaps wish I had got insured for exemption." Howell guessed right, he was drafted, but the next month, he returned to Ann Arbor after having arranged for a substitute. By early 1864, Howell seemed carefree, declaring to his brother, "I am in the most excellent health, and the world moves here pretty much in consonance with my wishes." Students could have chosen to return home to enlist in their local regiment or to join Ann Arbor residents in attempting to fulfill the community's soldier quota and avoid a draft. Yet, despite Ann Arbor's offers of bounties for this purpose, many students stayed in school. If drafted, it appears that some found ways, probably through their parents, to pay for a substitute. The rest did not find the country's apparent need for more soldiers in the field compelling enough to leave what they increasingly considered their own patriotic work as university students.[22]

Other students viewed conscription with dread because they had already served a term in the army and were in no hurry to return. Quarles, the underclassman who had begged his mother to allow him to enlist early in the war, served in a Hundred Days' regiment in the summer of 1864. As his term was ending, Quarles decided not to reenlist and instead to return to school. In a letter to his mother, the young man wrote disdainfully about the draft, remarking that it would be "just my fortune" to have to serve under those circumstances. He feared that the chances of finding a substitute were hopeless, causing "a poor fellow [to] 'tote' a musket." Disillusionment with the prospect of soldiering plagued students on the home front as it did other Northerners by the end of the war.[23]

In addition to the threat of the draft, students at the University of Michigan also dealt with how their decision to remain in school affected the "quest for manhood." Historian Lorien Foote calls this pursuit "a central question . . . in the Civil War era" and argues that manhood "indicated an achievement rather than an innate nature that all biological males possessed." These students surely felt that their education symbolized a significant level of personal accomplishment, but the war complicated this notion. Suddenly, the successes for which they strove may not have been the feats and triumphs valued by the larger American society. By late summer 1861, the young men who had been motivated to join the war from their hearts, or for other reasons, had already done so. Others waited, perhaps for parental permission, while some considered their decision regarding enlistment from a different perspective. Spurred not by a hatred of slavery or a sense of duty, these students, like many other American men, instead waited to determine the level of personal benefit that would come from fighting in the war. What they sought was associations with the war that would further the public's perception of them as gentlemen. Charles L. Watrous, a junior at University of Michigan from Freetown, New York, implored White, his professor and fellow Empire State native, regarding an officer commission in August 1861. Despite a letter of recommendation from Tappan, Watrous had failed to obtain a commission from the state of Michigan. If he enlisted in Michigan, Watrous would face "carrying a musket, which I don't feel just ready to do." Quite sure that he "had the material of which officers are made," Watrous wrote to White to see if the professor had any connections back in their home state. Although it was obvious that the young man sought individual recognition before he would lower himself to join the military rank and file, he tried to persuade White to respond quickly, as "at present, it is very hard to work to 'keep cool' and study." Soon, however, students who remained at the university argued that they were still developing the traits of those who left to fight.[24]

Indeed, by 1863, students came to assert that their involvement in the University of Michigan's achievements was an accomplishment equal to that of valor on the battlefield. *Palladium* editors Farr and Kinne boasted that year that though some may consider the students a "less patriotic and ambitious class" than those in the ranks of the army, "the fact that our zeal continues unabated, the labors of our several Professors untiring and successful, and that our number, although somewhat diminished, exceeds that of many institutions located nearer the Atlantic;—these facts speak eloquently in commendation of the present flourishing condition, and the encouraging prospects of our University." They even linked the courage former students demonstrated on the battlefield as inspiring those who remained in Ann Arbor to rededicate themselves to their studies in order to prove that "college life has not yet 'begun to swoon.'" These descriptive choices highlight the negotiation underway by the students to ally themselves with the manly characteristics ascribed to their compatriots on the battlefield. The students also refuted any suggestions that remaining on campus challenged their manhood. They described life on campus in ways that conjured up images of strength and endurance and used gendered language to emphasize further that their continued presence on the home front was not feminizing them. In fact, they shaped an argument by which their education provided them the manly qualities that they perceived the public likely believed they could only obtain by fighting.[25]

In 1864, this assertion about the increasing prestige of the university became more explicit. Confidence replaced self-consciousness regarding the attention of these young men to their education rather than to their possible national military duty in wartime. "Though the nation may be struggling for life," stated that year's *Palladium* editors, Scovel Stacy of Michigan and Schuyler Grant of Connecticut, "though the din of arms and roar of battle may greet us from without, though the noble sons of our Alma Mater are falling by scores in defence of their country's flag, yet the University of Michigan rides proudly on, buffeting the stormy waves, acquiring continually, strength, beauty and renown, an honor to the State, a center of learning for the great north-west, and an object of pride and reverence to her sons." This kind of prose encompassed the characteristics of manhood so sought by the young men of this generation; a university education now symbolized more than intellectual accomplishment. It provided strength, honor, pride, and beauty—all attributes of gentlemen and specifically during the Civil War terms used to pay tribute to Union officers and gloried soldiers.[26]

Whether for political or personal reasons, the initial hesitation students had about their role in the conflict was replaced by new ideas concerning their contributions to the nation's conflict. As the war passed its midpoint, the persistent theme in the students' discourse on patriotism, duty, and honor revolved specifically around their individual education at the University of Michigan. These young men believed that they were to become members of the future generation of leaders who would help the nation reconcile after the war. As the conflict progressed, the students spent less time bemoaning their dilemma regarding the choice between education and military duty and more time boasting of the invaluable role they would play in returning the country to greatness. In 1863, the *Palladium* described the students as "gratified, that in this the hour of our country's peril . . . the sons of Michigan, and of her sister States gathered together at this 'Western Athens,' are not found recreant to their sacred duties and obligations, as scholars, true patriots, and as sharers of the common blessings that our Government bestows." The fraternity members proclaimed confidently toward the end of the war that despite the failure to yet achieve peace, "the country is alive to her educational interests, and the coming generation will not be wanting in strong and cultivated minds." Hendryx filled his *Sibyl* article with inspirational prose about the destiny that undoubtedly lay ahead for University of Michigan graduates: "A shattered society will have to be reconstructed. . . . To shape the future destinies of this nation aright we shall need men of sterling worth and integrity . . . always supporting the cause of truth and justice upon the shoulders of the young men of to-day fall the burden. Let us prepare to receive it."[27]

Soon after the Union victory in 1865, the *Palladium*'s editor, Henry Smith of Johnstown, Ohio, spoke even more passionately regarding the advantages derived from an education at the University of Michigan. He argued that no school offered a better opportunity for someone who wanted to participate in the "profound knowledge and deep research" that would be necessary during Reconstruction. "No period of a young man's life is so important and critical as his years at college," the editor insisted. "Here is the turning point to future prosperity and usefulness, or to oblivion." According to these ambitious young Americans, four years spent in the military, defending the nation's Constitution, did not apparently measure up to a college education. And by way of further convincing themselves that their efforts in the classroom were as demanding and manly as time spent in uniform, the editor remarked that veterans who enrolled in the university in the fall of 1865 "have proved themselves as strenuous in the pursuits of education as they were valiant in war."[28]

During the war years, University of Michigan extracurricular clubs and organizations threw themselves into their patriotic public responsibilities. Literary societies especially concentrated their attention on current events, routinely staging rigorous debates and formal votes about contentious topics of the day. Essentially, University of Michigan students utilized these venues as a means by which to practice and hone their leadership skills. Their debates allowed them to examine and pass judgment on the political, economic, and military decisions made by their incumbent national government. By pretending to stand in the shoes of a Union general, President Lincoln, or Congress, these young men rehearsed how they would scrutinize and react to similar situations and began to build their agendas and ideas regarding the future direction of the country. Considering the changing patterns of their views also reveals how Michigan students actively shaped their involvement in the war despite their distance from it.

The Alpha Nu literary society followed a largely conservative Republican ideology. In 1860, the young men agreed that the concept of popular sovereignty was "unsound in theory and unsafe in practice." Following Lincoln's inauguration, they called for his government to end the secession movement with military force and supported the administration's request that General John C. Frémont modify his proclamation that liberated slaves in Missouri in 1861. Members of Alpha Nu did not accept emancipation as a military tactic but did believe that it should be required of the Southern states following their eventual defeat. Students debated several major national political decisions from the Trent Affair to foreign intervention in the war. In December 1862, they believed that separation from the South was better than a Union with slavery but the next month denied that the federal government should assume more centralized power during the war. Their position on slavery held the Republican line in 1862, as they found the abolition of slavery in Washington, D.C., acceptable and declared that the Emancipation Proclamation was "demanded by the exigencies of the times."

Alpha Nu members also supported Lincoln in the limitations he placed on the Northern press and his decision to withhold speedy trials for some of those arrested and imprisoned during the war.[29]

Military matters held special interest for these young men. For example, they debated the propriety of prisoner exchanges with the Confederacy, the decision to remove General George Brinton McClellan, and General William Tecumseh Sherman's order to evacuate civilians in Atlanta, Georgia. Abstract military ideas also piqued their attention. In May 1863, the students defeated a resolution that "a monarchy is better adapted than a Republic for successfully waging war." The next year, students disagreed that "victories are due more to the bravery of the soldier than to the skill of the general." One wonders whether their former classmates-turned-soldiers would have agreed. Foreign policy also received thoughtful attention; in April 1865, for example, the students resolved that the U.S. government should enforce the Monroe Doctrine against Maximilian's regime in Mexico.[30]

The Alpha Nu students' dedication to Lincoln was unwavering, and they agreed that he should retain his position in 1864. During the war and following Lincoln's assassination, the Alpha Nu *Sibyl* contained many poems and articles in tribute to their leader. "The Honest Man, our Saviour and our Friend, the Great Emancipator," one contributor mourned on April 21, 1865, "now lies enshrined. . . . Nature might stand up and say to all the world, <u>This was a man</u>." These young men consistently supported both Lincoln's political and military policies but clearly remained aloof from the more far-reaching aims of the left wing of his party. As the war came to a close and Republicans started to divide over questions of Reconstruction policies toward the rebellious states and the freed slaves, the conservative character of the Alpha Nu members' Republicanism became apparent. Twice in 1865 (February and September), members voted that blacks should not be granted the franchise. That fall, they voted against the idea that the Southern states formerly in rebellion should be reorganized as territories.[31]

Literary Adelphi followed an unmistakably different trajectory during the war era. These students began the secession period from a chiefly Democratic standpoint. Despite adopting a resolution that "neither Congress nor the legislature of a territory have the right to protect slave property in the territory," they upheld the decision to execute John Brown and contended that it was appropriate for states to nullify federal laws that they deemed unconstitutional. As 1861 opened, the students of this group called on the president to prepare Washington, D.C., for invasion but did not support the use of arms to put down the rebellion. Instead, the Literary Adelphi decided against the idea that "the separation of the gulf states would be detrimental to civilization." They declared that the Union should be preserved "as it is and the constitution as our fathers bequeathed it."[32]

Interestingly, though, the results of Literary Adelphi debates began to take a clear turn toward a Republican stance in the fall of 1861. At the start of the new term in October, these members declared support for Frémont's proclamation. Although they did not encourage wholesale emancipation when debated later that month, they decided by April 1862 "that the present condition and future prosperity of the country demand that the constitution be amended as to entirely exclude slavery within its limits." Again in April 1863, the students agreed that immediate abolition was necessary, and in October, they insisted that Congress should not accept a peace at war's end without complete emancipation. While their position on freedom appears consistent by the middle of the war, the students voted in March 1864 to support a prisoner exchange with the South "without regard to colored troops." Their political perspective, therefore, still adhered to the more moderate elements of the Republican Party.[33]

Throughout the war, Literary Adelphi members also debated military affairs and twice in 1862 declared that Lincoln should not remove McClellan from command of the Army of the Potomac. General Ambrose Everett Burnside, however, did not receive similar tolerance, as his failure at Fredericksburg prompted the students to encourage his dismissal in December of that year. They supported Lincoln in his suppression of the freedom of the press, in his suspension of the writ of habeas corpus, and in his decision to arrest and then banish Vallandigham. Only in May 1864 did this group finally decide that McClellan's removal was justified. Despite these pro-Lincoln tendencies, there appears to be a decided shift towards a Radical Republican stance in the Literary Adelphi hall during the last year of the war. In the fall of 1864, the students denounced the proposal that the government should arrange a peace conference to end the hostilities and, for the first time, took a critical position on a question about Lincoln: They found him at fault for the failures of McClellan's Peninsula campaign. Unlike their counterparts in the Alpha Nu, these young men twice voted in 1865 (April and November) to extend the right to vote to black men. In March 1866, the students sided with Radical Republicans in their denial of admission to representatives sent to Congress from the former Confederate states. These Literary Adelphi members traveled the furthest ground politically during the war era, from a Democratic viewpoint to that of the Radical Republicans.[34]

Both literary societies offered their members the opportunity to express their developing opinions in written form. Individual students wrote articles, poems, and stories to share with each other. During the war years, themes about the nation's plight dominated the pages. In 1861, one Literary Adelphi student outlined "our nation's duty" in his persuasive commentary on the need for immediate emancipation. He called slavery a "heaven-closing and man-degrading institution" and identified it as the cause of the war. These views were already somewhat ahead of the general opinion regarding abolition so early in the war, but the student leapt in front of popular discourse when he insisted, "[E]mancipate every negro and if need be put arms into their hands." His tone was confident, his demands clear, and his awareness of historical and current political exigencies exhibits the characteristics of leadership that these young men felt they needed to master. As the fall term commenced in 1865 and the postwar period started to take shape, Alpha Nu members began to articulate their self-proclaimed importance to the new era. "Armed resistance is vanquished," the students declared in their journal, "but reconstruction is not effected. Time alone can solve the problem; meanwhile we may exercise the right of American citizens—the privilege of recommending and suggesting our own views."[35]

When debating current events, members of both literary societies explored their positions on questions that would have been facing them had they been leaders in the national government, their own towns, or churches at that time. Their belief that an educated citizenry would guide the masses through Reconstruction drove their consistent return to these issues. They argued, played devil's advocate, prepared and gave speeches, and conducted their meetings in a manner that they felt would prepare them for their future responsibilities. Admittedly, throughout the period, these young men also entertained topics that had nothing to do with the war. They frequently deliberated on subjects such as the character of Oliver Cromwell, the intentions of the Church of Rome, the historical benefit of the Crusades, and whether "man is greater in his affection than in his intellect." The literary societies chose subjects from a broad spectrum of personal enhancement, economics, political history, and religion, to name a few. The propriety of protective tariffs, for example, repeatedly appeared for debate. But their regular interest in contemporary themes of national concern demonstrates that they considered themselves involved in the affairs of their country and engaged in those real-world situations as best they could from Ann Arbor. It is intriguing to note that although these young men agreed that their education and participation in debate societies like the Alpha Nu or Literary Adelphi shaped them for their inevitable positions among the highly regarded of their generation, these two groups came to represent the two opposing factions of the Republican Party. By the end of the war, the University of Michigan sent into the world educated and talented men who would essentially populate at least two of the major viewpoints on the political landscape.[36]

The demographic makeup of each organization may have played a significant role in the differing and shifting political positions of these two groups of young men at the University of Michigan. In considering the six school years from 1860–61 to 1865–66, the percentage of members in the Alpha Nu literary society who originally hailed from Michigan significantly outnumbered the same category in the Literary Adelphi society. For example, in the 1860–61 school year, 73 percent of Alpha Nu's members identified a town in Michigan as their primary residence, compared to 57 percent of Literary Adelphi's membership. The following year, the ratio was even more drastic, as Alpha Nu remained about even at 72 percent, while Literary Adelphi claimed 48 percent of its members from within Michigan's borders. This pattern continued throughout the war. Michigan residents constituted more than half of Alpha Nu's membership each year until 1865–66, while Literary Adelphi attracted at least half or a majority from outside the state every year after 1861. By 1865–66, only 33 percent of Literary Adelphi's membership cited Michigan residency. It is potentially a large generalization to draw conclusions based on these figures, but it appears that the influence of larger numbers of non-Michigan residents may have affected the perspective of the Literary Adelphi in swinging it to a more Radical Republican political stance as the war continued. The catalogues show that more students from the East began to enroll in the University of Michigan as the war progressed, and these students would have eventually come to sway or offset those of the midwestern students who may have been more susceptible to the volatile political loyalties of their region. That Alpha Nu remained Republican but leaned more toward the Conservative side is also explainable by the fact that large majorities of their membership came from within the state until the war was over. Even in this Northern, Midwest state, Democrats had regained some political power during the midwar years, and Republicans found themselves needing to moderate controversial positions. Michigan youth who took their oath to Alpha Nu at the University of Michigan, not surprisingly, reflected their state's wartime ambivalence to the political agenda of the Radical Republicans.[37]

Beyond the practice that literary societies afforded them in preparing for their future positions of leadership in the country, the students sought and created other opportunities to build upon their roles as student-patriots and hone skills that they might need upon graduation. Hosts of other student-run organizations existed, with elected leadership positions and plenty of chances to develop and hold large public events, social affairs, or ceremonies that represented occasions these young men could use to gain important experiences. For example, in a January 1864 letter to his brother, Charles B. Howell wrote about a speech he gave in the law school's moot congress regarding Lincoln's Proclamation of Amnesty and Reconstruction. In another instance one morning after chapel, close to the election of 1864, the students in the Literary Department took a vote on Lincoln versus McClellan. Lincoln garnered 131 votes, while McClellan polled 24. William H. Boardman gleefully wrote home to his father in Illinois, "It was the first time I ever had the pleasure of casting a vote for old Abe."[38]

Quarles recognized the importance of the presidential election in his November 9, 1864, speech. He called it "one of the great dates in history" because both Europe and the soldiers of the rebellious states were waiting in "breathless suspense for the result." Quarles clearly delineated what the American people were choosing between—either to continue the war or seek immediate peace. He was confident that Lincoln would win because "we prefer <u>war</u>, bitter war to such a peace as our enemies declare they will alone accept." The speech is remarkable in its lucid analysis of the political and military consequences of the election. Quarles drew parallels between this event and other historical moments in American history to help make his argument about the date's significance. Interestingly, though, there are clear similarities in prose between Quarles's oration and the Gettysburg Address. The young man obviously invoked Lincoln as his muse while lifting phrases, such as "mystic chords," directly from the president's inaugural message. In seeking to earn the right to someday replace their idols and lead the country, University of Michigan students learned by mimicking these men.[39]

Brothers in the Delta Kappa Epsilon fraternity (Omicron chapter at the University of Michigan) had the opportunity to practice their own formula for communication between North and South when, in March 1862, they replied to a letter from the Gamma chapter at Vanderbilt University in Tennessee. The Omicron members extended their "promises of sincere and eternal fidelity" to the Southern chapter despite location, political party, or "whether they owe allegiance to Lincoln or to [Jefferson] Davis." The author's superior attitude is apparent despite his best attempts to make statements of brotherhood; it is as if he cannot bring himself be truly pleasant without reminding the Gamma members of the current situation. "I hope you will be able to prosper as well as you always have deserved," one part of the letter begins, "notwithstanding the trials which beset you and your state. It does not become me to allude to the causes which have brought on the trouble in our country whatever they may be." Later, there is a reference to a conversation between Delta Kappa Epsilon soldiers on opposing sides in the eastern theater of the war. The condescension is obvious in the remark that "we were very much pleased to hear from them and to hear of their regret for the necessity which compels them to take up arms against their brothers in ΔKE." This clearly places blame for the war on Southern shoulders. The overall tone of the letter is warm, but it was obvious that the Omicron brothers in Michigan wanted to subtly indicate that the relationship was, and would continue to be, affected by the war's circumstances.[40]

Whether hosting a national figure for a public speech, practicing arguing a point in a moot court, or participating in a mock election, these young men found a variety of ways to train for their future endeavors. Through these forms of practice, students ultimately defined their ideas of patriotism and their understanding of their role in the war. Their function as citizens of the nation in this time of martial conflict was to prepare themselves to hold positions of leadership as the country began its inevitable rebuilding process. Their active intellectual engagement in the most pivotal issues facing their government, including their concentrated attention to the possible needs of the Reconstruction period, makes it evident that the University of Michigan became not just a place to obtain an education in the classics or prepare for a certain standing in society. These young men expanded the purpose of the university to suit their specific needs, through these clubs and organizations, and shaped their developing ideologies regarding the nation's future. In the end, their understanding of their role encompassed not only the verbal expressions of loyalty to the country expected from home-front citizens but also the utilization of the resources at their fingertips in a way that would label them as patriots and, thus, as men, despite the shadow cast by not wearing a military uniform.

It is true that during many days at the University of Michigan, the battlefield seemed little more than a distant concept. The students, of course, saw the disabled and deceased soldiers returning to their towns, watched families mourn the loss of loved ones, and felt the contrasting thrill of final victory followed by the grief over Lincoln's assassination. But for these young men who each at some point contemplated going to war, their daily lives in the "circumscribed college world" essentially intertwined with the way that they experienced the conflict. Granted, for a few days following the fall of Fort Sumter, the university cancelled classes, and the students spent most of their time drilling on the campus greens and attending Union mass meetings. However, there was hardly the same type of paralyzing response long term that so many other universities, North and South, experienced during the war era. In Ann Arbor, students, faculty, and residents managed to integrate the immense changes wrought by the nation's civil war into their daily lives. Often, the hours were passed in mundane ways and lacked drama despite the national crisis. Albert Farley captured the reality of their isolation from immediate physical harm in his January 7, 1864, diary entry: "Nothing wonderful has happened today. Nothing is expected and consequently there is no disappointment." Because daily life at the University of Michigan offered this combination of normalcy and the ability to shape and express one's grasp of worldly affairs in an academic setting, students who attended this Ann Arbor campus had the unique opportunity of being intellectually and emotionally engaged in the Civil War while being effectively sheltered from its military aspects. This distinct combination of elements significantly affected their front experience.[41]

Ultimately, because of their seclusion from the battlefield in the northern part of the Midwest and because of the increasing prestige of the university they attended, most Michigan students came to declare loyalty to both their nation and their college in equal measure. In fact, in some instances, they put drama associated with events transpiring within their midst ahead of the attention they gave to wartime news. University of Michigan students took such pride in their institution that often their patriotism, their understanding of their role in shaping the nation's course during this war, was indistinguishable from their understanding of what it meant to be a student on that campus. They characterized patriotism within a narrow spectrum of their contemporary experience, effectively enabling them to justify their continued presence in Ann Arbor. Rather than literally engaging in martial combat to save the country, these students considered themselves patriots by their intellectual contributions at the university and dedication to education in general. Staying in school became the equivalent of fighting the rebels. Michigan students embraced gendered rhetoric to highlight the manly qualities of obtaining an education, and they benefited from this altered portrait of the university experience. Even if they could not always agree on the political motivations for their ideas of patriotism, as the rise and decline of Copperhead rhetoric and activity colored the campus during the middle of the war, students at the University of Michigan argued for a Union that they hoped would remain strong and command respect. Especially as the war turned from months into years and talk of entering the army instead of getting a degree lessened, these students felt that they performed their patriotic duty by helping the university thrive and by intentionally participating in the prosperity of their immediate home front.

Another fascinating aspect of the home-front experience at the University of Michigan is that the way that these students molded their ideas about patriotism and duty was through their focus on their future contributions to the nation's reconstruction period. Yes, they were currently not offering their lives on the battlefield, but in their minds, their education was just as important because soon after the war, they would take seats next to the most important local and national politicians, lawyers, and clergymen to help influence the way the country moved forward. Those students who disagreed with the Lincoln administration earned valuable experience in being the voice of opposition during this period, although largely overshadowed in the end by those who pledged their loyalties to the president's agenda. These years in Ann Arbor were more than class pranks or reciting Greek; the students actively engaged and took charge of how they developed their individual characters with the intention of being informed and contributing citizens in the postwar era. They mobilized their extracurricular organizations around questions of wartime policy, including all aspects of political, economic, military, and intellectual issues. In both verbal and written forms, these students sharpened their debating skills, practiced articulating their emotions and opinions in poems or speeches, and learned to hear, respect, and consider the beliefs of others. The University of Michigan continued to grant degrees during the Civil War, with perhaps one of the most impressive records in higher education given the circumstances. The school also grew to notable new heights in national prestige. More than this, though, the young men who took advantage of the opportunities associated with the institution came of age in a time when they may have faced criticism in order to be there and yet defiantly sought fulfillment of the role they deemed was their destiny.

Notes

I thank Dr. Leonne M. Hudson, Dr. Lesley J. Gordon, Dr. J. Matthew Gallman, Monika Flaschka, Brenda Faverty, and Anthony Mujic for their insightful comments on this essay. I also extend my deepest appreciation to the Bentley Historical Library at the University of Michigan for the generous Bordin-Gillette Researcher Travel Fellowship, which supported my research for this essay.

1. *Peninsular Courier* (Ann Arbor, Michigan), February 18, 1862, quoted in F. Clever Bald, "The University of Michigan in the Civil War," in Willis F. Dunbar, ed., *Michigan Institutions of Higher Education in the Civil War* (Lansing: Michigan Civil War Centennial Observance Commission, 1964), 21–22.

2. Henry M. Utley and Byron M. Cutcheon, *The Class of Sixty-One: University of Michigan and Something about What "the Boys" Have Been Doing during Forty Years from 1861 to 1901* (Detroit, MI: John Bornman, 1902), 40; Bald, "University of Michigan," 19. Enrollment dropped slightly for the 1861–62 and 1862–63 school years but rose to over 850 by 1863–64. The University experienced another impressive increase to more than 950 students in 1864–65. State University of Michigan, *Catalogue of the Officers and Students* (Ann Arbor: University of Michigan), 1860–1866, Bentley Historical Library, University of Michigan (hereafter Bentley Library).

Three main departments at the university during the war era were the Literary, Medical, and Law Departments. Enrollment in the Literary Department, which offered courses to undergraduates in the classics, the sciences, and civil engineering, remained below 300 students until the year after the war ended. The Medical and Law Departments contributed the most to the university's overall expansion. The Law Department grew from 156 students in 1860–61 to 386 in 1865–66. The Medical Department saw student registrations jump from 166 in 1859–60 to 465 in 1865–66. Thus, the Literary Department declined from contributing 41 percent of total enrollment to 29 percent over the war period, while the Medical and Law Departments rose from 36 percent and 23 percent to 39 percent and 32 percent, respectively. See State University of Michigan, *Catalogue of the Officers and Students,* for more details. Emerson David Fite attributes the increase in the Medical Department to a larger interest in related professional opportunities in the military but offers no explanation regarding the increases in the Law Department. Fite, *Social and Industrial Conditions in the North during the Civil War* (New York: Frederick Ungar, 1963), 238. My current research has not been able to deny or prove his claim, but it seems more likely that the increased enrollments were related to the growing popularity of professional degrees. The University of Michigan was on the cutting edge of offering programs that "responded more directly to the specific problems of society" rather than teaching ancient languages and philosophy. Alan Creutz, *From College Teacher to University Scholar: The Evolution and Professionalization of Academics at the University of Michigan* (PhD diss., University of Michigan, 1981), 503; Howard H. Peckham, *The Making of the University of Michigan, 1817–1967* (Ann Arbor: University of Michigan Press, 1967), 57.

Historians have considered some aspects of the impact of the war on higher education, but their work usually focuses on student experiences as soldiers or includes brief analyses of the war period in a larger institutional analysis. Their research does reinforce the unique nature, however, of circumstances at the University of Michigan, where the war period saw increases in enrollment and the expansion of curriculum. For example, Richard F. Miller contends that "within a few days [of the fall of Fort Sumter] Harvard itself had almost ceased to function." Miami University in Oxford, Ohio, suffered such enrollment and financial difficulties that they struggled to recover even after the war and closed in 1873 for more than ten years. Many Southern universities closed their doors when the war began and either never reopened or later appeared in a form much different than originally intended. In his institutional history of Tulane University, John P. Dyer asserts that the "parsimonious legislatures and lethargic citizens of New Orleans had failed to kill the university, but the war now administered the *coup de grâce*." Tulane ceased to operate during the four years of war, and its buildings stood "silent and deserted." Richard F. Miller, *Harvard's Civil War: A History of the Twentieth Massachusetts Volunteer Infantry* (Lebanon, NH: University Press of New England, 2005), 16; John D. Millett, *Higher Education in Ohio* (Ohio Interim Commission on Education, 1962), 33; Willis Rudy, *The Campus and a Nation in Crisis: From the American Revolution to Vietnam* (Madison: Fairleigh Dickenson University Press, 1996), 60; John P. Dyer, *Tulane: The Biography of a University, 1834–1965* (New York: Harper and Row, 1966), 28.

Additionally, in 1964, the Michigan Civil War Centennial Observance Committee published a book of essays regarding the wartime experience of the state's colleges and its one university. No other college in Michigan had as many students as did the University of Michigan, but many were established institutions that weathered the conflict despite significantly decreased numbers in the student body. Kalamazoo College, for example, reached upwards of 400 students in the 1850s but had no students enrolled in the senior class by the middle of the war. In two of the war years, Michigan State Agricultural College graduated no students. Several colleges saw increases in the number of enrolled female students, who were not admitted to the University of Michigan until 1870. Beyond enrollment numbers, administrative decisions, or stories of former students serving in battle, these essays continued the pattern of not providing insight into how the students who remained on campus viewed themselves during the war. Granted, some of this neglect is due to a severe lack of sources from the period. The sheer quantity and quality of sources for University of Michigan students make a more thorough analysis of the ideology of its student body during the Civil War all the more important. See Michigan Civil War Centennial Observance Commission, *Michigan Institutions of Higher Education in the Civil War* (Lansing, MI, 1964).

3. Melinda Lawson, *Patriot Fires: Forging a New American Nationalism in the Civil War North* (Lawrence: University Press of Kansas, 2002), 163, 9. Several historians have addressed patriotism as a concept and as a motivation for enlistment in the Civil War. In addition to Lawson, see also James M. McPherson, *For Cause and Comrades: Why Men Fought in the Civil War* (New York: Oxford University Press, 1997); Earl J. Hess, *The Union Soldier in Battle: Enduring the Ordeal of Combat* (Lawrence: University Press of Kansas, 1997); Gerald F. Linderman, *Embattled Courage: The Experience of Combat*

in the American Civil War (New York: Free Press, 1987); Merle Curti, *Roots of American Loyalty* (New York: Columbia University Press, 1946).

4. Donald George Tewksbury, *The Founding of American Colleges and Universities before the Civil War* (Hamden, CT: Archon, 1965), 215. Students native to states other than Michigan came to the University of Michigan for the 1860–61 school year from Connecticut, Illinois, Indiana, Iowa, Kentucky, Maine, Massachusetts, Mississippi, New Hampshire, New Jersey, New York, Ohio, Pennsylvania, Tennessee, Vermont, Wisconsin, and Canada. State University of Michigan, *Catalogue of the Officers and Students, 1860*; Frank W. Blackmar, *The History of Federal and State Aid to Higher Education in the United States* (Washington, DC: GPO, 1890), 239–41; Bald, "University of Michigan," 16; *History of Washtenaw County, Michigan; Together with Sketches of Its Cities, Villages and Townships, Educational, Religious, Civil, Military, and Political History; Portraits of Prominent Persons, and Biographies of Representative Citizens,* (Chicago: Chapman, 1881), 2:879, 887; John Edward Shay Jr., *Residence Halls in the Age of the University: Their Development at Harvard and Michigan, 1850–1930*, PhD diss., University of Michigan, 1966, 51, 52, 52n2; New York Society Records (1860–63), New York Society (Ann Arbor, MI), Bentley Library.

It is important to distinguish between being pro-Southern and being an adherent of the Democratic party's conservative wing, who were labeled Copperheads during the Civil War. In characterizing Copperheads, Jennifer L. Weber argues that they "were consistent, and constant in their demand for an immediate peace settlement. At times they were willing to trade victory for peace. . . . It remains unclear to this day how they expected the nation to return to the *status quo ante bellum*. . . . [The] peace wing never acknowledged Confederate wishes [for independence]. . . . Besides the desire for peace, the common denominator for all conservatives was their concern about personal liberties. Peace men were strict constructionists about the constitution. . . . Peace Democrats universally supported slavery, believing it to be the best situation for a degraded race. . . . Many conservatives blamed the abolitionists for starting the war. Southerners, by this account, were the innocent victims. . . . For their many faults, though, most Copperheads were not traitors. Though some made no bones about their Southern sympathies, most were genuinely committed to the well-being of the nation. . . . [T]he vast majority were loyal to the Union. . . . They did not want the Confederacy to win or the Union to split." When considering the pro-Southern actions and posturing of many communities in the southern Ohio River border regions of Ohio, Indiana, and Illinois during the Civil War, it is clear that the Copperhead activity of Michigan generally falls short of being overtly pro-Southern. Weber's work, as just one example, illustrates the range of Copperhead activity in the North and does not identify Michigan as being among the most virulent states in its support of either the Copperhead agenda or pro-Southern activities. Weber, *Copperheads: The Rise and Fall of Lincoln's Opponents in the North* (Oxford: Oxford University Press, 2006), 3–7.

The state of Michigan polled 57 percent of its popular vote for Lincoln in the 1860 presidential election. For more information on the early development of the university, its characteristics, and its relationship with Ann Arbor, see Peckham, *Making of the University of Michigan*; Burke Hinsdale, *History of the University of Michigan* (Ann Arbor: University of Michigan Press, 1906); Wilfred B. Shaw, *A Short History of the University of Michigan* (Ann Arbor, MI: George Wahr, 1937); Elizabeth M. Farrand, *History of the University of Michigan* (Ann Arbor, MI: Register, 1885); Kent Sagendorph, *Michigan: The Story of the University* (New York: Dutton, 1948); Richard Rees Price, *The*

Financial Support of the University of Michigan: Its Origin and Development (Cambridge, MA: Harvard University, 1923); Jonathan Marwil, *A History of Ann Arbor* (Ann Arbor: University of Michigan Press, 1987); George S. May, "Ann Arbor and the Coming of the Civil War," *Michigan History* 36 (1952): 241–59.

5. Ike Elliot, "Stepped from Class Room to Ranks of Union Army," in Class of 1861 (University of Michigan) records, 1861 and 1910, Bentley Library; Bald, "University of Michigan," 18–20; Charles M. Perry, *Henry Philip Tappan: Philosopher and University President* (New York: Arno, 1971), 271–72; Andrew D. White, *Autobiography of Andrew Dickson White* (1905; New York: Century, 1922), 1:90; Robert Beasecker, ed., *"I Hope to Do My Country Service": The Civil War Letters of John Bennitt, M.D.* (Detroit, MI: Wayne State University Press, 2005), 10–11. Bennitt did enlist in the summer of 1862, but it appears that it was more for the financial benefit to his family than for patriotic reasons.

6. Stanton B. Thomas to Mother, April 16, 1861, folder Thomas, Correspondence, 1860–64, box 1, Nathan M. Thomas Papers, Bentley Library; State University of Michigan, *Catalogue of the Officers and Students, 1864*; Joseph V. Quarles to Mother, November 23, 1862, folder Correspondence 1860–62, box 2, Joseph V. Quarles Papers, 1843–1911, Wisconsin Historical Society, Madison.

7. Editorial, *University Palladium*, December 1861, 3, Bentley Library (hereafter cited as *Palladium*). This magazine lists the names of members of the Greek societies, literary societies, religious clubs, departmental organizations, and nonacademic extracurricular activities, such as choir, chess, or cricket. Beginning in 1861, the magazine also published the army roll of alumni and past students. While available evidence seems to indicate that the students were debating their role in the war among themselves and writing primarily for an audience of their peers, it is also possible that they were reacting to pressure to enlist from the outside. Whether they were feeling compelled to join the military effort from fellow students or Ann Arbor residents or friends and family at home, it remains plausible that some portion of their concern for justifying their decision to remain in school stems from the very publicized pressure that the home front was placing on all able-bodied men when the war first broke out. For more, see James M. McPherson, *Battle Cry of Freedom: The Civil War Era* (New York: Ballantine Books, 1989), 311; Linderman, *Embattled Courage*, 87–90; Jeanie Attie, *Patriotic Toil: Northern Women and the American Civil War* (Ithaca, NY: Cornell University Press, 1998), 28. Regarding reenlistment pressure, see John Robertson, "Re-Enlistment Patterns of Civil War Soldiers," *Journal of Interdisciplinary History* 32, no. 1 (2001): 15–35.

8. *Palladium*, December 1861.

9. *Hesperian*, February 7, 1862, box 1, Records, 1857–1939, Literary Adelphi (University of Michigan), Bentley Library; *Sibyl*, November 6, 1863, box 3, Records, 1843–1931, Alpha Nu Literary Society (University of Michigan), Bentley Library (hereafter Alpha Nu's *Sibyl* cited as *Sibyl*). The *Hesperian* and the *Sibyl* are bound volumes kept by the literary societies in the fashion of the day. These are internal literary papers that were read aloud within the society meetings on a regular basis. They were not intended for outside eyes, nor were they published for public consumption. They were often collections of essays, poems, arguments, or other literary expressions meant as another opportunity for personal intellectual growth of members. Francis Thomas to Beulah L. Hailes, March 5, 1865, Francis Thomas Letters, 1864–65, Bentley Library.

10. *Sibyl*, May 8, 1863; *Hesperian*, February 7, 1862, box 1, Records, 1857–1939, Literary Adelphi (University of Michigan), Bentley Library.

11. *Sibyl*, May 8, 1863, October 21, 1865.

12. *Palladium*, 1863, 1864, 1865; Bald, "University of Michigan," 23.

13. *Palladium*, 1861.

14. *Sibyl*, November 6, 1863; *Palladium*, 1864, 1865.

15. *Palladium*, 1864; *Sibyl*, November 6, 1863; William M. Hayes to Parents, December 6, 1863, William Mordecai Hayes papers, 1862–64, Bentley Library. Clement L. Vallandigham was an Ohio politician during the war who led the Copperhead movement in the Midwest. In May 1863, he was arrested and sent behind Confederate lines. He escaped to Canada and led a failed attempt to win the gubernatorial seat in Ohio from exile. He continued to cause trouble for the Lincoln administration and serve as an inspiration to Copperheads until the decline of the movement after the 1864 election. Vallandigham returned to Ohio after the war and continued to practice law until his death in 1871. See Frank Klement, *The Limits of Dissent: Clement L. Vallandigham and the Civil War*, as well as Brett Barker's essay in the current volume.

16. Gideon Winan Allen to Annie Cox, December 12, 1863, Gideon Winan Allen correspondence, 1862–67, 1872, State Historical Society of Wisconsin, Madison (hereafter cited as Allen correspondence). Copperheads on the University of Michigan campus most likely felt very comfortable by 1863 expressing their views because the county surrounding the school swayed in that direction politically during the middle of the war. While in 1860, Washtenaw County voted across the board for Republican candidates, Democrats by 1862 won the county's support in every major political contest, including governor and sheriff. These results did little to offset the rest of the state that still continued to support the Republican incumbents, like Governor Austin Blair, but they do reveal political discord on the home front. This movement climaxed in 1864 when the county gave the Democratic presidential candidate, George Brinton McClellan, their majority over Lincoln by more than two hundred votes. Again, they tried but failed to replace the Republican governor with the Democratic candidate who won their voting support in that contest. *History of Washtenaw County, Michigan*, 2:255–56; anonymous letter, November 14, 1863, Bentley Library.

17. Gideon Winan Allen to Annie Cox, October 15, 1863, Allen correspondence; "Foreign Intervention," January 15, 1864, box 1, records, Michigan University Literary Adelphi, Bentley Library; Weber, *Copperheads*, 4. See, for example, letters from Gideon Winan Allen to Annie Cox between April and November 1863, Allen correspondence.

18. Northern volunteerism for the military had waned significantly following the Union's Peninsula campaign in the summer of 1862. Congress therefore found it necessary to pass the first draft law in 1863, the Enrollment Act of 1863. With this first attempt at conscription, a young man could avoid service either by paying $300 or by finding a substitute. Eugene C. Murdock, *One Million Men: The Civil War Draft in the North* (Madison: State Historical Society of Wisconsin, 1971), 6–7; William M. Hayes to Parents, Sister, and Cousin, December 27, 1863, William Mordecai Hayes papers, 1862–64, Bentley Library.

19. Dunbar, *Michigan Institutions*, 11; Joseph B. Steere to [a friend], July 9, 1864, box 4, folder Letters 1860–64, Bentley Library; John Marshall Hinchman to Mother, April 26, 1863, and May 10, 1863, John Marshall Hinchman letters, 1861–64, Bentley Library; undated 1863, box 1, minute book 1859–68, Alpha Nu Literary Society (University of Michigan) records, 1843–1931, Bentley Library; May 29, 1863, box 1, Record Book, 1857–91, Literary Adelphi University of Michigan, Bentley Library.

20. Anonymous letter, November 14, 1863, Bentley Library; Annie Cox to Gideon Winan Allen, March 2, 1863, Cox to Allen, June 16, 1863, and C. J. Cox to Allen, November 12, 1863, all Allen correspondence.

21. Gideon Winan Allen to Annie Cox, June 9, 1863, and Allen to Cox, September 20, 1863, Allen correspondence.

22. Charles B. Howell to Brother, October 27, 1863, and January 26, 1864, Howell Family Papers, 1856–84, Bentley Library. Students made their decisions about the personal implications of the draft in an environment that did not fully support the conscription measures. On August 12, 1862, the *Ann Arbor (MI) Journal* criticized the "large numbers of the 'courageous' young men" in Michigan who had "suddenly been seized with a great desire for travel" and headed north in Canada to avoid the draft. The author of the segment scolded the men for "romantically idling away their time at the great cataract of Niagara, when their country and their homes are imperiled." The newspaper demanded, "Let them volunteer, or stand their draft like true men."

23. Joseph V. Quarles to Mother, August 4, 1864, box 2, folder Correspondence 1863–64, Joseph V. Quarles Papers, 1843–1911, Wisconsin Historical Society, Madison.

24. Charles L. Watrous to Andrew D. White, August 6, 1861, Andrew D. White Papers, Bentley Library; Lorien Foote, *The Gentleman and the Roughs: Manhood, Honor, and Violence in the Union Army* (New York: New York University Press, 2010), 3. Scholarship using gender as a category of analysis for Civil War studies is not as prevalent yet as in other fields of history, but Civil War historians are making significant progress. See LeeAnn Whites, *Gender Matters: Civil War, Reconstruction, and the Making of the New South* (New York: Palgrave Macmillan, 2005); LeeAnn Whites and Alecia P. Long, eds., *Occupied Women: Gender, Military Occupation, and the American Civil War* (Baton Rouge: Louisiana State University Press, 2009); Catherine Clinton and Nina Silber, eds., *Battle Scars: Gender and Sexuality in the American Civil War* (Oxford: Oxford University Press, 2006); Thomas E. Rodgers, "Billy Yank and G.I. Joe: An Exploratory Essay on the Sociopolitical Dimensions of Soldier Motivation," *Journal of Military History* 69, no. 1 (2005): 93–121; Michael T. Smith, "The Beast Unleashed: Benjamin F. Butler and Conceptions of Masculinity in the Civil War North," *New England Quarterly* 79, no. 2 (2006): 248–76. The foundational work on gender as a category of analysis is Joan Scott, "Gender: A Useful Category of Historical Analysis," *American Historical Review* 91, no. 5 (1986).

25. *Palladium*, 1863.

26. Ibid., 1864. See Foote, *Gentleman and the Roughs*, 4–6.

27. Philip Shaw Paludan may give us insight into what provoked this growing confidence in earning a college education rather than going to war. In his seminal work on the North, Paludan asserts that the passage of the Morrill Act in 1862 "increased the trained leadership of the nation and thereby encouraged the continued growth for the economy. Both were endorsed by the deep patriotism shown in existing colleges and universities of the nation." The Morrill Act granted each state large tracts of public land to sell for profit that would, in turn, be used to fund higher education specifically aimed at agricultural programs, mechanical arts, and military tactics. As is usually the case when referring to colleges during this era, Paludan relies on statistics from the aristocratic universities, such as Harvard, Yale, Amherst, Bowdoin, and like, to make his point about the high rate of educated participation in the military but does mention that Michigan "was unique among larger schools in gaining students." Sources from faculty and the board of regents at the University of Michigan do indeed reveal

an intense preoccupation during the war with obtaining the grant money from the Morrill Act in order to expand their institution. Ultimately, the money went instead to Michigan State University in East Lansing. It is plausible then that Michigan students were well aware of the increased attention on colleges during the Civil War and embraced the rhetoric surrounding the Morrill Act to help build their justification for the link between patriotism and education. The interest of the government in improving and enriching higher education during a war might very well have given the students the impression that their contribution to the nation's future was equal to that of the soldiers who were fighting at the same time. However, nowhere in available sources from students found to date do they directly mention the Morrill Act or the struggle that the university was going through in the state legislature to obtain those funds. As intriguing as it would be to identify the passage of the Morrill Act as the impetus for growing student confidence, the sources do not allow that conclusion at this time. Paludan, *"A People's Contest": The Union and Civil War, 1861–1865* (New York: Harper and Row, 1988), 132–33; *Palladium*, 1863, 1865; *Sibyl*, May 8, 1863.

28. *Palladium*, 1866.

29. March 16, 1860, March 8, 1861, October 18, 1861, May 3, 1861, October 25, 1861, February 21, 1862, March 21, 1863, December 12, 1862, January 30, 1863, May 2, 1862, November 14, 1862, March 21, 1862, May 30, 1862, box 1, minute book, 1859–68, Alpha Nu Literary Society (University of Michigan) records, 1843–1931, Bentley Library.

30. January 20, 1862, January 23, 1863, October 7, 1864, May 8, 1863, May 27, 1864, April 28, 1865, box 1, minute book 1859–68, Alpha Nu Literary Society (University of Michigan) records, 1843–1931, Bentley Library.

31. *Sibyl*, April 21, 1865; November 4, 1864, February 17, 1865, September 29, 1865, October 13, 1865, box 1, minute book 1859–68, Alpha Nu Literary Society (University of Michigan) records, 1843–1931, Bentley Library.

32. March 9, 1860, October 19, 1860, November 2, 1860, January 11, 1861, April 21, 1861, April 3, 1861, box 1, minutes 1857–60, Literary Adelphi (University of Michigan) Records, 1857–1939, Bentley Library.

33. October 11, 1861, October 25, 1861, box 1, minutes 1857–60, Literary Adelphi, Literary Adelphi (University of Michigan) Records, 1857–1939, Bentley Library; April 25, 1862, April 17, 1863, October 28, 1863, November 13, 1863, box 1, Record Book, 1857–91, Literary Adelphi (University of Michigan Records) 1857–1939, Bentley Library. On November 13, 1863, only a few weeks after the first vote, the Literary Adelphi members again voted on the proposition that "the southern states be admitted into the Union only on the condition that they become Free." This resolution lost, but this appears to be an aberration in the pattern. March 11, 1864, box 1, Record Book, 1857–91, Literary Adelphi (University of Michigan) Records, 1857–1939, Bentley Library.

34. April 4, 1862, November 7, 1862, December 19, 1862, April 15, 1864, November 18, 1864, January 27, 1865, May 27, 1864, October 7, 1864, October 28, 1864, April 21, 1865, November 24, 1865, March 9, 1866, box 1, Record Book, 1857–91, Literary Adelphi (University of Michigan) Records, 1857–1939, Bentley Library.

35. *Hesperian*, December 6, 1861, box 1, Literary Adelphi (University of Michigan) Records, 1857–1939, Bentley Library. For more information on how support for emancipation and arming blacks developed in the Midwest during the war, see Victor Jacque Voegeli, *Free but Not Equal: The Midwest and the Negro during the Civil War* (Chicago: University of Chicago Press, 1967); *Sibyl*, October 21, 1865.

36. See, for example, December 7, 1860, April 27, 1865, box 1, minute book 1859–68, Alpha Nu Literary Society (University of Michigan), Bentley Library; May 20, 1864, box 1, Record Book, 1857–91, Literary Adelphi (University of Michigan) Records, 1857–1939, Bentley Library; June 14, 1861, June 6, 1862, March 3, 1865, box 1, minute book 1859–68, Alpha Nu Literary Society (University of Michigan), Bentley Library; May 29, 1863, box 1, Record Book, 1857–91, Literary Adelphi (University of Michigan) Records, 1857–1939, Bentley Library. See, for example, December 7, 1860, April 27, 1865, box 1, minute book 1859–68, Alpha Nu Literary Society; May 20, 1864, box 1, Record Book, 1857–91, Literary Adelphi.

37. These calculations are based on a comparison of the Alpha Nu and Literary Adelphi membership rosters in the *Palladium* for each school year between 1860–61 and 1865–66, with residential identifications from the *Catalogue of Officers and Students*, which was officially published annually by the university. Students who were listed in the society membership rosters as being in the army were not included in the calculations, nor were the few students for whom no hometown could be identified. The question for the calculation was what percentage of each society identified their residence as being within the state of Michigan, and the breakdown of the results is as follows:

School Year	Alpha Nu	Literary Adelphi
1860–61	73	57
1861–62	72	48
1862–63	68	50
1863–64	66	44
1864–65	52	34
1865–66	43	33

38. Charles B. Howell to Brother, January 26, 1864, Howell Family Papers, 1856–84, Bentley Library; William H. Boardman to Father, October 30, 1864, Boardman Family Papers, 1864–65, Bentley Library.

39. Joseph Quarles, November 9, 1864, box 1, folder Quarles Speeches 1864–70, Wisconsin Historical Society. It is unclear what the speech was for, but it was likely for a literary society event or some other student activity. It is a part of his papers found at the Wisconsin Historical Society.

40. March 5, 1862, folder Correspondence of Scriptors, Delta Kappa Epsilon, Omicron Chapter (University of Michigan) Records, 1855–1927, Bentley Library.

41. *Palladium*, 1865; Albert William Farley, diary, January 7, 1864, Albert William Farley diary, 1864–65, Bentley Library. Alumni from the class of 1861 remembered that one of their favorite college pastimes was leapfrog. In their book honoring the 1861 graduates, alumni Henry M. Utley and Byron M. Cutcheon recalled, "It was no unusual spectacle to see future college professors and presidents, congressmen, and clergymen, progressing from the University toward the post-office by means of this exhilarating, if not dignified, game." The students also played practical jokes on each other or took part in pranks among the undergraduate classes. In one instance, the sophomores thought it good sport to go around pulling freshmen out of their beds during the night. A week later, the freshmen responded by stacking benches in front of the classroom in which the sophomores were doing recitations. Then, as the sophomores tried to climb over the barricade to exit, the freshmen pulled the pile of benches

down the stairwell, taking the older students with it. There were the usual course of fistfights, and groups of students routinely stole the campus bell that announced the changing of classes. Like others, John Hinchman reveled in the social opportunities of the surrounding community. "I am enjoying myself more than usual," he wrote in 1864 to his mother. "Ann Arbor will be very gay this winter, as each church has a social once in two weeks. College goes on about as usual." Utley and Cutcheon, *Class of Sixty-One*, 38; William H. Boardman to Father, November 20, 1864, November 27, 1864; John Marshall Hinchman to Mother, October 25, 1863, October 24, 1864, John Marshall Hinchman letters, 1861–64, Bentley Library.

THE AGRICULTURAL POWER OF THE
MIDWEST DURING THE CIVIL WAR

R. Douglas Hurt

It sounded like distant thunder in the mid-October twilight. As the moments passed, Elvira Badger heard the rumble growing louder, far faster than an approaching storm. She looked at the clock. The hands held at 7 P.M. Then, in the street before her window, "a very large drove of horses went by." Unable to count them, she wrote, "I think there must have been more than a thousand." This Charleston, South Carolina, born-and-raised woman, who had lived in the North since June, did not realize that the herd of well-shod horses pounding toward a nearby army camp represented the agricultural power of the Midwest. Most of those horses, like many of the men who would drive them from supply wagons and caissons or who rode them as cavalry, would be dead long before the guns fell silent at Appomattox more than three years later. Others of these horses would become injured, worn out, or diseased and sold back to civilians, but more would follow in a seemingly endless supply gathered by army contractors from the farms across the Midwest.[1]

During the American Civil War, Illinois farmers furnished not fewer than 150,000 horses to the various branches of the army as well as "a large number of serviceable mules." With the Southern market closed, midwestern farmers welcomed army contractors while they waited for it to respond favorably as the war progressed. They knew that Yankee and Confederate armies would confiscate farm horses, and Southerners would need more horses and mules when the war ended. The midwestern farmers expected that Southern farmers would be limited "only by their ability to pay for the animals needed." For midwestern farmers with horses and mules to sell, the war brought quick and considerable cash into their households. In 1861, one Ohio farmer believed that army demands along with growing urban and agricultural markets meant "probably more profit breeding horses than cattle," and given the demand, he contended that even greater profits could be earned from better breeding practices.[2]

The early and great supply of midwestern horses to the army, however, did not mean that all or even most of those animals were fit for the heavy and dangerous work that awaited them. Many farm and carriage horses sold to the army had neither the strength nor stamina to meet military needs. Still, army contractors paid good money, and they did not look too carefully at a farmer's stock because they received their commissions on the number not the quality of the horses purchased for the government. Or, contractors bought low and sold for the maximum army price, which by the end of 1861 reached $119 for cavalry horses and which escalated to $185 per head in 1865. This policy embarrassed the editor of the farm paper *Ohio Cultivator*, who complained that the horses in the Buckeye state lacked the size, strength, and weight "to throw into the collar and provide a good days work plowing." Yet, with the army at first wanting horses for transportation, Ohio farmers reportedly "took notice that [their] stock was bad enough, and thought it a good way to get it used up so the country would be rid of such stuff." Seeing opportunity and profit where none had existed before, they welcomed army horse buyers.[3]

The large number of poor-quality horses that midwestern farmers sold to the army stemmed from breeding practices that did not produce strength but rather small, sleek, stylish horses for buggies. As a result, one Ohioan observed that "ewe-necked nags" provided the draft power for a battery of light artillery from Cleveland, but it should have had a "thundering troop of horse" to keep it from getting "knocked hither and yon, whenever the gun carriages crossed a gully or struck a mole hill." But army contractors cared little about the quality of horses purchased, and midwestern farmers relished the opportunity to sell "mean" horses that would soon be worth only the value of their hides and shoes to skinners who worked the battlefields. Although the call for better breeding would take time to meet the needs of both farm and military, the army needed horses, and the War Department had money to spend. Midwestern farmers had horses to sell, regardless of quality, and they wanted cash. Only the purists complained. In August 1861, a Cincinnati resident observed, "The streets swarm with horses and mules for the army, which are rapidly gathered up and sent to Virginia." Indeed, Ohio and Indiana horses flooded the Cincinnati market, where government agents paid $100 per head for good horses while "fair" ones brought $60 each.[4]

By 1864, a report from Johnson County, Ohio, indicates that the army bought all the "large stout horses," while another contends that nearly all the good horses had disappeared from Auglaize County during the war because farmers accepted "round prices" from army contractors. The heavy demand for horses provided the opportunity for farmers to breed larger animals once the small stock, particularly Morgans, had been sold. Throughout the war, midwestern farmers also needed larger horses for draft power, that is, for plowing, harrowing, and planting, as well as cultivating, mowing, and hauling wagon loads of grain and hay to market. By the end of the war, however, they had done little to breed for strength alone. High prices continued to encourage farmers to sell extra horses and keep only those needed for farm work. They did not concern themselves with improved breeding practices because they could sell their horses without difficulty.[5]

By November 1864, one observer noted that since April 1861, the army had purchased approximately 416,000 horses, and it required 110,000 head annually, or more than 10 percent of all marketable stock. Urbanites also needed horses for carriages and wagons, and these consumers willingly paid more for horses than government contractors. Moreover, the army did not purchase more than one-third of the mares on the market because they were more "ticklish" than geldings, and the mares had a reputation for being noisy and dangerous to men and other horses when in heat. Given this demand, one contemporary estimated that midwestern farmers would need to furnish 144,018 horses for civilians and 108,742 horses to the army for a total of 252,760, or about one-fourth of the marketable stock annually. Yet, farmers produced only an estimated 250,690 horses yearly for a deficit of more than 2,000 head, which accounted for a "scarcity of horse flesh" in town and country, particularly since the army preferred four-year-old horses, that is, full-grown animals. As a result, horses from midwestern farms remained in demand with their prices high during the war.[6]

While midwestern farmers garnered considerable income throughout the war and while they waited for the railroads and commission men to untangle the snarl of agricultural trade after the navy closed the Mississippi River to downstream commerce in April 1861, they also capitalized on their ability to increase corn production to fatten more hogs, which the army also needed as salt pork, hams, and bacon. Since the earliest settlements across the Midwest, farmers had fed their corn crop to hogs and either slaughtered their swine and packed the meat at home for sale to local merchants engaged in the river trade or they sold their hogs to contractors who drove them to slaughter and packinghouses in the towns and cities along the major rivers that provided access to Southern and eastern markets. The Civil War, however, closed the Ohio River and its tributaries to Southern and eastern buyers, and pork packers quickly worked to realign their businesses with railroads that gave quick access to markets. During the Civil War, pork packing became inextricably linked to railroads and provided the main source of freight in the Midwest. Pork packers in the railroad terminal cities of Chicago and Milwaukee thrived as their business mushroomed while the industry in the river towns, such as Cincinnati, declined.[7]

Army contractors preferred to purchase pork from large-scale packers in cities with railroad transportation to expedite the shipment of hogs from farm to packer and from packer to the army. Civilian buyers also preferred railroad transport to urban markets and dinner tables. More than 1.5 million men were serving in the army, and meat furnished the essential protein and energy that sustained the high-caloric diet needed by fighting men. Hogs provided meat the quickest, the cheapest, and in the greatest quantity. With midwestern farmers raising two hog litters annually under the right conditions, the war-driven meatpacking industry provided steady income.[8]

The 1861–62 pork-packing season exceeded previous years. Ohio led the region with 787,439 hogs packed, up from 627,131 the year before. In Indiana, the pack increased from 382,616 to 486,243, in Illinois from 509,750 to 841,473, in Iowa from 153,241 to 196,373, and in Wisconsin from 53,260 to 100,556 head. One contemporary observed that Ohio Valley producers received large numbers of hogs, resulting from "the feeling of insecurity consequent upon the existing rebellion," which seems to indicate that they wanted to sell their hogs before prices declined from the loss of Southern markets. Midwestern farmers need not have worried because the army purchased a large volume of pork annually. Although prices fluctuated during the war, hog production remained profitable. Not only were more hogs packed during the 1861–62 season than before but also informed observers noted that heavier hogs that produced greater yields of lard reached the packers, although this characteristic would not continue.[9]

Cincinnati packers adjusted to the reality of war by the 1861–62 packing season. With downriver markets closed, they shipped their hog pack to Atlantic and military markets by canal and rail. Despite a location less favorable than Chicago's to draw upon the hog crops of the Midwest, Queen City packers still increased their output during the first two packing seasons of the war, peaking at 110.4 million pounds of pork and bacon in 1862–63. Thereafter, the Cincinnati pack declined due to war, railroad transportation, and the emergence of Chicago as the pork-packing center or "Porkopolis of the West." Small-scale packers in Keokuk, Iowa, Peoria, Illinois, and Terre Haute, Indiana, as well as Dayton, Ohio, Logansport, Indiana, and Decatur, Illinois, among others, could not compete with the large-scale packers in Chicago and Milwaukee, which used the railroads and financial reserves to draw upon the farms in Minnesota, Iowa, Illinois, and Indiana for the annual hog pack each autumn and winter. As a result, during the Civil War, the midwestern packers grew larger in size but also smaller in number. Midwestern farmers, however, did not suffer economic losses in that transition because the railroads provided quick access to markets, and government contracts kept prices profitable.[10]

Prior to 1860, midwestern packers had not processed more than 2.5 million hogs during a season, but the pack increased to 4 million for the 1862–63 season before declining to 3 million for the 1863–64 pack due to a weather-reduced corn crop. At that time, the hog pack fell short of early estimates by approximately 25 percent, with weights down 12 percent because the corn crop failed in Indiana and Illinois due to drought and frost. Throughout the war, however, farmers rushed their hogs to market to gain good prices and increase their income while providing more meat for the army, and the amount of meat packed usually increased because of the larger volume of hogs sold, even though those pigs averaged less weight than before.[11]

Although the regional pack in Cincinnati declined from approximately 18.49 percent to 14.27 percent of the hogs slaughtered from 1861 to 1864, packing cities, such as Indianapolis and Milwaukee, also increased the number of hogs packed during the war due to improved railroad service resulting from the consolidation of lines. In August 1863, pork packers in Indianapolis prepared for a busy season. One reporter noted, "The time was when the river towns monopolized the packing of pork. Railroads have changed all that—now the most eligible locations both for receiving and shipping are to be found in just such towns as Indianapolis." By 1863, the hog pack had become so great that the army and domestic markets could be easily met. As a result, Indianapolis entrepreneurs, financed by British investors in Liverpool, planned a brick slaughterhouse alongside the White River and Terre Haute Railroad to pack 180,000 hogs for the English market during the coming season.[12]

In Chicago, cattle sales also increased from approximately 140,300 to 343,726 head between the 1860–61 and 1864–65 seasons with 62 and 76 percent of the cattle, respectively, shipped elsewhere by rail for slaughter. Overall, Chicago's pork and beef packers increased from twenty-one during the 1859–60 season to fifty-four by the end of the war. During the war, the largest packers processed more than 30,000 hogs and several thousand cattle each. Spurred by military needs, many individually owned and small-scale packinghouses became major companies that provided convenient markets as well as profitable prices for midwestern farmers. By the end of the war, the Chicago firm of Craigen and Co., drawing on army contracts while expanding sales in northeastern markets, packed 2.2 percent of the hogs processed in the Midwest, more than the output of all packers in Indianapolis. By drawing on the volume of hogs produced in the Midwest, Chicago earned the sobriquet "Hog Butcher to the World." Before the war ended, Chicago packed 24.8 percent of the region's pork.[13]

The agricultural power of the Midwest can also be seen in crop production, particularly grain. Although farmers produced large crops in 1860 and 1861, the wheat crop of 1862 exceeded all records. In the grain states of Indiana, Illinois, Wisconsin, and Iowa, farmers harvested 83 million bushels of wheat for a 33 percent increase, 290 million bushels of corn for a 25 percent increase, and 43 million bushels of oats for a 15 percent increase from 1859. Although frost and drought ruined much of the corn crop in 1863 and drought the wheat crop of 1864 in some areas, midwestern grain production remained high during the war years. During each year, Chicago merchants shipped 20 million bushels of wheat and flour, up from a prewar high of 10 million bushels. Prior to 1860, they shipped a high of 11 million bushels of corn but averaged 25 million bushels during the war years. Grain shipments from Chicago totaled 31 million bushels in 1860, 50 million bushels in 1861, and 56 million bushels in 1862 before declining to 54 million bushels in 1863 due to short crops and again to 46 million bushel shipments in 1864 before increasing to 52 million bushels in 1865, still more than 20 million total bushels of grain shipped than on the eve of the Civil War. The other lake ports of Milwaukee, Detroit, and Toledo had similar increases in grain shipments, which also reached British and French markets via the Erie Canal. During the war, then, midwestern farmers not only produced enough grain to meet civilian and military needs but also foreign demands, the latter two, military needs and foreign demands, of which kept prices high despite what otherwise would have been years of price-depressing surplus production. In 1863 when the Mississippi River reopened, farmers and grain merchants preferred the safe, quick, and direct railroad transportation to Chicago and the other lake ports. By the end of the war, ninety trains entered Chicago daily, up from one in 1859 and seven lines in 1861. During the war, however, farmers complained about high and unreasonable shipping rates.[14]

The war also caused commodity prices to rise across the Midwest. In mid-April 1861, wheat sold for 87 cents and corn 31 cents per bushel while cattle brought between $2.80 and $3.40 and hogs $4.40 to $4.60 per hundredweight on the Chicago market. After the firing on Fort Sumter on April 12–14, 1861, wheat brought 95 cents and corn 83 cents per bushel. Cattle prices increased slightly, but hog prices jumped from $5.00 to $5.25 per hundred pounds. By early May, flour had risen to $17 per barrel, up from $4.60 a month earlier. One observer attributed the price rise to the war: "Some anxiety has been felt lest there be a scarcity of provisions at Washington in consequence of the large numbers of troops being sent there." The editor of the *Prairie Farmer* told midwestern farmers that armies needed food and urged the farmers to produce "every bushel of grain that can be grown, every pound of pork and beef that can be fattened, every colt that can be raised." He also believed that England would want more grain and flour in the days ahead, and farming would be "very remunerative." With the troops in Washington, D.C., consuming 76 barrels of pork or 25,000 pounds of fresh beef on alternate days and 115 barrels of flour and 50 bushels of beans daily, the editor's optimism seemed warranted. Indeed, the *Prairie Farmer* ventured, "There is a certainty of a fair, if not a large, price for every farm product. This aside from all considerations of patriotism will stimulate the extra exertions to increase the number of tilled acres."[15]

During the early months of the war, however, the closure of the Mississippi River kept agricultural prices low because farmers who relied on river transportation could not get their produce to market. In the autumn of 1861, for example, Iowa farmers sold their wheat for 50 cents per bushel while corn brought 10 cents, oats 12 cents, and potatoes 12 to 20 cents per bushel. Butter sold for 10 cents per pound and eggs for

8 cents per dozen. Chickens brought 10 cents each, and cattle and hogs sold for $2.00 per hundred weight. When a rumor spread that Vicksburg had been taken and the Mississippi River reopened, prices rose rapidly only to fall back when the news proved untrue. After more than eight months of fighting, one Indiana farmer reported, "Very few here can pay their debts—many cannot pay taxes—We had a cold wet spring— drouth in summer, army worm and hog cholera—all combined fall on with crushing effect." He also complained, "Many things that farmers have to sell have no cash price here—corn hauled 18 miles to market brings 15cts per bushel—pork if good $2.25 per hundred—wheat 50 to 60 cts—potatoes 15 to 20 cents" per bushel.[16]

In Illinois, wheat also declined to 80 cents and corn to 25 cents per bushel because merchants often rejected paper money from Illinois banks, and farmers refused to sell wheat, corn, and other produce unless paid in cash, that is, gold coin. As a result, one eastern correspondent noted that "many commission men are sending gold to their country correspondents with which to purchase grain." Midwestern farmers distrusted eastern paper as much as notes from western "wild cat" banks, and they took a wait-and-see approach to market demand even though cattle and hog prices remained high and eastern currency allegedly sound. By midsummer 1861, an Indiana farmer reported that "times is hard and money is scarce. [I]n fact you can sell anything here for money." He meant, of course, gold coin, because the federal government had not yet begun printing sound paper money to help pay for the war and facilitate the necessary trade, including agricultural products, required to conduct it.[17]

Speculators and banks began hoarding gold coin by December 1861, and the circulation of sound money nearly ceased. In February 1862, Congress responded by passing the Legal Tender Act, which authorized the federal government to print paper money. These "greenbacks" began circulating in April, but they were not backed at face value with gold or silver. The value of these greenbacks fluctuated depending on the conversion market between greenbacks and gold dollars, but the U.S. Treasury would redeem them on demand. This legal tender restored public confidence in the circulating currency, but it took time. By May 1864, midwestern businessmen and bankers also agreed to accept only greenbacks and national bank notes for all transactions. As a result, "wild cat" bank notes soon disappeared from circulation. Farmers welcomed this monetary standardization because they believed that the greenbacks had a reliable value. When farmers, often of necessity, accepted "wild cat" bank notes, that is, unsecured paper money, they received considerably less than face value if they exchanged it for greenbacks, national bank notes, or gold.[18]

The problem, however, was that farmers received payment for their produce in paper money, not specie, that is, gold coin, and in 1862, $200 in paper money was worth only $150 in specie at the current exchange rate. Midwestern farmers complained about depreciated paper money, low agricultural prices, increased expenses, and manufacturers that passed their costs on to them. In the autumn, midwestern farmers contended the "great bulk" of their produce had declined in price from 35 to 70 percent for an average of 43 percent during the past two years. Only oats, rye, and barley increased in price, but other than oats, which proved a "short crop," these crops were essentially insignificant. Illinois farmers believed they received only 64 cents in depreciated money for every $1.00 earned, for a 36 percent decline due to paper currency. At the same time, they paid $1.77 in inflated prices for manufactured goods that should have cost only $1.00. The difference was $1.13 against the farmer for every dollar exchanged for purchases. One observer complained that a farm expenditure that cost seven bushels of corn in 1860 cost nearly thirty bushels by late 1862. Although prices on the Chicago and local markets had increased, midwestern farmers calculated that they only kept about one-third of their income from sales because of commission men, transportation costs, and other expenses. These farmers wanted manufacturers to freeze prices and "abstain from increasing the pressure on the shoulders of the overburdened farmers." And, with a veiled threat that would be more sharply articulated during the thirty years following the war, one editor spoke for many midwestern farmers: "Unless there is a great rise in their produce . . . they must to a very considerable extent, forego the use of many comforts they have heretofore been accustomed to, and also of farm machinery and labor. . . . The consequences will be a curtailment of farm operations. And perhaps, after all, only in this way can the prices of farm produce be made reasonably remunerating."[19]

Some agricultural observers, however, considered deflated paper money a benefit, and many farmers welcomed high wartime commodity prices and used their income in depreciated paper dollars to pay off mortgages contracted in gold. In February 1862, S. D. Harris, editor of the *Ohio Cultivator*, urged farmers to take "government notes and good currency freely this year." As long as they operated on a "pay as you go" basis, he argued, they could expand or improve their farms. Federal troops needed food, and as soon as the army and navy reopened the Mississippi River, "a million hungry humans will open their mouths like young robins to get a taste of our cheap bacon and beef and corn and wheat and whiskey." In July 1864, one Indiana farmer observed that "eatables is enormously high." Another Indiana farmer reported that "times is good" if a farmer had commodities to sell with wheat bringing $1.80 to $1.90 and corn $1.00 to $1.25 per bushel and pork 12 cents to 14 cents per pound on local markets. With high prices such as these, he mused that "even a hen's cackle in a barnyard is worth five cents." Despite complaints, then, midwestern farmers enjoyed prosperity rather than hard times during the war.[20]

Indeed, by autumn 1864, many farm experts believed something was "radically wrong" with a farmer who could not free himself from debt. "Never in the lifetime of the present generation will such another opportunity present itself," one observer said. Everything that a midwestern farmer raised commanded a "highly remunerative price" and a "ready purchaser." Many farmers now operated on the principle that a dollar cancelled a dollar's worth of debt, and since those debts could be paid with paper money, they profited considerably, even though their expenses for labor, implements, and seed as well as transportation rose during the war. Moreover, high wartime prices gave higher profits than earned from greater productivity before the war.[21]

The establishment of a reliable currency and the expansion of railroad transportation soon caused prices to rise and commodities to reach the market, encouraging midwestern farmers to increase wheat and corn production for domestic, military, and international customers. Many midwestern farmers, however, often planted fewer acres or at best maintained their prewar acreage due to bad weather (including drought and frost), insects, and crop disease. Drought, frost, and insects sometimes caused crop damage and reduced harvests in some locations, but good weather, high prices, and diverse crops in other areas helped make up any general crop shortfall across the Midwest.[22]

Near the end of the war, an Ohio observer reflected on cattle prices, "[I]t is very doubtful whether or not beef cattle will ever be as low again as in old times." In 1861, cattle brought $2.50 per hundredweight in Madison County, Ohio, and rose to $4.50 in 1865. By May 1864, the *Prairie Farmer* reported, "Government contractors find it hard work to fill contracts at ruling prices, and are constantly dragging down the market, which . . . must continue to advance as long as the large army is in the field." A month later, cattle brought from $7.00 to $8.50 per hundredweight on the Chicago market. In August, the editor reported, "There is now in store here about double the amount of wheat and corn that there was a year ago, notwithstanding the short supply of corn last year." Wheat brought $2.20 per bushel on the Chicago and Milwaukee markets and $2.27 in Ohio. Contractors paid $5.00 to $6.25 for "army grades" of beef while civilian buyers paid more for better cattle. Hogs brought $8.50 to $12.00 per hundredweight.[23]

High prices, then, made the Civil War profitable for midwestern farmers. In 1861, Louis P. Harvey, governor of Wisconsin, had recognized the wartime economic opportunity for farmers. They would prosper, he wrote, due to their "immunity from the desolations liable to fall upon the border States . . . and largely due to the fact that we are an agricultural people, producing immense quantities of great food staples which must always sell at some price, and which are usually enhanced in value in time of war." An Illinois farmer agreed, "Your market is certain, and all history is a lie if it shall not be remunerative." By 1863, one observer commented, "Every agricultural product has met with a ready sale and at greatly augmented prices."[24]

Most midwestern farmers who had not lost a son or family member agreed that war paid. In January 1864, an Iowa farmer reported, "[T]imes are pretty good here now, evry thing brings a good price." Another contemporary stated, "Fortunes are being made in a day every where over the land. . . . The country is full of money." Production and market prices, of course, fluctuated during the war depending on drought, army worms, and government purchases as well as civilian demand, but prices rose and remained consistently high during the war. One observer reported that even though paper bank and treasury notes might contribute to higher agricultural prices, the real reason for inflation was that "war prices always were and always must be high prices."[25]

As early as spring 1862, then, midwestern farmers produced for a war-time market, and large supplies of meat, flour, and grain filled warehouses in Ohio, Indiana, Illinois, and Iowa while lesser quantities accumulated in Michigan, Wisconsin, and Minnesota. Some observers calculated the agricultural power of the Midwest by claiming that Ohio alone could export 50 percent of its crops without causing an "absolute want for food." In August, a soldier at Camp Denison, Ohio, made his own report in a letter home on the agricultural abundance of the Midwest: "We got plenty to eat, good light soft bread, beans, pork, rice, beef, good coffee sweetened." With the exception of the rice and coffee, which reflected the prewar supplies of the quartermaster, the men of the 50th Ohio Infantry consumed food produced on Ohio farms. At the same time, a member of the 97th Illinois Volunteer Infantry reported from Camp Butler near Springfield, Illinois, "Supper consisted of fat pork roasted on a stick, bakers bread and coffee." Breakfast consisted of fresh beef, bread, and coffee. While at Camp Butler, soldiers purchased sweet potatoes, onions, apples, and milk from local farmers, which they consumed with their rations of fresh beef, pickled pork, and smoked meat.[26]

In 1863, one traveler reported that the agricultural productivity of the Midwest was great: "On the whole, so far as the eye can measure the West could continue the war for the next ten years, and not feel it vitally." Southerners did not have the luxury or safety net of this agricultural productivity, that is, agricultural power. As early as June 1861, confederate troops in Virginia reportedly suffered from inadequate provisions, which made hunger a daily trial. During the war, several Southern cities also experienced bread riots, and when Union and Confederate armies marched, hungry men pillaged farms at will.[27]

The most serious problem confronting midwestern farmers, however, that limited their ability to capitalize on high wartime prices was the loss of tens of thousands of farmers and agricultural workers to the army, where they became consumers rather than producers of food. Approximately 2.1 million Northerners fought for the Union, and the Old Northwest provided about 1 million soldiers of whom approximately 48 percent were farmers or farmworkers. Yet, here, too, the agricultural power of the Midwest can be seen in the rapid adoption of horse-powered implements. The great number of volunteers and draftees from the Midwest created a severe labor shortage during the war that midwestern farmers largely solved by increasing their use of horse-drawn machinery, particularly for the production of small grains, such as wheat. Although midwestern farmers had begun using a host of implements, such as reapers and mowers, during the 1850s, the Civil War hastened the adoption of agricultural technology not only because high wartime agricultural prices provided the capital for such investment but also because labor shortages necessitated the substitution of implements for expensive and scarce human-labor power. Not every farmer, however, could instantly afford a reaper when the war began. In 1861, some Iowa farmers still used cradle scythes to harvest their wheat. A year later, some Wisconsin farmers attributed the failure of the wheat harvest to their inability to harvest the crop due to a labor shortage military enlistments caused.[28]

In June 1861, with wheat at 65 cents per bushel on some local markets, midwestern farmers complained that grain prices did not permit them to pay high wages for agricultural workers, and they questioned the patriotism, decency, and Christianity of those who demanded more than $1.50 per day with board. By autumn 1862, Indiana farmers paid $1.00 per day for plowing and 75 cents per day for threshing wheat. Experienced farmhands earned from $120 to $150 per year with room and board. A year later, some Indiana farmers only paid 75 cents per day, but they expected to pay higher wages at harvest time. In 1864, Illinois farmers paid workers $2 per acre at harvest time and $1.25 per acre for plowing. When the war ended, farmworkers often earned $200 to $250 annually.[29]

In 1862, one farmer reported cutting wheat with a reaper at the rate of five acres per day, and he also threshed with a steam engine, which he probably hired along with the threshing machine and an itinerant threshing crew. In November, while farmers busily harvested corn by hand, some threshed their wheat with machines, thereby completing two harvesting tasks during the same season. One editor reported that an "unprecedented quantity of reapers and mowers" had been sold in the Badger State for the wheat harvest. At that time, the *Prairie Farmer* reported that approximately thirty-three thousand reapers had been built for the grain harvest. In 1863, the Ohio firm of C. Aultman and Co. manufactured thirty-one hundred Buckeye mowers and reapers, and W. H. Loomis, secretary of the Indiana State Fair, estimated that at least five thousand combined reapers and mowers and ten thousand mowers would be used to gather the wheat and hay crops. He believed that these implements would replace the more than twenty thousand men required for the wheat harvest only eight years earlier. The U.S. commissioner of patents also reported the manufacture of forty thousand harvesting machines and estimated that as many as ninety thousand reapers and mowers would be built for sale to midwestern farmers in 1864, more than twice the number manufactured two years earlier.[30]

During the war, one observer reported, "At least from one-third to one-fourth of the ordinary farm laborers were transferred to the battlefields, and in many instances the farmers themselves, and the entire amount of farm labor was performed by those who remained at home," that is, boys too young or men too old for military service as well as farm wives and daughters. He also said, "Machinery and improved implements have been employed to a much greater extent during the years of rebellion than ever before. . . . Without drills, corn planters, reapers and mowers, horse-rakes, hay elevators, and threshing machines, it would have been impossible to have seeded and gathered the crops of 1863 with the implements in use forty or fifty years ago, by the same laborers that really performed the labor in 1863." An Illinois wheat farmer also contended that a "fifteen year old boy or an old man of sixty" conducted the work of two men by using a reaper with no more exertion required than driving a team of horses while reducing costs and increasing production. An Indianan reported, "It takes about half as long to harvest now as it used to. They get almost everything done by machinery." Horse-drawn farm implements saved time and labor.[31]

In 1863, in order to meet the farm worker shortage, the *Davenport Gazette* suggested that farmers look to the "Sunny South" for labor. In October, however, one Northern correspondent reported that the wheat crop had been a "good one" and that "throughout many sections of the country it would have been altogether impossible to gather the crops had it not been for the recently invented mowing and reaping machines." The next spring, the *Prairie Farmer* editor related that the oats crop was "immense" and that the high price of corn at $1.09 per bushel would encourage farmers to plant as much acreage as possible. He believed that with gang plows and wheeled cultivators, more could be done with the same help than usual because the young and the old could operate those implements, and "it is not uncommon to see a lady operating farm machinery now." Even with the increased use of reapers, mowers, and threshing machines, however, insufficient labor often required farmers to postpone nonessential work. In 1864, for example, an observer said that in Huron County, Ohio, "no improvements worthy of mention have been made by farmers in draining their farms or in cultivation for the past year, on account of the absence of their sons in the service of the country. . . . Farmers have all they can do to hold their own. . . . [I]t is difficult to obtain labor sufficient for the <u>seedtime</u> and <u>harvest</u>."[32]

Certainly by the summer of 1864, the agricultural labor problem became severe. The editor of the *Prairie Farmer* stated, "It is a year of great scarcity of labor and consequently high wages. . . . If we may judge the amount of grains planted, it will not be a year of deficient harvests," provided drought, frost, and insects did not ruin the crops. Farmers had money to purchase implements, more so than any other year in the war, and he did not expect the agricultural labor shortage and high wages demanded to inordinately interfere with farm operations because of new machinery and its availability. He also believed that "with such a progressive people that can wield the dreadful weapons of war with one hand while they feed themselves and the world with the other, we fear no great backward movement in these matters." Even though peace came with the spring of 1865, the agricultural labor problem worsened in the region because many men did not receive discharge from the army until summer, far too late for the spring plowing and planting seasons. One Iowa farm woman complained to her army-bound husband that "to get a man to do anything is out of the question."[33]

Overall, midwestern industrial power translated to agricultural power. During the war, farmers used reapers and mowers to reduce their labor needs. One Ohio farmer contended, "The nearer home farmers can procure a good machine, the more likely they are to own one." And, in 1862, the Ohio State Board of Agriculture reported that 175,000 men had left for the war but that agricultural machinery replaced 154,771 for a labor deficiency of approximately only 20,000 men. One contemporary commented that "machines have been introduced as substitutes for laborers." As a result, "Ohio can readily contribute 100,000 men for the suppression of the rebellion, without serious embarrassment in her agricultural operations." Consequently, he contended, "enough bread stuffs can be grown by those remaining at home, to subsist at least twice the present population of the State."[34]

By the end of the war, the midwestern farmers had increased their agricultural implements threefold since 1860. In 1864, many of the 187 agricultural implement manufacturers that had built $15 million worth of harvesting machines operated in the Midwest, and those implement companies produced at full capacity. Yet, they still could not fill all orders during the war. The Fish Brothers in Racine, Wisconsin, now built approximately three thousand wagons valued at $300,000 annually. J. I. Case and Co. in Racine also manufactured one thousand threshing machines along with horse powers, wagons, straw stackers, and other implements for $1 million annual sales. Observers reported that reapers and mowers were "very extensively manufactured" at Beloit, Janesville, Madison, and Whitewater, all in Wisconsin, and that the Whitewater Plow Company conducted a "great business." In Wisconsin, George Easterly built more than five thousand seeders and cultivators valued at $400,000. One observer commented that the number of reapers and mowers annually sold in Wisconsin during the war was "really marvelous" and that "there must be very few farmers unsupplied." Moreover, he wrote that "many of our farmers are raising such large cereal crops as to be forced from motives of economy, to throw aside their old implements at the moment an unmistakably improved one comes to their knowledge." Throughout the war, agricultural-implement dealers in Wisconsin reportedly sold grain drills, "sulky" cultivators, revolving steel-toothed rakes, and horse hay-forks in the "most incredible numbers."[35]

Other implement companies, particularly in Ohio and Illinois, also manufactured a variety of horse-drawn agricultural implements, all designed to save labor and reduce operating costs, provided the farmers could afford the implement. No shortage of metal occurred that required limitations on the manufacture of agricultural equipment. Southern armies did not destroy midwestern agricultural-implement factories or iron works, and the expanding railroad network transported new implements to waiting farmers. In 1863, the editor of the La Crosse, Wisconsin, *Democrat* noted, "The several agricultural shops in this city are driven with work and hardly able to meet the demands on them for threshing machines, reapers, fanning mills, etc. Millions more dollars could be profitably invested here in the manufacturing of farm tools and labor saving implements of all kinds. There is no end to the demand which increases each year in astonishing ratio." Southern farmers did not have the industrial resources that helped create and became a part of midwestern agricultural power.[36]

During the war years, the increased adoption of farm implements, particularly the reaper, which replaced four to six men at harvest time, made the expansion of wheat acreage and production possible. One Wisconsin farmer remarked that "under the stimulus of necessity during the war, very great improvements have been made in nearly every class of machines and implements. . . . There seems but little more wanting to give the farmer comparative independence of the slow manual labor on which but one or two decades since he was compelled to rely altogether." He believed that "for the incalculable service they have rendered during our national struggle . . . the American inventor, manufacturer . . . and vender of agricultural implements and machines, are entitled to rich material reward and the gratitude of the nation and world." The agricultural newspapers ran numerous advertisements for reapers, mowers, and other implements throughout the war.[37]

Certainly, the wartime military and consumer demands for food increased commodity prices and encouraged farmers to adopt new technology in order to plant and harvest more acres or maintain prewar acreage and cultivate it more intensively. By so doing, they increased their income from the harvest of more bushels of grain at high prices, which, in turn, provided the profits for investment in new farm implements. The rapid and widespread adoption of farm implements during the Civil War also marked the change from hand power to horse power. Midwestern farmers became increasingly reliant, even dependent, on horse-powered implements thereafter until the early twentieth century. Certainly, the Civil War served as a catalyst for the adoption of new agricultural technology. More important, the rapid adoption of horse-powered implements in the Midwest meant the expansion of the region's agricultural power. The Confederacy did not have that technological luxury.[38]

The adoption of horse-powered implements to replace the normal farm labor force also meant that others, often women, would be required to operate that technology. Few farms could become successful without partnerships between men and women, usually in marriage. Men and women had traditionally shared farm labor, although by the Civil War, many American-born women did not conduct fieldwork. Still, most farm women knew how to do it, and some took up that burden when their husbands left for the army or to compensate for a lack of money to hire workers. In 1861, an Iowa farm woman and her children raked and bound twenty acres of wheat that her husband had cut with a cradle scythe. The temperature was more than 100 degrees, she wrote, and "I wore a dress with my sunbonnet wrong [wrung] out in water every few minutes and my dress wet also. [T]his was all that . . . I wore. . . . Our hired man left just as corn planting commenced so I shouldered my hoe and have worked ever since and I guess my services are just as acceptable as his or will be." She and her daughter also picked and husked corn, dug potatoes and carrots, and pulled rutabagas. With labor scarce and wages high at $1.50 to $2.00 per day, plus board, the mother and daughter necessarily conducted the farm work as a family. Her husband commented, "I don't know what I should [do] without them."[39]

Technology in the form of farm implements lightened their labors and enabled farm women to maintain and sometimes increase agricultural production. In March 1863, an Indiana farmer's daughter, who lived near Fort Wayne, harrowed ground for planting wheat. She also helped "thrash" the previous year's crop with a horse-powered machine. She wrote, "When we thrash he has my younger sister drive the horses and my brother rake the straw from the machine and my oldest sister to pitch the sheaves to me and I have to unbind them and get them up on a table so he can get them and he feeds the machine himself. . . . I do not know what he would do if it was not for his girls." During the summer of 1863, a correspondent for the *Cleveland Herald* also observed, "It is a very common affair to see a bright eyed young woman seated on a reaper driving a four-horse team." He also reported women in Lake County raking, pitching, loading hay, and driving the hay wagon as well as cultivating with a hoe. Across the Midwest, farm women helped their husbands by using horse-drawn cultivators and rollers to prepare their fields for crops.[40]

Still, reaping machines required workers to follow and bind the cut grain into sheaves and place them in shocks until threshing time. In the absence of male labor, midwestern farm wives and daughters often trailed the reapers. In 1863, for example, a woman said, "The men have all gone to the war, so that my man can't hire any help at any price, and I told my girls that we must turn out and give him a lift in the harvesting." Somewhere in Wisconsin or eastern Iowa, an observer reported, "Women were in the field everywhere, driving the reapers, binding and shocking, and loading the grain," and she was amazed at "how skillfully they drove the horses." She also watched women follow the reapers and bind and shock, and "although they did not keep up with the men, their work was done with more precision and nicety, and their sheaves had an artistic finish that those lacked made by the men." These women wore "stout boots," Shaker bonnets, and dresses without hoops. Another farm wife considered herself "as good a binder as a man" and could keep up with the "best of 'em." One Iowa farmer was so proud of his daughter's ability to bind sheaves of wheat that he offered a ten-dollar bet in the local newspaper that his daughter could "beat any one binding wheat that will enter the field with her as a contestant." But, he warned, "She weighs 205 pounds, and carries no extra flesh."[41]

In September 1863, the agricultural-implement committee of the Illinois State Agricultural Society stated that farm wives and daughters were "ready and anxious to lend a helping hand, if they can do it consistent with their strength and womanly feelings and not compromise their dignity and sense of propriety by so doing." Although this comment reveals more about the opinion of the male committee members concerning propriety, Illinois farm women did not shirk from work. Moreover, the committee urged farmers' daughters to "put on their high heeled, thick soled shoes, shaker bonnet, 'the other dress,' and . . . leave their hoops in the dark bed room, and . . . with a proud step and patriotic heart, mount on to a good, clean, painted and varnished two-horse cultivator, reaper or mower, and have the satisfaction at night of having had a fine day's ride, and saving their dear fathers two dollars per day." One Ohioan contended, "We shall have a more efficient race of women when the war is over," and an Iowa farmer urged women to abandon "corsets, belts, and cosmetics." Fieldwork would "strengthen their frames" and enable them to "grow robust instead of slender, rosy instead of pallid, brown rather than delicate." No doubt, many Iowa farm women disagreed with his premise, and they conducted fieldwork from necessity rather than for reasons of health and appearance. Even so, Southern women did not have the luxury of these burdens because many families fled their farms or operated them on a subsistence basis until the war ended. They had little opportunity for the agricultural work that enabled commercial production that translated into regional agricultural power.[42]

In Iowa, foreign-born farm women held American-born women who refused to plow, plant, cultivate, or harvest in contempt and contended that American-born women only cared for frivolous things, such as clothing. Most midwestern farm women would not take up the plow unless no other option availed for getting the work done. Gender divisions for farm labor prevailed, but exceptions occurred. In August 1864, a Des Moines newspaper editor said that "female labor in the corn fields" could be observed all across the state, and in Wisconsin, "German, Norwegian, and Bohemian servant girls" reportedly brought in the grain harvest. The editor of the Green Bay, Wisconsin, *Advocate* wrote, "We have a great element of strength up here which goes far toward repairing the loss of farm hands by the war. The sturdy, muscular German and Belgium women plough and sow and reap with all the skill and activity of men, and we believe are fully their equals in strength." The Milwaukee *Daily News* also reported, "A grown man at work in the field is a rare sight. The farm labor is mostly being done by women and children."[43]

Many midwestern women, however, did not work in the fields but shifted farm operations from the heavy work of raising corn, which required cultivating, picking, and shelling, to the comparatively lighter work of raising wheat, which required less physical labor if a reaper cut the grain. Some had sufficient help from older and young men, sons, or other family members, or they rented their farms and moved back to parental homes. Moreover, farm women with small children often could not work in the fields, and family household chores usually proved full-time jobs, considering these women customarily had responsibility for the chickens and garden and the canning that the latter brought with it. Time and family responsibilities not the lack of ability or desire kept many women from fieldwork. But if they could not drive a reaper, they could supervise the harvest hands and threshing crews, and farm women managed the financial accounts and paid debts. They also made decisions about raising crops, acquiring land, and renting their farms until their husbands returned. By October 1861, observers saw Ohio women "superintending the farm, overseeing the workshop, hunting up buyers for the garden and orchard products, and laying in their winter stores with care and economy."[44]

Still, even with the increased use of new or improved farm implements, the productivity of midwestern farms generally remained at prewar levels or decreased. At the same time, most farms, though small, had acreage available for crop expansion. Ohio farms, for example, averaged only 114 acres with about 70 acres, or 61 percent, improved, that is, under cultivation. If those farmers could acquire the labor or implements to permit the planting and harvesting of more acres, they could increase their production of corn and wheat. Midwestern farmers emphasized wheat and corn as well as hogs and beef and sheep for wool along with poultry, hay, and some dairying. This diversification met home food needs but also enabled farmers to pursue agricultural production for commercial gain. The marketplace had become important to farmers in Ohio, Indiana, and Illinois before the war, and Iowa, Wisconsin, Minnesota, and Michigan farmers found cash outlets for their crops, livestock, and dairy products as the war continued. Farmers had relatively easy access to urban markets via railroads, and they began to specialize along those rail lines. Indeed, the war encouraged specialization, and farmers increasingly produced more of the commodities that they could raise the most efficiently and cheaply and in the greatest volume. The agricultural productivity and wealth of the Midwest also permitted some farmers to experiment with a few select crops, even in wartime, so great were their economic comfort and security.[45]

With the closure of the Mississippi River, for example, sugar from the Louisiana plantations disappeared from merchants' shelves. Midwestern farmers compensated, however, not by doing without but by producing more sorghum molasses for a sugar and maple-syrup substitute. The production of sorghum molasses was less labor intensive than tapping maple trees and collecting and boiling the sap. Although sorghum required pressing the stalks and boiling the juice, this early autumn activity could be conducted on more farms than those that had a stand of maple trees. Moreover, an acre of sorghum required no more labor than an acre of corn to plant, cultivate, and harvest, and it returned at least $60 per acre for the production of sorghum molasses. In 1861, midwestern farmers sold a thousand barrels of sorghum molasses to dealers in Chicago and ten thousand barrels a year later. The market potential seemed unlimited, which encouraged Ohio farmers to hold a "state sorghum convention" and later to organize the Ohio Sorghum Association to help improve production of sorghum sugar and molasses. Although no one would mistake the dark-brown sorghum molasses for maple syrup, midwesterners used it to sweeten tea and coffee and as syrup for cornbread and hot cakes. In 1863, when sugar from captured plantations in Louisiana began moving north with the reopening of the Mississippi River, together with increased imports from Cuba and a killing frost that damaged the crop, sorghum acreage declined rapidly.[46]

Yet, the failure to produce a sugar and syrup substitute that consumers found tasteful did not mean that midwestern farmers had turned to sorghum production in desperation. Rather, the raising of sorghum for molasses indicates that midwestern farmers produced enough wheat, corn, and livestock for civilian and military needs that also brought sufficient profit so that they could plant other acres in sorghum. In some cases, their optimism proved boundless. In November 1862, one Indianan predicted that sorghum molasses would soon be the state's most valuable export: "Intelligent farmers in Southern Indiana say that in a few years they will ship sugar down the river in larger quantities than now ascends the Ohio." Not much sugar, of course, ascended the Ohio at that time, but he, surely, made the comparison to the past. The Civil War fostered desires to overpower Southern agricultural production, at least regarding sugar. In the end, peace and taste dictated a different outcome, but for a while, optimism reigned supreme among the producers of sorghum molasses. Some midwestern farmers, particularly in Illinois, also experimented with raising sugar beets, but the conversion of beets to sugar remained in the future with the development of new technology. The luxury of time, money, and labor to experiment, however, indicated an agricultural power that Southern farms never enjoyed.[47]

Midwestern farmers along the Ohio River also experimented with cotton. Many farmers in Southern Illinois brought the cotton culture with them when they migrated from the South prior to the Civil War. They used their small crops for home use, but most farm families preferred to purchase their clothing rather than spin and weave cotton for pants, dresses, and shirts. With cotton ranging in price from twenty-seven to forty cents per pound, however, some farmers in Southern Illinois believed the gamble in labor costs merited the risk. William H. Osborn, president of the Illinois Central Railroad, encouraged these efforts and gained a $3,000 congressional appropriation for the distribution of cotton seed in Ohio, Indiana, and Illinois. Osborn, of course, wanted to sell Illinois Central Railroad lands to farmers who would produce a crop that required transport to market. He advertised Illinois Central lands as being well-suited for the "perfection" of cotton that he contended would yield "a most profitable account." One contemporary also believed that southern Indiana farmers could raise cotton profitably if the price held about fifty cents per pound and crops yielded 100 pounds of "clean" cotton per acre and with one hand producing two bales or 800 pounds per year. He reasoned that cotton could be produced cheaper in Indiana than in the South because the crop would be lighter thereby reducing the cost of picking, which he said was "the greatest part of the work." He also contended, "Anybody who can pick berries, can pick cotton." Cotton, however, required about two hundred frost-free days, and even the southern fringes of the Midwest proved marginal at best for cotton production. In Southern Illinois, farmers produced only 6,770 pounds, or about 13.5, 500-hundred-pound bales, in 1862 but increased production to 384,480 pounds, or approximately 7,609 bales, from 12,835 acres during the last harvest of the war.[48]

Three-fourths of the Illinois cotton crop reached local markets along the Illinois Central Railroad where gins stripped the seed, and presses baled the fiber. Carbondale, which had eleven gins and four presses, became the cotton center of the Midwest. Illinois cotton reached New York City through Chicago with the freight rates at $2.40 per hundredweight. Small-scale farmers produced most of this cotton although a few farmers cultivated from twenty-five to one hundred acres with hired labor at wage rates for picking ranging from one to two and a half cents per pound. With cotton bringing eight to eleven cents per pound and "ordinary" pickers gathering 100 pounds and "good" pickers averaging 150 to 200 pounds per day, cotton proved a profitable crop, more so than tobacco. Still, knowledgeable observers considered cotton a risky crop. One Illinois farmer advised small-scale operators to plant corn, wheat, and potatoes for family needs and "then put the extra labor on cotton, which will be likely to line the pocket well with greenbacks." With the 1864 cotton crop paying Illinois farmers $1,125,396, they planned to expand cotton production for the next season. Still, cotton required considerable labor for plowing, planting, cultivating, and picking, and it quickly became scarce and expensive in the Midwest. Moreover, before cotton could be sold for manufacture, the seeds had to be separated from the fiber by a gin. With gins costing between $100 and $500 during the war, few farmers or others believed the crop merited that investment.[49]

With a good cotton crop producing about 250 pounds of ginned fiber per acre in Southern Illinois, similar to cotton crops planted on more extensive acreage in the Deep South before the war, the danger of economic failure would come with the peace. One farmer urged caution: "If we attempt to grow cotton in Illinois for market, at rates that have formerly ruled, we shall find it an uphill business, requiring the greatest energy, skill and improved machinery." Few doubted the profitability of cotton as long as the blockade kept prices high. But one farmer warned, "That must soon melt away before the progress of events and the march of armies." Moreover, cotton farming required year-round labor and more of it than needed for raising corn. All things considered, midwestern farmers welcomed wartime opportunities to make money, but farmers in Southern Illinois knew a bad risk when they saw one, and few took their chances with cotton. In the end, Illinois farmers considered hemp and flax "more remunerative" crops for the Prairie State, and tobacco farming seemed a less risky and better opportunity.[50]

Prior to the war, farmers had raised tobacco along the Ohio River where the temperatures proved moderate and where many farmers had cultural ties to the South and knew something about raising this time-consuming crop. When the war quickly prevented Southern tobacco from reaching Northern consumers, some farmers attempted to meet the demand that increased tobacco from three cents per pound on the eve of the war to as high as thirty-five cents per pound by the end of the conflict. By late November 1862, tobacco had become one of the staple products of Indiana. Warrick, Spencer, and Dubois Counties each marketed $200,000 of tobacco that year, while other counties also produced "large amounts." Farmers in southern Indiana reportedly showed "unusual excitement" as they planned to seed a larger tobacco crop in the spring. Knowledgeable observers believed that tobacco would pay better than any other crop as long as the war disrupted access to Southern markets. One Indianan, however, remarked, "If it enriches the man who produces it, it impoverishes the soil that grows it and the man who consumes it." Most southern Indiana farmers, no doubt, agreed with the first two contentions.

By summer, one contemporary reported that farmers in southern Indiana had a "great deal" of tobacco, far more than before the war.[51]

In 1863, farmers in Sangamon County, Illinois, reportedly raised 50,000 pounds of tobacco valued at $125,000, and a tobacco factory opened in Springfield. In the absence of Southern tobacco, this crop brought substantial new income to Sangamon farmers. Adams County farmers also considered tobacco a "paying crop." In Quincy, three large tobacco manufacturers purchased the leaf from nearby farmers, and they planned to increase production to take advantage of this market. Illinois farmers increased their tobacco production more than farmers in southern Ohio and Indiana during the course of the war. They produced 6.8 million pounds in 1859 and 20.3 million pounds in 1863 before the crop declined to 18.8 million pounds for the remainder of the war.[52]

Ohio farmers, primarily in the Miami Valley, produced 37 million pounds of tobacco in 1863, but they saturated the market, causing prices to tumble. Production declined to 17 million pounds a year later. Still, some Ohio farmers hoped that tobacco would become the cotton of the North when Brown County leaf reportedly sold at forty cents per pound on the Cincinnati Market. Based on that hope, Ohio farmers increased tobacco production from 25 million to 29 million pounds, while Indiana farmers increased production from 7.9 million pounds in 1859 to 10.4 million pounds in 1863 before production declined to 8.78 million pounds the next year. During the war, the U.S. commissioner of agriculture reportedly received numerous letters from midwestern farmers requesting tobacco seeds. By 1864, however, production declines resulted, in part, from speculators already at work in the Upper South purchasing tobacco as well as cotton in areas federal troops seized.[53]

Yet, here, too, the leisure to experiment with cotton and tobacco on the part of some farmers further marked the agricultural reserves of the Midwest. Farmers do not experiment when hunger plagues armies and civilians. Northerners, whether in uniform or urbanites at the dinner table, did not suffer hunger and want, at least not due to inadequate agricultural production. Midwestern farmers had money in their pockets from their increasingly specialized and commercial crops and livestock. High wartime income gave some farmers the freedom for "cautious experiments," knowing full well that Southern cotton, tobacco, and sugar would someday once again reach Northern markets.

By spring 1864, sound money and high wartime prices had encouraged midwestern farmers to push their acreage and livestock to the limits of production. In May, the *Prairie Farmer* editor commented, "It is almost certain that teams will be worked beyond their real capacity. Men are scarce, and wages high, so that each driver will be expected to accomplish more work than formerly. . . . Horses are high priced, and farmers do not generally feel like keeping more team than is barely sufficient to do the work." He did not envy workhorses under these circumstances, and he hoped that farmers would treat them with more than ordinary care, even mercy. The last full year of the war would be one of feverish work for man and beast across the Midwest.[54]

By April 20, 1865, eleven days after Robert E. Lee surrendered at Appomattox, midwestern farmers felt the impact of the peace. A farmer near Xenia, Illinois, expressed its appearance as well as anyone when he reported that prices had fallen to sixty cents for corn and eighty-one cents per bushel for wheat: "I think that the war is over." For midwestern farmers, the Civil War had brought prosperity that would not come again soon. Looking back from the vantage point of peace in July 1865, one newspaper reported that as early as 1861, the agricultural productivity of the Midwest strengthened the nation in its "gigantic work" and prevented England from recognizing the Confederacy, so great was Great Britain's need for American wheat and flour. Certainly, it had been a profitable war for midwestern farmers. As early as February 1862, the editor of the *Ohio Cultivator* told his readers, "If you know how to ride this wave, it will bring you to plenty, and while you are thus sustaining the best interests of the government, work also for yourselves a good recompense of reward." Most midwestern farmers took his advice and profited by war's end.[55]

With the peace established, agriculturalists anticipated a bountiful grain harvest. Surplus production would not only enable an increase in agricultural exports and diminish the national debt but also "relieve the South from the terrible privation brought upon it by the war." One commentator asserted, "Our ability to supply the wants of the South will greatly promote the speedy renewal of the commercial intercourse and all the old ties of the two sections." Midwestern farmers anticipated the opening of Southern markets and continued high prices. Whether the coming years would continue the wartime prosperity free from sectional politics and postwar economic adjustment problems remained to be seen. But what had been seen during the course of the war was the agricultural power of the Midwest, a power that sustained armies and civilians alike while men and women fought and labored to determine whether two nations would reunite as one Union.[56]

Notes

1. Elvira Sheridan Badger, diary, October 13, 1861, Elvira Sheridan Badger Papers, Newberry Library, Chicago. For a comprehensive study of the Union army's use of horses for the cavalry, see David J. Gerleman, "Unchronicled Heroes: A Study of the Union Cavalry Horses in the Eastern Theater: Care, Treatment, and Use, 1861–1865" (PhD diss., Southern Illinois University, 1999).

2. *Transactions of the Illinois Agricultural Society*, 1861–64 (Springfield: Baker and Phillips, 1865), 5:20–21; *Sixteenth Annual Report of the Ohio State Board of Agriculture*, 1861 (Columbus: Richard Nevins, 1862), xvii, xix–xx.

3. *Ohio Cultivator* (Columbus), September 1861; Gerleman, "Unchronicled Heroes," 77–78.

4. *Ohio Cultivator* (Columbus), August, September, and October 1861.

5. *Nineteenth Annual Report of the Ohio State Board of Agriculture*, 1864 (Columbus: Richard Nevins, 1865), 169; *Twenty-Fifth Annual Report of the Ohio State Board of Agriculture*, 1870 (Columbus: Nevins and Meyers, 1871), 416; *Prairie Farmer* (Chicago), May 28, 1864.

6. *Prairie Farmer* (Chicago), November 19, 1864.

7. Margaret Walsh, *The Rise of the Midwestern Meat Packing Industry* (Lexington: University Press of Kentucky, 1982), 55, 57.

8. Ibid., 57.

9. Ibid., 20; *Daily State Sentinel* (Indianapolis, IN), April 17, 1862.

10. Emerson D. Fite, "The Agricultural Development of the West during the Civil War," in *The Economic Impact of the Civil War*, ed. Ralph Andreano (Cambridge, MA: Schenkman, 1962), 53; Walsh, *Rise of the Midwestern Meat Packing Industry*, 34, 61–64, 67–69; *Twentieth Annual Report of the Ohio State Board of Agriculture*, 1865 (Columbus: Richard Nevins, 1866), 292.

11. Fite, "Agricultural Development," 53; *Daily State Sentinel* (Indianapolis, IN), January 23 and December 24, 1863; *Indiana Daily Gazette* (Indianapolis, IN), September 11, 1863.

12. Walsh, *Rise of the Midwestern Meat Packing Industry*, 59; Frank L. Klement, *Wisconsin and the Civil War* (Madison: State Historical Society of Wisconsin, 1963), 99; *Daily State Sentinel* (Indianapolis, IN), August 17, 1863.

13. Walsh, *Rise of the Midwestern Meat Packing Industry*, 57, 59–60; Robert L. Jones, *Ohio Agriculture during the Civil War* (Columbus: Ohio State University Press, 1962), 9. For technical changes among the Chicago packers, including the use of ice cut during the winter to cool carcasses processed during the summer, see William Cronon, *Nature's Metropolis: Chicago and the Great West* (New York: Norton, 1991), 230–35.

14. Fite, "Agricultural Development," 48–49, 52–53, 59; *Indiana Daily Gazette* (Indianapolis, IN), July 2, 1863; *Prairie Farmer* (Chicago), May 28, 1864; William Trumble, "Historical Aspects of Food Production of the United States, 1862–1902," *Annual Report of the American Historical Association for 1918* (Washington, DC: GPO, 1921), 1:223. For railroad development into Chicago, see Cronon, *Nature's Metropolis*, 63–74.

15. *Prairie Farmer* (Chicago), April 18 and 25 and May 2, 19, and 30, 1861.

16. "Iowa Farm Letters, 1856–1865," *Iowa Journal of History* 58 (January 1960): 83; James and Susan Ferguson to Dear Cousin, December 22, 1861, James Ferguson Letter, Indiana State Library, Indianapolis.

17. *Prairie Farmer* (Chicago), May 30, 1861; John Watts Hamilton to James D. Crandall, July 1, 1861, John Watts Hamilton Papers, Indiana Historical Society, Indianapolis. Hereafter cited as IHS.

18. Kristen L. Willard, Timothy W. Guinnane, and Harvey S. Rosen, "Turning Points in the Civil War: Views from the Greenback Market," *American Economic Review* 86 (September 1996): 1001–2; *Prairie Farmer* (Chicago), May 21, 1864.

19. *Daily State Sentinel* (Indianapolis, IN), October 15 and November 12, 1862.

20. *Ohio Cultivator* (Columbus), February 1862; Isaac Clements to Powell Howland, July 16, 1864, and Isaac Clements to Powell Howland, September 21, 1864, folder 5, box 1, Howland Papers, IHS; C. M. M. Hamilton to G. A. Crandle, January 1, 1865, John Watts Hamilton Papers, IHS.

21. *Prairie Farmer* (Chicago), September 10, 1864.

22. *Twentieth Annual Report of the Ohio State Board of Agriculture*, 1865, 210, 216; *Twenty-First Annual Report of the Ohio State Board of Agriculture* 1866 (Columbus: L. D. Myers and Bro., 1867), 173; *Daily State Sentinel* (Indianapolis, IN), September 3 and November 2, 3, and 5, 1863; *New York Times*, July 21 and September 10, 1864; John Griffin Thompson, "The Rise and Decline of the Wheat Growing Industry in Wisconsin," *Bulletin of the University of Wisconsin*, no. 292 (1909; repr., New York: Arno Press, 1972), 58.

23. *Twentieth Annual Report of the Ohio State Board of Agriculture*, 1865, 309, 320, 326, 332; *Prairie Farmer* (Chicago), May 21, June 4, August 6 and 13, and December 17, 1864.

24. *Transactions of the Wisconsin State Agricultural Society*, 1861–68 (Madison: Atwood and Rublee, 1868), 8:83; *Transactions of the Illinois Agricultural Society*, 1861–64, 12; *Eighteenth Annual Report of the Ohio State Board of Agriculture*, 1863 (Columbus: Richard Nevins, 1864), xxv.

25. W. F. Snoddy to Philip Schrader, December 14, 1863, Schrader-Weaver Family Papers, Indiana State Library; Thorne, "Iowa Farm Letters," 86–87; *Prairie Farmer* (Chicago), January 16, February 20, June 18, and July 2, 1864.

26. Charles T. Kruse to Dear Parents, August 24, 1862, Charles T. Kruse Letters, Newberry Library; Charles W. Colby to Dear Folks, September 7, 1862, Charles W. Colby Papers, Newberry Library.

27. *New York Times*, July 23, 1863; *Prairie Farmer* (Chicago), June 27, 1861; Michael B. Chesson, "Harlots or Heroines? A New Look at the Richmond Bread Riot," *Virginia Magazine of History* 92 (April 1984): 131–75.

28. *Ohio Cultivator* (Columbus), April 1862; Wayne D. Rasmussen, "The Civil War: A Catalyst of Agricultural Revolution," *Agricultural History* 39 (October 1965): 187, 195; Thorne, "Iowa Farm Letters," 82; *Report of the Commissioner of Agriculture for the Year 1862* (Washington, DC: GPO, 1863), 421; *Transactions of the Wisconsin State Agricultural Society*, 1861–68, 99; Thompson, "Rise and Decline," 355–56; Stanley L. Engerman and J. Matthew Gallman, "The Civil War Economy: A Modern View," in Steig Forster and Jorg Nagler, eds., *On the Road to War: The American Civil War and the German Wars of Unification, 1861–1871* (Washington, DC: German Historical Institute, 1997), 220. James M. McPherson has calculated that approximately 48 percent of the Union soldiers were farmers or farm laborers. McPherson, *Battle Cry of Freedom: The Civil War Era* (New York: Oxford University Press, 1988), 688. See Paul W. Gates, *Agriculture and the Civil War* (New York: Knopf, 1965), 229.

29. *Prairie Farmer* (Chicago), June 13, 1861; Account Book, 1856–1863, entries April 5 and 16, 1862, and Samuel Ashton Diary, entry March [?] 1863, Thomas Beeson Papers, IHS; *Transactions of the Illinois Agricultural Society*, 1861–64, 284–85; *Twenty-First Annual Report* . . . 1866, 134–35.

30. Samuel Ashton, diary, entries July 8, 9, and 21 and September 9, 1862, Beeson Papers, IHS; George Kerber to R. M. Banta, November 14, 1862, folder 5, Robert M. Banta Papers, IHS; Thompson, "Rise and Decline," 356; Leo Rogin, *The Introduction of Farm Machinery in Its Relation to the Productivity of Labor in the Agriculture of the United States during the Nineteenth Century* (Berkeley: University of California Press, 1931), 91, 93; *Indiana Daily Gazette* (Indianapolis), June 17, 1863; Jones, *Ohio Agriculture*, 21.

31. *Eighteenth Annual Report* . . . 1863, xix–xx; *Transactions of the Illinois State Agricultural Society*, 1861–64, 100; J. C. Repine to Dear Uncle, August [?] 1863, J. C. Repine Papers, Indiana State Library.

32. *Indiana Daily Gazette* (Indianapolis), July 2, 1863; *Daily State Sentinel* (Indianapolis), October 31, 1863; *Prairie Farmer* (Chicago), May 21, 1864; *Nineteenth Annual Report* . . . 1864, 168–69.

33. *Prairie Farmer* (Chicago), June 18, 1864; J. L. Anderson, "The Vacant Chair on the Farm: Soldier Husbands, Farm Wives, and the Iowa Home Front, 1861–1865," *Annals of Iowa* 66 (Summer–Fall, 2007): 247; George Mills, ed., "The Sharp Family Civil War Letters," *Annals of Iowa* 34 (January 1959): 527, 532.

34. *Sixteenth Annual Report* . . . 1861, lviii; *Seventeenth Annual Report of the Ohio State Board of Agriculture for the Year 1862* (Columbus: Richard Nevins, 1863), xviii; *Ohio Cultivator* (Columbus), February 1862.

35. Rasmussen, "Civil War," 194; *Prairie Farmer* (Chicago), July 23, 1864; Rogin, *Introduction of Farm Machinery*, 93; *Transactions of the Wisconsin State Agricultural Society*, 1861–68, 39–40.

36. *Transactions of the Wisconsin State Agricultural Society*, 1861–68, 53–54; Klement, *Wisconsin and the Civil War*, 98; *Seventeenth Annual Report* . . . 1862, lvi.

37. *Transactions for the Wisconsin State Agricultural Society*, 1861–68, 38–39.

38. Lee A. Croy and Thomas Weiss, "Agricultural Productivity Growth during the Decade of the Civil War," *Journal of Economic History* 53 (1993): 527–48; Rasmussen, "Civil War," 194.

39. Thorne, "Iowa Farm Letters," 82–84, 86. For a study of the relationships between farm women and their husbands, see Anderson, "Vacant Chair on the Farm," 241–65.

40. Anderson, "Vacant Chair on the Farm," 242; Mary Hamilton to Adelia Hamilton, March 20, 1863, Mary Hamilton Letters, Indiana State Library; *Daily State Sentinel* (Indianapolis), August 29, 1863; *Prairie Farmer* (Chicago), April 8, 1865.

41. Anderson, "Vacant Chair on the Farm," 247, 249; Mary A. Livermore, *My Story of the War* (Hartford, CT: Worthington, 1888), 145–49.

42. *Transactions of the Illinois Agricultural Society*, 1861–64, 255–56; Anderson, "Vacant Chair on the Farm," 262–64; *Ohio Cultivator* (Columbus), October 1861.

43. Thomas E. Rodgers, "Hoosier Women and the Civil War Home Front," *Indiana Magazine of History* 97 (June 2001): 107, 112; Anderson, "Vacant Chair on the Farm," 262–64; Frederick Merk, *Economic History of Wisconsin during the Civil War Decade* (Madison: State Historical Society of Wisconsin, 1916), 55.

44. Anderson, "Vacant Chair on the Farm," 249, 251, 253–55, 257, 262; Rodgers, "Hoosier Women and the Civil War Home Front," 113; *Ohio Cultivator* (Columbus), October 1861.

45. Gates, *Agriculture and the Civil War*, 129, 131, 135.

46. Ibid., 142; *Ohio Cultivator* (Columbus), January 1862; Klement, *Wisconsin and the Civil War*, 96.

47. Gates, *Agriculture and the Civil War*, 146–50; *Daily State Sentinel* (Indianapolis, IN), November 27, 1862.

48. *Transactions of the Illinois Agricultural Society*, 1861–64, 514; Gates, *Agriculture and the Civil War*, 151–53; *Daily State Sentinel* (Indianapolis, IN), March 26, 1863; *Transactions of the Illinois Agricultural Society*, 1865–66 (Springfield: Baker, Bailache, 1868), 6:66.

49. *Transactions of the Illinois Agricultural Society*, 1865–66, 67–68; *Transactions for the Illinois Agricultural Society*, 1861–64, 519.

50. *Transactions of the Illinois Agricultural Society*, 1861–65, 518–19.

51. Gates, *Agriculture and the Civil War*, 142–43; *Daily State Sentinel* (Indianapolis, IN), November 27, 1862; *Indiana Daily Gazette* (Indianapolis), July 29, 1863.

52. *Prairie Farmer* (Chicago), June 18, 1864; *Transactions of the Illinois Agricultural Society*, 1861–64, 319.

53. *Seventeenth Annual Report . . .* 1862, 143, 163; *Eighteenth Annual Report . . .* 1863, 140, 144, 148; *Nineteenth Annual Report . . .* 1864, 177; *Indiana Daily Gazette* (Indianapolis), April 17, 1863, and March 17, 1864; *Ohio Cultivator* (Columbus), July 1862.

54. *Prairie Farmer* (Chicago), May 28, 1864.

55. J. M. Copeland to Dear Cousin, April 20, 1865, Mrs. West Hedrick Papers, Indiana State Library; *New York Times*, July 27, 1865; *Ohio Cultivator* (Columbus), February 1862.

56. *New York Times*, July 27, 1865.

"Bellevue Soldiers Leaving for the War in 1861," Bellevue, Iowa. Scenes like this gathering were common at steamboat landings across the Midwest. Newly enlisted soldiers from the Midwest, of Yankee, Southern, and midwestern origins, came together to fight for the Union. Events leading to their departure signified the beginning of the home-front war. Cotton Collection, State Historical Society of Iowa, Iowa City.

Johnson's Island, Sandusky Bay, Ohio. This was the view of the prison that excursionists encountered in hopes of glimpsing Confederate prisoners. Charles E. Frohman Collection, Sandusky Library, Sandusky, Ohio.

(*Left to right*) Charles Kendall Adams, Isaac H. Elliott, and Albert Nye, 1861. These three men led the three student military companies that formed on the University of Michigan campus in 1861. Adams, like some other college men, did not serve in the war. Elliott joined the 33rd Illinois Infantry as a company captain in September 1861 and rose to the rank of colonel. He survived the war. Nye enlisted one year short of his graduation and died in Murfreesboro, Tennessee, in 1862, just as the faculty had decreed to award his degree despite his absence. University of Michigan Photographs, BL003711, Bentley Historical Library, University of Michigan.

PRAIRIE FARMER.

NEW SERIES, VOL. 7—NO. 19.]   CHICAGO, ILL., THURSDAY, MAY 9, 1861.   OLD SERIES, VOL. 23—NO. 19.

FARM ECONOMY.

Plant! Plant!

Do not mistake your calling. It is as important that armies should be fed as that they should fight. It is not for want of patriotism or doubting that of any one, that we would urge the farmers not to neglect the plow and cultivator, upon the uncertainties of his services being needed in the defence of the country. In the present stagnation of manufacturing, mining and general business interests, there are sufficient numbers offering to answer present calls, and every bushel of grain that can be grown, every pound of pork and beef that can be fattened, every colt that can be raised, will all be wanted in our own country, and if, as is now the prospect, England's drafts on us will be large for grain and flour, farming must for the next season be very remunerative. Plant corn—all you can possibly take good care of. Plant beans—they are a nutritious food, and will command good prices. Where not too late, put in small grains, all that the land can be prepared for. Put in root crops—they are easily grown, and will afford a large return for the labor bestowed. Plant a patch of sugar cane, which, have manufactured into syrup if practicable, if not, cut in season, it makes an excellent fodder.

A Corn Stalk Rake.

EDS. PRAIRIE FARMER:—There is such an immense quantity of corn stalks to be got rid of this spring, that almost every conceivable kind of rake is being used to gather them together. I have made one for myself which I like better than any other I have seen, and having never seen or heard of one like it, I will send you a description of it.

The head and teeth are the same as used in the revolving hay rake, except that they are heavier and stronger, to hold two horses instead of one, and when used, the teeth stand upright, instead of lying flat.

The frame is very simple: two side pieces 2 by 5 inches, 4½ feet long, with two cross pieces 5 feet long. The pole is bolted to the middle of the cross pieces on the under side.

The handles are about 7 feet long, 1½ inches thick, and 4 inches wide at the largest place, where they are bolted to the rear cross piece, and tapered towards both ends, the forward end running into auger holes in the forward cross piece. On the outside of each handle, directly over the head of the rake is a small projection of iron which catches on a corresponding piece of iron on two of the teeth when they are in a perpendicular position. Then by a sudden jerk of the handles, springing them together, the catches are loosened, and the rake revolves the same as the hay rake. There are two false teeth put in crosswise to the others, of the same length, to keep the head from falling on the ground when it revolves.

The handles are made thin, so that it will be easy to spring them together. The doubletree should be attached to the under side of the pole to prevent too much pressure upon the horses necks.

The size of the head is 5 by 6 inches, 9 feet long; and the teeth of best hickory, 2 inches in diameter, 3 feet 9 inches long.   J. M.

TROY GROVE, March, 1861.

Jerusalem Artichokes—Squashes.

EDS. PRAIRIE FARMER:—In your paper of the 4th inst., the inquiry is raised relative to the Jerusalem Artichokes. Last Spring I succeeded in procuring about a half of a common water bucket of seed of the white variety (much resembling Neshanock Potatoes.) I planted them after cutting into small pieces about the size of common hickory nuts, in two rows, each 24 rods long, in about the middle of May. The seed had been left in the ground during the winter, and from some cause a part of it had got out of the ground in the open air and had been frozen, and in consequence failed to grow, making the hills missing, the field and trimmed most of them well to the ground.

I cultivated them the same as corn, having corn upon each side, but between the artichokes and corn I planted a row of Sweet Potato Squashes.

After clearing the field of corn this Spring I turned in my stock, and when they had remained in a few days my boys gave notice that the hogs, cattle and sheep had fell on to the artichokes and were making sad havoc. I immediately took the wagon and four tined hay forks, and another hand and myself pitched into them, expecting to get five or six bushels perhaps, but to my great surprise we got a large, wide, two horse wagon bed nearly full. I basined a hole a spade deep and buried them, covering well, and still had to fence them to keep the hogs and other stock from digging them out. I think that a root which seems so palatable, and which stock seek after with so much avidity, must have some virtue in it, for nature will not lie, and I think in a case of this kind, mislead. And it must not be supposed that my stock were starving, unless it were for roots, for I aver that no man has wintered his stock better than myself. I am a great friend of roots. I have fed turnips, potatoes, carrots and beets, but not many artichokes. I believe one bushel of corn fed with one half bushel of roots is a much better feed for any kind of stock than two bushels of corn and no roots. I know that all kinds of stock will keep in better health and condition with the root feeding. I do not think it of so much consequence as to the amount of nutriment in the root used and the specific action of roots upon the digestive organs, keeping them in an open healthy tone, removing that costive condition consequent upon feeding them dry and concentrated food during six long months of winter, is not duly appreciated by our Western farmers.

With intelligent farmers it is unnecessary to argue the point. I am fully satisfied that with more roots and less corn we would have healthier cattle and sounder horses. Well, here is a root as easily planted as potatoes, (indeed it will plant itself) and as easily cultivated as corn, can be gathered in the Fall, or remain in the ground during Winter, and dug at any time when the frost is out of the ground. No hill had less than a peck and a half in it; they beat any thing I ever saw; the ground was literally full of them. I do not think the yield less than at the rate of 2,000 bushels to the acre. This may seem large, but our season was good for all kinds of roots.—I shall plant from one to two acres this season, four rows of artichokes and one row of squashes, and so on. Nothing makes horses and cattle fat faster than squashes. I have quit pumpkins altogether; one load of squashes is worth two of pumpkins, and will out yield them with me.

The carrot and beet are delicate plants when small, and with the potato are very sensitive to Jack Frost; but here is a root in the artichoke that bids defiance to flood, draught or frost. It will grow in the fence corner and by-places, but will doubtless do better with good cultivation, and make better and richer feed. My neighbors, who have grown it some years speak well of it, and say that sheep and hogs will exterminate it entirely when necessary. I am myself well pleased with it, and think for the future I will be well supplied with plenty of roots to mix with corn and other dry feed during the long and tedious winter months; let the season be wet or dry, I am confident with fair cultivation they will certainly produce an abundant crop. Another season will enable me to speak with more certainty, or at least with more experience. I think it well worthy the consideration of Western farmers.

W. G. CLARK.

SELECT GOOD SEED CORN.—Remember that pure white or pure yellow, will bring in market several cents per bushel more than mixed varieties; get pure seed if it costs a little more, and requires some time to procure it.

Easterly reaper operating in a grain field near St. Paul, Minnesota, 1860, photograph. The war was a catalyst for farm mechanization, thanks to rising prices for farm commodities and lack of labor. Many farm families purchased machines for the first time or replaced old equipment. ID # SA4.52 r59, Minnesota Historical Society.

William and Mary Vermilion of Indiana, undated, photographs. The Vermilions were like many Union couples and families. To lessen the burden when William left after enlisting, Mary moved in with his family, who happened to be Copperheads. Combining households created security—as well as new tensions.

Iowan Harriet Jane Thompson and her husband, William, undated. Harriet experienced the war as an intense and restless separation from her beloved. Although she contributed to the home-front war effort, she was one of those who chose not to join a soldiers' aid society. William G. Thompson Papers, State Historical Society of Iowa, Des Moines.

Ladies Sanitary Aid Society, Fairfield, Iowa, 1863. Rural midwestern women were more inclined to contribute foodstuffs for Union soldiers than nonfoodstuffs. Original image, Fairfield Public Museum, Fairfield, Iowa; copy courtesy of State Historical Society of Iowa, Iowa City.

"News from the War," Winslow Homer, engraving, *Harper's Weekly*, June 14, 1862. Homer poignantly shows the war's grief and anguish in the figure of a woman (*upper center*) slumped forward over the table, a notification letter in hand. For farmwives, these letters carried also the prospect of losing the farm and the way of life they knew. "The Civil War Art of Winslow Homer from *Harper's Weekly*," (New York: Applewood Books, 2001), CD-ROM.

Hollingsworth's sulky hay rake, *Prairie Farmer*, June 10, 1865, advertisement. A woman operates a hay rake because her "brother has gone to the war."

"Women Working in the Fields in War-Times," Thomas Nast, 1865, sketch. Women with young children in the harvest field likely were the exception rather than the rule for midwestern farm women whose husbands were in the army. In Iowa, farmwives with young children and absent husbands were more likely to manage or leave the farm rather than remain and conduct fieldwork. F. B. Goodrich, *The Tribute Book* (New York, 1865), 461.

"The Soldier's Song—Unionism vs. Copperheadism," political cartoon, 1864. The cartoon carries a warning at the bottom about the so-called home traitors. Opposition to the war was widespread throughout the Midwest. In Ohio, partisan Republicans attempted to silence opposition by intimidating Democratic newspaper editors by way of boycotts, threats, and violence in advance of the 1863 and 1864 elections. American Cartoon Print Filing Series, Prints and Photographs Division, Library of Congress.

NO FIT WIFE

SOLDIERS' WIVES AND THEIR IN-LAWS
ON THE INDIANA HOME FRONT

Nicole Etcheson

W hen her husband joined the Union army, Alice Chapin was a young wife with two small children. Both she and her baby son were sick in early 1862 when Lucius Chapin enlisted. Unlike most enlistees' wives, who accepted their husbands' decisions, Alice's reaction was anguished: "now my dear husband let me tell you I do not <u>verily</u> believe I could live & bid you good bye to go in the <u>Army</u> how can you for a moment think of such a thing, can you leave <u>me</u>? <u>can</u> you leave our babes? <u>no</u>, no, <u>no</u>, ever since the idea has got into my brain I'm like a foolish one, I cry & cant help it most all the time." Lucius had not consulted with his wife about enlisting, and they had very different ideas of his duty. While Alice focused on the need for Lucius's physical presence at home, where he could care for her and their children, Lucius and his father-in-law emphasized the need for Lucius to make a living. Although Lucius Chapin would later achieve considerable success in life, he was not doing well in the 1850s.[1]

Alice's father, newspaperman John Willson Osborn, spoke of the army as a new start for Alice and Lucius's family: "It has been said that <u>she tied your hands</u>, so that you could not make anything. For this the present arrangement has been made for her support, úntil you can make a start. I know at the present time, when money matters are so stringent, and under your depressed state of feeling, it will be hard. But we must bear hardship as good soldiers."[2] Lucius himself wrote to Alice of the practical disposition of his pay and bounty money: "We were mustered in on yesterday—will have to wait a day or two for our money—You will be compelled to use the most of it for provision for winter supplies as it maybe some time before I draw any more money—and I did want to save our Bounty money but we will not be able to do so and must pay up as fast as possible."[3] Clearly, Lucius had enlisted at a difficult time for his family, however much it eased certain financial pressures. He repeatedly avowed his love for his family and asked after the children, especially their seven-month-old boy, who was ill. Lucius assured Alice, "Many times in the day my <u>heart</u> turns to the dear ones at home[.]"[4] The conflicting pressures on him are revealed in another letter: "I am detirmined to do my best for my dear family My little Boys sick. Please write how he is often as you can—"[5]

Lucius was still at Camp Morton in Indianapolis, where Indiana's regiments were being formed, when his son's condition worsened. At Alice's urging, Lucius returned home to Putnamville, Indiana. Their son died an hour after Lucius arrived. The emotional turmoil surrounding the infant's death and Lucius's enlistment precipitated a tumultuous scene. Lucius's sister Sue turned upon Alice with accusations that cut to the heart of her marriage.[6] Alice did not truly love Lucius, for she had not named their son after him. She was lazy and not a "<u>fit wife</u>" for Lucius. And perhaps most hurtful of all, Sue insisted that the family had sent Lucius into the service in order to get him away from Alice. Sue was particularly anguished by the way the family troubles had affected her mother. She said, "That in giving up <u>George</u> [another son who had gone into the army] her husband dying & <u>all</u> the trouble her Mother had ever had did not begin to compare with her sorrow at the <u>wreck</u> of Lu, 'That they had got Lu to go to the Army on purpose to get him away from me & hoped he <u>never</u> would come <u>back</u> to <u>me</u>.'" Ruth Osborn, Alice's mother, told Sue, "If these were her feelings towards me [Alice] I <u>never</u> should step my foot in their house[.]" Sue "immediately cooled down & said they did not feel so <u>now</u>." Sue's evident dislike of Alice and Sue's feeling of family grievance against her warred with the need for Lucius's wife and daughter to have a home during the war. And Alice may have related these events not just because of the emotional anguish, "sorrow and excitement" she felt but to justify a desire not to live at her in-laws.[7] For much of the war, Alice lived with her parents in Terre Haute, Indiana, but Lucius wanted her to live with his mother in Putnamville, particularly after his brother's death.[8]

Another family crisis, the battlefield death of Lucius's brother Cowgill, permitted a reconciliation between Alice and her in-laws. Alice and her Osborn relations joined the Chapins for the funeral. Afterwards, Lucius's mother wrote him, "I do not wish you to feel any uneasiness about Alice in the future as I intend to take care of her myself and see that she does not have to do her housework[.]"[9] Alice remembered that when she first arrived at the Chapin house, her mother-in-law "threw her arms around me, kissed me, and said she would henceforth love me as one of her own children—and desired the past should be buried. . . . We had a real long talk and many tears were shed."[10] The good feelings resulted in part from the recognition that Lucius had incurred some financial hardship by sending his brother's body back to Putnamville, Indiana. Freight for the coffin cost $15, exceeding a month's pay for a soldier. The Chapins acknowledged that this meant he could not send money for the support of his wife and child and, further, that Alice had heartily endorsed his course of action. Lucius's siblings were glad that Cowgill could be buried near their father in Greencastle. His sister Anna promised, "We will do all we can to help Alice along & I am sure you will not lose any thing by the course you took. John [another brother] says he will send Alice some money as soon as he can collect." Still, Mother Chapin's embrace and protestations of affection could not erase Alice's memories of how she had been treated.[11]

American Civil War historians have considered whether the war advanced women's rights, either by encouraging women to seek a wider political role or by causing men to acknowledge women's contributions. Studying women's relations with their in-laws offers insight into how men preserved their authority even when absent from the home. Husbands and wives occasionally disagreed on whether the wife should live with her parents or his during a soldier-husband's absence. Even when wives did not get along with their in-laws, husbands preferred to have wives reside with their relatives. Although these arrangements did not work out, they revealed husbands' continued efforts to exert their authority and wives' deference to that authority. As Nancy F. Cott writes, marriage was an unequal relationship. At best, women consented to inferior status and chose their superior when they married. Studies of abolitionist marriages show that even when husbands valued women's autonomy, the demands of caring for a household and children made it difficult for women, such as Angelina Grimké Weld, to maintain a public role. Some wives, such as Julia Dent Grant and Sallie Pickett, were content with their dependency.

Husbands, such as Confederate general Richard S. Ewell, who had assertive wives were seen as weak. While no one accused William Tecumseh Sherman of weakness, he was famously unable to detach his wife, Ellen, from her preference for living with her parents. Most of these accounts, however, concentrate on the spousal relationship with less discussion of the wider in-law networks of which the couples were a part. Amy Murrell Taylor's discussion of families divided between Unionist and Confederate members touches on women's efforts to span the gap between their own families' loyalties and that of a lover or husband. And Stephen Berry has provided a fascinating account of Abraham Lincoln's troublesome Confederate in-laws, the Todd family. But Mary Todd Lincoln's loyalties were not in doubt, except in the minds of suspicious observers. Carolyn J. Stefanco's account of Nelly Kinzie Gordon's wartime experience notes that the northern-born Gordon chose to emphasize her loyalty as wife to her Confederate husband. Even her mother urged her to accept her husband's authority, including his political choices even though Gordon had difficulty doing so. Biographer Joan E. Cashin describes Confederate First Lady Varina Davis as regularly losing arguments with her brother-in-law Joseph Davis, including one over the sensitive matter of Jefferson Davis's will, which, at Joseph's urging, left Varina unprovided for if she should be widowed. Davis's marriage to Jefferson Davis nearly foundered because of her independence and assertiveness.[12]

The experiences of soldiers' wives in Putnam County, Indiana, reveal similar tensions between women and their in-laws. Some of the tensions resulted from personality and familial disputes, such as those that caused Sue Chapin to explode at her sister-in-law. But others resulted from issues of political loyalty. During the war, Mary Vermilion lived with her husband's family in Putnam County, who were Copperheads, Northern Democrats sympathetic to the South. Mary felt torn between loyalty to her husband's Unionist principles—William Vermilion was a Union officer—and loyalty to his disloyal family. Money played a role in the family dynamics. Jennie Fletcher as a wife and then widow found her in-law relations were complicated by the wealth and power of her father-in-law, Indianapolis banker Calvin Fletcher. Yet, other wives, such as Matilda Cavins and Elizabeth Applegate, came under less pressure to submit to patriarchal authority, either from their husbands or in-laws.

According to nineteenth-century ideology, the woman should have primacy in her domestic sphere. But, in reality, young families often had to live with parents while they sought to become established, as did

Ohioan Celestia Rice Colby, whose experiences Tina Stewart Brakebill documents. The Colbys lived with the husband's parents early in their marriage. After her first ten years of marriage, Celestia reflected that she had not had a "true home." She felt that she had been "repressed and dwarfed by the opinions, prejudices, and cold mercenary spirit of others." Brakebill sees in this the distance that had grown between Colby and her husband, but it was also the case that Colby never became close to her in-laws. Her mother had died when she was young, yet she did not turn to either her stepmother or mother-in-law for advice or comfort with a young wife's travails but rather to her older sister. Colby's mother-in-law may have even mocked her views on women's rights and her writing. Brakebill concludes that Colby's relationship with her in-laws was one of the "most restrictive impediments on her path to contentment."[13] As Brakebill's account indicates, the ideal of kin networks seamlessly integrated through marriage was often unrealized.

In *True Sisterhood*, Marilyn Ferris Motz argues that women and men hoped to marry those "who would be a congenial member of the kin network" as well as good spouses. Married women often hoped to love their female in-laws as dearly as they loved their own mothers or sisters. Women's similar roles across families and women's needs for care in childbirth or with young children created the framework for such close relationships with in-laws. Motz sees women as mediators between kin networks, able to play off the claims of competing families and gaining some status from that role, rather than as being subject to patriarchal males. But the experience of Putnam County women indicates that women, even when mediating or counterpoising one family against another, found themselves submitting more often than they might have liked to the husband's family. Motz's women lived with their own families when their husbands were away. Putnam women whose husbands had gone to war, however, by contrast, just as often found themselves living with the husband's family. Whereas Motz sees the woman's ties to her family as a counterweight to the husband's authority, this was not the case for Putnam women.[14] Instead, in-law relations were frequently a power struggle between husband and wife, and the husband's authority often prevailed.

Like Alice Chapin, Mary Vermilion was a young wife when her husband, William, joined the army. Wed in 1858, they had no children. William was born in Kentucky, but when he was only a few months old, his parents moved to Putnam County. His father, Joel Vermilion, bought a farm and preached at a Baptist church. Mary recalled that a favorite phrase of Joel was to call someone an "unhallowed scamp." She described her father-in-law as mentally unstable and said he would "rave . . . publickly in his preaching, as he does sometimes when he is troubled about anything."[15] Although the young Vermilions were staunch Republicans, William's father, who had been a Whig, passed through the Know-Nothing party and joined the Democrats the year before William and Mary wed. The elder Vermilion virulently opposed the Republican administration. William's political views left him isolated in the family. This isolation may have been obscured because William left Putnam County a decade before the war broke out. William, who had been a student at Indiana Asbury University in Greencastle, moved to Illinois to study medicine and later lived and established a practice in Iowa. Like William's family, Mary's had moved to Putnam County shortly after her birth in 1831. She taught school in Putnam County in the early 1850s and in 1855 moved with her family to Iowa, where she continued teaching school until she married William. When the war broke out, William joined an Iowa regiment.[16]

Although Mary's family lived in Iowa, William took her back to Putnam County to live with his parents, a decision that ultimately caused Mary much unhappiness. William had not even left for the front before he was learning of these woes: "I fear my dear from the tone of your letter you are not satisfied—not comfortable. . . . I know how it is at fathers. They live a different way to what I want you to live if I can help. I am sorry almost every time I think of it."[17] Even before the war, William had apparently grown discontented with his family: "The error was my taking you there, but there I thought you would get along better than I used to. I thought they were doing better. But such people seldom improve Dollie."[18] Of all William's relatives, Mary liked his sister Jane and brother Henry the best. But Mary found the family unloving toward Jane and blamed Henry's "rough" demeanor on his parents. It was, Mary concluded, "a most unhappy household." Whether it was a lack of love and kindness that Mary perceived in the family or political divisions, none of the family except for Jane and Henry had written to William while he was in the army. Perhaps, the Vermilions had decided Mary should live with her in-laws because her parental home was not a happy one either. Mary's mother, who was going deaf and had "almost lost her mind," could neither run her household nor even make dinner. Her father had not been "good" to Mary when she lived at home. She never intended to live with her parents again.[19]

For whatever reason, Mary went to spend the war in Putnam County. Although she was miserable at her in-laws, William's approval was necessary for any change in her situation, for he considered it his decision to make, not Mary's. He insisted that she go live with her aunt Anna McCarty: "You must not stay at father's if it can possibly be helped. . . . Go to Mrs. McCarty's & tell her that I want her to board you what time you stay in that country & you will pay her any fee she may see fit to charge. . . . I cannot stand it for you to stay at father's & know you don't want to go contrary to my wishes."[20] Aunt Anna, however, cautioned against a sudden break that would hurt the Vermilions' feelings. Mary agreed. She would tell William's family that she was going to visit her cousin Julia for a few weeks. Mary's conciliatory tone was fueled by the family's efforts to make amends. While running errands, Mary stopped by William's older brother's store at Mount Meridian, intending to pick up a schoolbook for the younger brother, Reason. Tom Vermilion chatted with Mary for only a few minutes, but even that was more than he had spoken to her since she moved back to Putnam County. Further, he inquired about William. Mary told her husband, "The change in his manner was so marked that I know mother has told him that I said I didn't believe they cared anything for you because you had gone to the war. It may be, love, that it really is their way and that they have not been so bad all the time as they seemed. I am willing to believe so darling and let it all go."[21] Despite Mary's entreaties, William was unimpressed: "You are too afraid of hurting father's folks feelings, Dollie. They have but little regard for our feelings. . . . I can't stand it & I won't stand it. . . . I am too proud to have you stay there."[22]

The difficulty between Mary and her in-laws went beyond the Vermilions' inability to express affection. The family blamed William's political deviancy on her. "I know they think me an 'unhallowed abolitionist,' and that I have turned you against them," she told William.[23] Certainly, William and Mary did not believe that their relatives could support the troops and yet despise the cause in which they fought. William replied, "I can't & will not stand it for you to stay among the people who hate the cause I am sacrificing and risking for. To say who they are, if they think anything of me, they can't like much of Jeff Davis's government. If they think anything of his confederacy I don't want them to think anything of me. And I don't want any person that does think anything of me to stay where rebel sympathizers are. . . . If you leave Indiana, it will be a very long time before I see that part of God's Earth again. I would not be likely to eat mother's turkey very soon." William wanted his family to know that "I hate Traitors both North & South."[24] Even after Tom's attempt to be cordial, William remained angry: "To think that my father is against the cause I am risking everything for. . . . Let them be traitors Dollie if they want to be. They are no relatives of mine. No person who wishes people well who are trying to take my heart's blood from me shall call me brother by my consent."[25] Even Mary's belief in conciliation wavered when like-minded neighbors conversed with the Vermilions. As the men discussed General Ambrose Everett Burnside's disastrous campaign at Fredericksburg, Mary said she "sat in the corner with my knitting and listened." The men's pessimism about the military situation and their concurrence that the South was right in fighting for their homes made Mary resolve "that I would go to Mrs. McCarty's as soon as I could."[26] But her resolve quickly faded: "You say I must not stay here any more. I want to do just as you tell me my darling, but I am in a delicate position. They have been kind to me in their way all the time, and now they are very kind to me. . . . They didn't think or know any better than to treat me as they did at first. I have forgiven it all. Won't you forgive them too, darling? . . . I don't want to hurt their feelings dear. It would be wrong, and would look very badly on me. But still I want above everything else to please you. You can tell me what you want me to do and I will do it. . . . I have tried to do right."[27]

Ultimately, Mary could stand it no longer. She moved in with Aunt Anna in the winter of 1862–63. William, ignoring her pleas for under-standing his family, ordered the move: "Let what I have said this time Dollie be the law. I am used to giving commands here Dollie, you know. You won't object to my giving them to you."[28] Even after the move, Mary urged William not to become estranged from his family. She feared exacerbating her father-in-law's insanity. Although he was somewhat recovered, any family strain "might throw him off balance and make him as wild as ever," Mary told William. "Let us be mindful darling of his grey hairs, and his shattered mind and do nothing that we can ever regret." She further insisted that she was forming a friendship with Jane and that William's mother had been kind to her. Mary was even willing to palliate the Vermilions' Copperheadism: "As to their disloyalty I feel as badly about that as you do, but they are just like a large majority of the people now in this country. Not a whit worse."[29]

Although Mary was comfortable at her aunt's, the marital tug-of-war over her residence continued. Mary evidently proposed coming to

Arkansas, but William opposed the idea. Mary argued that if she could not join him, she should at least go to Iowa: "It looks badly, dearest, for me to go anywhere else to stay after your leaving me at father's. People don't understand it, and if they knew the facts they would <u>all</u>, except 2 or 3 widow women, blame <u>us</u>, and not them." Since there was strong Copperhead sentiment in the county, Mary worried that people would blame her, rather than the Vermilions, for any discomfort between them. Mary's father was willing to have her come to him. But she deferred to William's wishes as he asserted his right to give the orders.[30]

Local public opinion would finally force Mary back to the Vermilions' house. Aunt Anna had become increasingly worried about a rift between her family and the Vermilions. Mary decided she was bringing too much trouble on her aunt. She returned to her in-laws for a couple months in the spring of 1863, but in April, she moved to her parents' farm in Iowa. Mary insisted that she had returned to her home out of consideration for William because the harsh things his family said against him drove her away. Having gone to stay with her husband's family indicated his patriarchal authority. By leaving, however, she did not reject that authority but affirmed it. She had left her husband's family because they did not respect him. Nonetheless, Mary insisted that she tried to distinguish between the Vermilions as "<u>traitors</u>" and as William's parents. As the latter, not the former, she urged William to forgive them and not to increase the hard feelings.[31]

Unlike Alice and Mary, Jennie Fletcher had no tumultuous fights with her in-laws, but she did apparently resist her father-in-law's authority. Few letters from Jane survive, but the family she married into—the Fletchers of Indianapolis—were copious diarists and letter writers. Her husband, Miles J. Fletcher, was the fourth son of banker Calvin Fletcher. The senior Fletcher, by virtue not only of his wealth but also of his strict Calvinist principles, dominated his many children. He sent almost all his sons to school in the east. After graduating from Brown University, Miles taught at Indiana Asbury University in Greencastle. He returned east to attend law school at Harvard and then took up a professorship of belles lettres and history again at Asbury. Like Lucius, Miles found it hard to make a start in life. In his diary for 1857, Calvin lamented that Miles had run up debts while handling his father's business affairs, had "abandoned the law when he should have pursued it," started projects on the farm but did not finish them, and became involved in many benevolent organizations. "Did everybodies business & neglected his own & mine. . . . & everything he undertook he failed in."[32] Calvin had opposed Miles's taking a position at Asbury, fearing that it had been offered not because of Miles's accomplishments but because of his father's importance. But by the outbreak of the Civil War, Miles had come a long way toward earning his father's respect. Over his father's objections, Miles accepted the nomination as Republican candidate for state superintendent of public instruction. (It was the third time that local men had solicited him to run for the office.) Father and son had a wager on the election, and despite his father's doubts, Miles won. Having agreed to pay Miles a bushel of corn for every vote he got over the state average, Calvin settled the "jest" with a note for $220. Although Miles saw this as payment for their wager, Calvin paid it in part because Miles "has a hard time to get along & meet his expenses[.]"[33]

On July 15, 1852, Miles married Jane "Jennie" Hoar. As Jennie was originally from Rhode Island, it seems likely that he had met her while at Brown. They apparently had become engaged in 1849, but Miles broke off the engagement the following year. Calvin, as usual, did not quite approve, and Calvin accused Miles of also having made advances to a girl in Indianapolis. "Wrote Miles," Calvin entered into his diary soon after Miles announced the broken engagement and "gave him my opinion of a young man who makes love to evry girl he meets." Miles denied the accusation.[34] Calvin also disapproved because both the engagement and the breaking of it had been "entered into without parental advice." Calvin was perhaps worried that Miles sought a rich wife. Of the broken engagement, Calvin wrote, "I regret this rupture. If it was in consequence of her standing so far as relates to poverty or obscurity I am decidedly opposed to the violation of their good understanding. He should have married her. I have not desired my sons should seek fortunes in their marriages—no far from it. I have no confidence in rich wives in goods &c but such as are rich in virtue in faith in Christ."[35] Whatever the quarrel may have been, Miles and Jennie reconciled and were married.

Just before their wedding and his graduation from Brown, Miles was offered the position at Asbury. He consulted his father about the wisdom of accepting. Once again, the men differed, but this time it was about Jennie's role in Miles's decision. Calvin thought she should be consulted; Miles emphatically did not. "I must certainly differ with you here," Miles wrote his father.

I think that no woman has a right to aid, or say one word in regard to the course her husband should pursue. Upon some things she may give her opinion, but then the husband should always decide according to his own judgement. Her prefferences should all be merged in that, which is for his good; knowing that what is for his good is for her own. A woman should decide before she marries a man, whether she is willing to leave home, friends, country prefferences and everything else, and submit all to the hands, and mind of her husband. If she is not willing to do this, she has no right to marry him. If she does, it is very evident she is moved and prompted by some other feeling than from love. There is however, I suppose an exception to this. If a husband is a ninny, and the wife sees that she is evidently "The Man," then let her assume the sway. If the husband submits, it is an evidence that they have both found their appro[p]riate place. When I engaged myself, it was with the understanding that my lady was to go wheverer I saw fit, and stay as long as I saw fit. I think I have one who loves me so well, and has so much respect for my judgement, that she will with pleasure submit to whatever I wish. If however, when I am married and removed to my home wherever it is, my wife mourns for her former home, and feels that she <u>loves her former home</u> more than the place, which in every way is a better home for me, then I will pay her expenses back to her home, and there she can stay supporting herself, untill she sees fit to return, and be happy with me. My wife shall ever be consulted. I shall ever be open to be influenced by her wishes; yet because she wishes a thing simply without my own judgment agreeing, I will never do, or leave undone a single thing. I anticipate much pleasure and happiness in my matrimonial relations. I feel that I have one, who thinks that I can accomplish or do anything. I have known her long enough to be convinced, that she has many—no, I should say some faults, and to be assured that she is not an angel.[36]

Although Miles was evidently aware of Jennie's imperfections, he was unwilling to let her find any in him or his judgment. In fact, to admit her judgment superior in anything would be to confess himself an emasculated "ninny." He apparently received from Jennie—or hoped to receive—the unqualified approbation his father never provided. Perhaps Miles was right that Jennie would derive her happiness from him, despite being far away from her family in Rhode Island. Soon after Miles started at Asbury, Jennie commented, "Miles is more uniformly cheerful than I have known him to be for a long time. Is always busy."[37]

Marriage evidently did not soften Miles's sense of primacy. In describing their room in Greencastle in a letter to his mother, Miles referred to the location of "my bookcase, my table, and my bed." Even the marital bed was his, not theirs.[38] Miles's interests seemed to dominate in the spring of 1853: "I yesterday took Jennie, and attended a horticultural meeting." He and Jennie "both joined," but it was "the first society I have connectd myself with since I came here." Although he owned no property in Putnam, he vowed to "take a deep interest in this society, and do all I can to promote its interests."[39] Miles was the driving force—taking Jennie, connecting himself with the society, working for its interests—and Jennie the appendage to his actions.

Even within the domestic sphere, Miles claimed to have better ideas as to the housekeeping. "Jennie is a good teacher and a fine seamstress," Miles said, perhaps having suggested that she instruct his younger sister Lucy.[40] But Miles wanted his mother to come instruct Jennie in house-wifery: "Jennie does well, firstrate, yet she lacks experience in many things. She works like a slave where if she only knew how, it would be done easily, and require but a moments time. She is cheerful and looks healthier every day. . . . Jennie had a good education in books, and in needle work, but her mother out of a mistaken kindness never initiated her into the mysteries of housekeeping. She needs showing in many little things."[41]

Like Alice, Jennie suffered from ill health. Historians have posited that illness was a socially acceptable way for women to resist and subvert men's authority. It allowed women to avoid domestic duties and even refocused the household's attentions on their needs.[42] It is impossible to know whether Alice's and Jennie's troubles were, indeed, physical, but, certainly, Jennie's health was a constant subject of Miles's letters. In Greencastle, Jennie attributed renewed good health to "the clear air of Greencastle, or the pleasure of being with Miles, and the contented feeling of being at home." Jennie suffered from the "chill" or "ague."[43] It recurred, however, along with "severe head ache." Miles, it seems, was not a good nurse: "You know that it gives me more pleasure to delve into a history, than to delve under a bed in search of a chamber. . . . I fear these feelings on my part does not make me the most agreable nurse in the world."[44] Miles evidently lacked sympathy with his wife's invalidism. He sent her to his parents to recover from an illness in 1857 with the admonition "Don't let her trouble you by hindering anyone."[45] Miles himself suffered an attack of typhoid fever in 1852 that provoked an anxious note from Jennie to her father-in-law. Lacking confidence in the local doctor, she wanted to send Miles to Indianapolis but could not accompany him as her school was having its public examination. Fortunately, Miles began to get better.[46] Unlike Miles, Jennie did not confess inadequacies or dislike of nursing—she did not focus on herself—but struggled to reconcile the competing practical imperatives of her employment with the needs of her patient.

Jennie and Miles had two children: William T., born in 1855, and Mary B., born in 1856. Mary's birth seems to have adversely affected Jennie's health. When Calvin went to see Jennie a month after the birth, he found her "very sick." When little Mary was two and a half months old, Jennie took her and Willy to visit her family in Rhode Island. Calvin still feared that Jennie was "rather feeble."[47] In early 1858, Willy stayed with his grandparents in Indianapolis while Jennie was ill. Miles, who was conducting business for his father in Putnamville, took the opportunity to consult with Daniel W. Layman, the Chapins' doctor. Layman thought Jennie's ailment "a combination of milk leg and neuralgia, following from cold taken in a puerperal fever."[48] A month later, Jennie seemed no better. She was unable to care for herself and had no use of her limbs. But by fall of 1859, when Calvin and Keziah Fletcher visited Miles and Jennie in Greencastle, her father-in-law thought she looked well.[49]

In addition to poor health, Jennie had a restless husband. Miles quickly grew bored with Asbury and Greencastle: "The history of one day here is the history of all." He wanted to go to Europe but didn't have the money. His threatened resignation secured him the raise he desired, and he stayed another year at Asbury.[50] But, in consultation with his father and older brother, Miles determined to leave Asbury "& either study law or go to Germany & prepare for a literary life." Jennie is not mentioned as having a part in these discussions, although Calvin considered Jennie in concluding, "At present I think he being married he best choose the law &c."[51] In fall 1856, Miles went to Cambridge, Massachusetts, for a year's study of law at Harvard. It is not clear where Jennie was during Miles's time at Harvard, but he sent his family away—perhaps to Indianapolis—because it was too expensive for them to live with him. By spring, Miles had been forced by "necessity" to return to Greencastle and again take up his professorship.[52]

Once again, Miles's financial affairs were in disarray. His father loaned him $100. He had taken in a young cousin, Eliza, but could no longer afford to keep her and noted that she required more patience than possessed by "a woman with two fretting babies," presumably thinking of Jennie.

Jennie does not seem to have been teaching, but the family had a lodger, which earned extra income for the family but added to Jennie's household work.[53] Miles's debt and his frequent changes of occupation and residence must have borne hard on Jennie, although only Calvin Fletcher seems to think that marriage should enter into Miles's calculations about his career. In addition, Miles apparently expected to maintain appearances as became a Fletcher, which perhaps contributed to his indebtedness. During his sister Lucy's visit, he became upset at finding her shoe was torn. Miles did not want her to appear as a "sloven." More than that, "[s]he did not seem to have remembered, that when here, she was not only 'Calvin Fletcher's daughter' but was also 'Prof Fletcher's sister.'"[54] One surmises that Jennie, too, was expected always to appear—and to keep house and children—in a fashion befitting Professor Fletcher's wife.

During the 1850s, Jennie frequently saw her in-laws. Calvin's diary contains many references to visits in Indianapolis by Miles, Jennie, and their children. For Jennie and the children, that relationship became more important after May 2, 1862, when Miles was killed in a railroad accident. After the Battle of Shiloh, Governor Oliver P. Morton had requested that Calvin accompany him on a trip to relieve the wounded soldiers. Calvin declined, preferring to help his son Elijah, who had just moved from New Albany, Indiana, get settled in Indianapolis. Miles took his father's place on the trip. On a lovely Sunday morning, Governor Morton's secretary arrived at Calvin's house to tell him that Miles had been killed at Sullivan, Indiana. As his train was moving through the rail yard at Sullivan, it was stopped by a freight car in its path. Miles leaned outside the window to see what was happening, and when the train sped up, his head struck a protruding plank. That night, Miles's body arrived by special train and was taken to the Fletcher house in Indianapolis. "We required no watch as is usually the custom," Calvin recorded. "He was safe in his fathers house, the last respect I could pay him." Jennie, the children, and the faculty from Greencastle arrived in Indianapolis that night. Miles was buried in Indianapolis next to his sister Maria. Calvin paid the fare of sixty-seven Asbury students who attended Miles's funeral. If Calvin consulted with Jennie about the funeral plans, he made no mention of it in his diary. The only indication of her distress at Miles's death comes from cryptic notes in letters from Miles's brothers to their father, then vacationing in New England. About six weeks after her husband's death, Jennie suffered a miscarriage. Miles's younger sister, Lucy, went to Greencastle to care for her.[55]

110

Although Jennie would remarry after the war, she was now a widow with two small children. Cooley, Miles's older brother, expected that Calvin would care for them: "I am thinking of you, &, more, that of his wife & of those two bereaved children—that bright boy, & that dear affectionate little girl, & I bow the knee & pray for them. I know, dear father, that you will be their earthly friend & their helper now that their earthly support is taken away." Cooley evidently did not write to Jennie himself but asked his father to send his condolences—still, his was the only condolence letter that even mentioned Jennie. Clearly, Calvin kept in touch with his widowed daughter-in-law. His diary records visits from Jennie and the children in October 1862. In November, Calvin reported, "Jenny, Miles wife, & 2 childrin & Baby [Fletcher] Hines [the son of Miles's sister Maria] came from Greencastle & were taken out to the farm house, now all furnished & ready for their reception." This would seem to indicate that Calvin was providing a permanent home for Jennie and her children. Diary entries in early 1863 refer to visits from Jennie, presumably coming from the farm to her father-in-law's house in Indianapolis.[56]

At the same time that Jennie moved to her father-in-law's farm in Indianapolis, Calvin provided some income for her. After Miles's election as superintendent of public instruction, Calvin had decided to deed him land. In November 1862, Calvin made the deed of nine hundred to a thousand acres in Martin County in trust to three of his sons "to pay Miles debts & to distribute residue to widow & heirs." Perhaps, the income gave Jennie the independence to separate from her father-in-law. In July 1863, a Greencastle newspaper ran a notice: "Mrs. J. Fletcher will open a SCHOOL, at her residence . . . Monday, September 13, 1863." Jennie had returned to Greencastle.[57] In the fall of 1863, visits from Jennie and her children were clearly visits from that town. The children frequently visited on their own. Nine-year-old Willy was "a smart boy, knows the prices at market—how to go & return on the R.R." Mary came for Christmas and awakened her grandfather's house "by hallowing Christmass gift & mery Christmass &c." Mary "will make a smart woman I trust. Strongly resembles her mother," Calvin predicted. His diary confirmed on New Year's Eve in 1863 that Miles's "wife & 2 childrin live at Greencastle."[58]

Although Calvin hoped that Willy "will make his mothers heart glad," he also wanted a male figure in the boy's life. Miles's brother Stephen Keyes Fletcher, known as Kid, had lived with Miles and Jennie while clerking in a Greencastle store in the late 1850s. Kid was now a soldier in the 115th Indiana Volunteers. While on leave, Calvin Fletcher confided to Kid, "I hoped he would come to the relief of his father & the charge of the farm & raise Miles' boy who wants to live on the farm 'with his uncle Kid.'" In early 1864, Calvin again spoke with Kid and with another son, Ingram, about bringing Jennie and her children to the farm in Indianapolis. They agreed with his idea. Kid was waiting to see if his regiment was called up again. If it was not, he would go to work on the farm. Kid was dispatched to Greencastle, evidently to speak to Jennie. Calvin was prepared to be generous but only if Jennie did as he wanted. "My advise is to take her to the farm. Give her childrin an out door life. Put Willy thro college at proper age but give him the musctle & strength of a country boy & Mary the little girl a good education—If they will comply with my suggestions I will if God permit Educate both childrin but She must comply with my terms." Although Jennie and the children arrived about a month later, it appears to have been for a visit rather than a permanent move, as there are references to Willy visiting from Greencastle throughout 1864. Although Willy liked the farm, Jennie was apparently less enthusiastic. In October 1864, Kid made another trip to Greencastle "to see Jennie Miles wife to see if She would come & live with him at the farm." He reported that Jennie had agreed to come in two months. In January, Jennie and Mary arrived from Greencastle—Willy was already in Indianapolis—and settled on the farm. But after that, Calvin did not mention Jennie in connection with the farm, although Kid was obviously living at and running it. In October 1865, Calvin paid another son, William B., $100 for boarding Jennie.[59] Billy was married and a physician. Perhaps Jennie had again been ill and was recuperating under Billy's care, but her father-in-law does not mention an illness. Perhaps, it was decided Jennie should live with the married brother rather than with the unmarried Kid. Calvin died in the spring of 1866, silencing even that incomplete record of Jennie's life. Although he had voiced more willingness to consult with Jennie about her—and her children's—future, he had proved as patriarchal in his own way as Miles. And, unlike Miles, he had the financial clout to get his way. He would help Jennie if she would "comply with my terms."

If Jennie had not already returned to Greencastle, perhaps she did so after her father-in-law's death. She married William D. Allen, a Greencastle grocer and Democratic politician, in 1868. Allen died in 1876, leaving three grown children from his previous marriage and a six-year-old son by Jennie. The 1870 census listed the value of Allen's real estate at $200 and his personal estate at $2,000. His wife, however, was much better off. Jennie owned real estate worth $19,000 and a personal estate of $13,000.[60] This probably reflected her, or her children's, share of Calvin's estate. Fletcher's will left "[t]wenty five thousand dollars to the wife & children of my son Miles J. Fletcher deceased, or to the survivor of them, having conveyed to trustees heretofore, over nine hundred acres of land in Martin County this State for their use & benefit[.]"[61] When she died in 1891, Jennie was buried with William Allen in Forest Hill Cemetery, outside Greencastle. The tombstone bears the name "J. M. H. Allen"—there is no *F* for Fletcher.[62]

If some wives, such as Alice, Mary, and Jennie, were unable to maintain independent households and struggled to deal with in-laws, others, like Elizabeth Applegate and Matilda Cavins, two wives whose husbands served in the Union army, did not move in with in-laws. Middle-aged husbands, such as John Applegate and Aden Cavins, exerted less pressure on their wives to live with the husbands' relatives. By the time the war broke out, Elizabeth and John Applegate were in their late thirties and had been married for fifteen years. Elizabeth and their daughter, Allie, who was six in 1861, lived in their own household. Both Elizabeth and John were from Putnam County, but Elizabeth maintained an independent household during the war. Both Elizabeth's father, John Lynch, and John's father, Peter W. Applegate, were old settlers in the county. Their properties were near each other in section 19 of Greencastle township. Lynch, a leading county Democrat, was proprietor of the Washington Hotel—a Democratic watering hole—and the local constable from the 1840s through the 1860s. Peter had also been constable briefly but was evidently not as successful as Lynch. Peter had been a merchant in Greencastle until "reverses" caused him to lose his property. He then worked as a tailor and hauled goods for express companies. Both Lynch and Applegate had numerous children. John Lynch had ten children, eight of whom survived him when he died in 1872. Peter Applegate also fathered ten, although only three were living when he died in 1877. (Weakened by captivity at Andersonville, John Applegate would not be one of the three.)[63] Elizabeth would have had no lack of kin on either side to turn to for help during the war. Aden Cavins was twelve years older and a widower with two young sons when he married Matilda Livingston in 1856. They had two more boys and a baby daughter when Aden joined the army in 1862. Aden's parents lived in Greene County, but rather than stay with them during the war, Matilda and the children moved in with her widowed mother, who lived in Greencastle. Aden paid for building an addition on his mother-in-law's house and for furniture to accommodate his family.[64]

Judging from the letters between spouses during the war, the Applegates' and Cavins' marriages were less romantic and companionate than the Chapins' and Vermilions'. Alice often signed her letters to Lucius "Wifey" and addressed him as "Dearie." William's pet name for Mary was "Dollie," and she called him "Peaches." By contrast, Elizabeth signed her letters "E. S. Applegate," and Matilda as "Ever Your Wife."[65] Although only in her twenties, Matilda was the second wife of an older man and a stepmother to his sons. This may have rendered their union less sentimental. The Chapins' relationship, at least in Alice's letters, was among the most openly sensual. Having her hair brushed caused Alice to reflect, "Now if you were here I would comb your hair—and help you fix up—and give visible demonstrations of—what? I am sure your heart can tell." She fantasized about his "rap at the door that wakes me so easily."[66] William and Mary were less explicit in their affections but did write about their longing for each other. "If I could only see you for one hour tonight what would I not give?" Mary asked. "I think of you every minute when I am awake and dream of you when I sleep. I long to see you more than I can tell. . . . Don't forget to write your Dollie and don't forget to love her."[67] William was more explicit: "Now Dollie . . . first of all things I would like to see you. . . . I would kiss Dollie and Dollie would pet me. I would love her and she would love me. I would hold Dollie's head on my bosom and she would pet me just as we used to do."[68] Although Elizabeth and John and Matilda and Aden missed each other—and the Cavins made arrangements to visit during the war, evidently resulting in yet another pregnancy—there are no comparable passages in their letters.[69] A companionate marriage and passionate intimacy, however, did not temper the need of Lucius, William, and Miles to wield authority. Perhaps, the younger husbands felt a stronger need to assert their newly gained authority than did husbands of longer standing.

Providing for the family became an area of contention between spouses. When men departed for war, women were left without a breadwinner. Alice borrowed money to buy groceries and spent the dollar her father had sent her on medicine and coal oil. John Willson Osborn had sent Lucius's mother another dollar, which went toward buying shoes.

By detailing the money she and her mother-in-law had received from Osborn, Alice emphasized Lucius's failure to provide for his female dependents. In the summer of 1863, the Chapins were particularly hard pressed for money. Lucius had expended funds needed by his family to return his brother's body to Indiana, and now Lucius was ill and in a hospital at Nashville. Then Alice was offered a job teaching school in Terre Haute, which would pay $40 per term and would permit Ally, their daughter, to accompany her.[70] But Lucius "veto[ed]" the idea, despite Alice's repeated mentioning of her need for money. "So you dont want a 'School Ma'am' for a Wifey? Well I suppose I'll have to give it up though I only had to get my Certificate perhaps I could not have passed muster," Alice wrote. Lucius's sisters were also teaching and boarding, but this was evidently not a reflection on Lucius's ability to provide, as they were the unmarried, young daughters of a widow.[71]

The war's close brought renewed concerns as to how Lucius would make a living. He toyed with the idea of moving to Illinois. Alice came up with a plan, in consultation with one of her family, for them to rent a farm near Chicago. Lucius's father-in-law wrote of a farm close to home that Lucius could buy.[72] While Lucius pronounced himself willing to "gladly avail myself of an opportunity to make a living," he invoked his authority as head of household, cautioning Alice against getting her heart set on one plan: "Do not become to[o] settled in any plan as your man might have to disappointment you and he does not want to do that he loves you too much[.]" For all his invocation of his love for her, it was clear that the decision would be his and his alone. Perhaps countering Alice's influence was the fact that Lucius's sister and mother hoped he would return to Putnamville rather than go to Chicago or farther west.[73]

The Vermilions were prosperous enough that the war did not provoke the economic concerns it did for the Chapins. "I think very little about our property back [in Iowa], not as much as I ought," William reflected.[74] But while he referred to "our" property, Mary called it his and worried that he would not think she spent it wisely. Because of the rift with her in-laws, Mary fretted about being under financial obligation for her stay with them: "I had nothing else but my board, and I think I worked enough to pay for that. I don't feel like we owe them anything in this way, darling. Sometimes I thought I would buy them several dollars worth of presents and send back to them, when I started home. Then I thought that we owed nothing, and I ought not to spend your money that way."[75] Mary paid her aunt board: "Aunt Anna is so good to me, and has so many women there now that it won't do for me to stay there without paying her well. And I hate to spend your money, darling."[76] Still, Mary did not hesitate to offer money to William's sister Jane. She gave Jane five dollars for a dress and insisted that William would be willing to pay for his sister to visit his wife in Iowa.[77] Her generosity was based on her assessment of what expenses William would approve.

Miles Fletcher's assertion that he would be the head of the household did not preclude Jennie's working. Since Miles was in debt, perhaps, the couple simply needed the extra income. Jennie taught school in Green-castle, often in spite of her ill health.[78] After his first year at Asbury, Miles acknowledged, "I do not know what I should have done had she not assisted me so much," perhaps referring to help she had given him with his teaching or with family finances. "She will not teach any more," he concluded, but whether that was a mutual decision or his dictate is not clear. Perhaps, he, or they, felt her health could not bear the strain. But Miles did have one regret: "I am sorry on her account that we cannot keep house." Although he blamed others for his inability to earn sufficient income to rent a house, he acknowledged how this deprived Jennie of her sphere in the home.[79]

Although the Applegates worried about money, John did not dictate to his wife—unlike the younger husbands. He sent Elizabeth forty dollars in late 1862 and instructed her, "I want you to do the best you can with as it will be sometime before I will get anymore."[80] Despite the extra expense, he wanted Elizabeth and Allie to rent a house near where he was stationed in the winter of 1863–64. But Elizabeth was not inclined to do so. John did not order her to come nor did she. The Cavins' ability to expend $300 in expanding his mother-in-law's house and $100 on furniture testifies to their affluence. And Aden saved at least $75 per month out of his officer's pay.[81]

In addition to their obligations as breadwinners, all but William Ver-milion were fathers as well. Even after Alice reconciled herself to Lucius's enlistment, she reminded him that he had abandoned his paternal re-sponsibilities and insisted that she was striving to preserve his daughter's attachment to him. She wrote Lucius that upon waking, Ally had been talking to herself: "'Got no Papa—poor Papa gone, gone to War? Gone fight Webels.'... Her Papa will be glad to know he has a place in her mind early in the morning and late at night; she always kisses me Goodnight for you." Alice expressed concern about Ally's development. Ally was "very intelligent and sweet" but capable occasionally of "the most ungovernable fits of passion." Alice's concerns about child-raising included a measure of guilt: "I do want her to grow up a good kind amiable woman. Oh how we need <u>home</u> and <u>Papa</u>!" Waking up in the morning, Ally said, "I so <u>mad</u> at Papa." When asked why, she said, "cause he no dont come <u>home</u> see <u>Ally</u>[.]" Lucius professed to love hearing that his daughter was talking about him. He may have been more reassured, however, by his brother's report that Ally "knew your picture & kissed it." Little Ally scrawled notes to her father in her mother's letters: "I must write to Papa I love my Papa Little Brother gone up heaven to God. Ally wants to see papa. Ally write papa letter[.]" Lucius sought to mold his child from afar: "Papa sorry to hear of his little daughter having to correct Mama. It does not look well She <u>must</u> obey her dear Mama whom she loves very much and I am sure she will if she lives [&] love her much soon if her faults are corrected now. But Papa . . . whiping you is only because to whip is just on all[.]" As the war continued, Lucius worried about the separation from his family: "If I am permitted to return home in peace to my family it will take something more than I now know of to induce me to <u>leave</u> my home again Though I perhaps will not regrett the past when it is once ended. My little girl will be in her sixth year will I know her[?]"[82]

Miles Fletcher seems to have been a concerned parent. When he spoke of governing Willy, who was mischievous, he gave no indication of consulting his wife, sister, or any other woman. Willy's mischief had led to injury. Four-year-old Willy overheard that one tied up a mule's leg to shoe it. He decided to try this and was kicked in the face. A young man brought the boy, whose face was covered with blood, to Miles, telling him the child was dead. Miles was able to resuscitate his son by putting Willy's head under the pump and washing off the blood. Willy had a two-inch cut under his chin and possibly a broken nose. Miles was obviously still distraught when he wrote to his father of the accident, but in his account of Willy, himself, the young man, the doctor, and the mule—Jennie is absent.[83]

Historian James Marten writes that men in the Civil War struggled to fit their ideas of duty, which took them away from their children, with their responsibilities for the daily care of the children. They reconciled these competing imperatives by "providing wide-ranging guidance and instruction." Marten notes that men provided more advice to sons than to daughters. Lucius may have refrained from advising his daughter because of her youth.[84] Aden's only daughter was an infant, but he wholeheartedly embraced the advisory role of a middle-class father to his sons.

Matilda prompted her absent husband to compliment their son on his generosity to her and to his half-brother, Hugh. He had spent his money to buy her a pretty vase and Hugh a "little heart." Aden hardly needed prompting. The following Christmas, he wrote a long letter to the children, exhorting them to improve their hearts as well as their heads: "You are now forming your characters for life. . . . Everything that you see, hear, say or think of or do has its influence in the formation of your characters." That character should be affectionate and self-controlled: "Remember that to have the character of a Christian gentleman is worth everything else in this world." Aden wanted to hear from the children and replied individually to the boys' letters. In addition to complimenting his son Charley on his academic progress, he included adjurations to patriotism and valor and instructions to "assist your mother all you can" and to always act so that Matilda would "give a good account of you." Throughout the war, Aden's letters to his children were filled with affectionate and didactic messages. Aden's own military service perhaps inclined him to think about the fitness of his sons for that life. He advised in late 1862, "Tell Charlie and Ed that they must be industrious and studious, so that when they grow up to manhood they may be men fit to take a prominent part in the defense of their country provided circumstances should require such a service of them. Willie likes war and it will be unnecessary to tell him more than to be studious and make a scholar of himself. As to Hugh you can tell him that he is already fit for the service." But his wishes for his only daughter were different. "My earnest wish for the little one, Jodie, is that war may never cloud her happiness and that life may be to her as mild as her infant slumber and as beautiful as the radiant sparkle of the dew drop hanging up flowers fresh and full-bloom in May." Aden did not limit himself to instructing the children. He also urged his ideas about childrearing on Matilda: "I am much rejoiced at the progress the boys are making and always like to have you make mention of it in your letters. A great deal will depend on their early training. . . . Correct ways of thinking and acting should be inculcated early. Energy, perseverance, industry, morality and independence should be among the first lessons in life. Teach them that a life of excellence and moral and intellectual worth will draw around them the sincere, ardent and lasting friendship of the better sort of people, while at the same time it will enable them to follow any career successfully, without any help from friends, and without dreading the hostility of the envious." Perhaps, ironically, from a father who was fighting a war—and sending home martial souvenirs to his sons—Aden also urged Matilda to "watch closely any feelings of restless or longing for adventure that may spring up in their minds, for many of the best natures have been brought to utter ruin by submitting to this vagrant spirit."[85]

John Applegate, a former blacksmith whose letters reveal him to be the least educated of the husbands, had more basic concerns. When Elizabeth reported that their daughter, Allie, was sick, John became distraught: "You promised when you left to let me hear from you everyday while Alli was sick but it seems that you have forgotten it or don't want me to hear from you I have not had a minutes peas since I received your last letter if I could get a furlough I would bin at home to day but as it is impossible at this time I will have to submit so Liz if you think any thing of me let me hear how Alli is[.]" Between 1848 and 1855, Elizabeth had borne four children, only one of whom—the youngest, Allie—had survived. The Applegates' first-born child, a boy, died on the day of his birth. A second child, a girl, died at fifteen months. In the spring of 1860, the third child, a seven-year-old boy, also died.[86] Even more than Lucius and Alice Chapin, the Applegates had felt the loss of children. This helps explain John's frantic need for information about Allie's illness.

John obviously missed his daughter greatly. He asked Elizabeth to "kiss Alle a thousands times for me[.]" His homesickness for Allie seemed to encompass all children, and he asked Allie to "giv my lov to all the children in the nebor hood[.]" John thought Allie should be thankful that she had been spared the hardships of war he saw around him: "I am well and hope that you and your Ma ar well and happy you ought to bee happy and thank god that you do not liv in this unhappy country I have seen little girles like you turned out of ther homes at mid knight and thar homes and every thing they [owned] burned up that is dun every few dayes hear on both sides[.]"Most of all, John wanted Allie to write: "I want you to bee a good girl and mind your ma in every thing and then you will pleas me I want you to wright as often as you can if it is only one line it will pleas me[.]"He desired that Allie "be a good girl and go to school every day until school is out," not because it would instill the characteristics that Aden might have valued but because education would enable her to write to him: "I want you to go to scool all the time and lern to read and wright so that you can wright to your Pa you must get your Ma to wright a few lines to me for you but I would rather you would wright it your self it would mak me so glad to her from My Little Daughter now alle bee a good girl until com home and do not forget your Pa[.]"

Like the other fathers, John tried to regulate Allie's conduct despite the distance. He reported to Allie that he had heard from her mother how she had been a good little girl—the best little girl in town—and that he wanted her to be good all her life. Although concerned with his daughter's behavior, John did not enumerate, as had Aden, the character traits that made up goodness. He did instruct her to "bee a good girl and Love and obay your Ma and pray for your Pa[.]" Miles left Jennie out of his discussions of childrearing. Like John, Lucius instructed his Ally to obey her mother, but he spoke of discipline—whipping—as his prerogative. Aden obviously viewed Matilda as an important conduit for carrying out his views of character formation. John more than any other father left the details of childrearing to his wife: "now alle I want you to be a good girl and mind your Ma obay her in every thing and then you will do right[.]"[87] But he did not instruct Elizabeth on what he considered right.

Within the marital household, the war liberated neither Alice Chapin nor Mary Vermilion nor Jennie Fletcher. Young husbands, such as Lucius and William, made it clear that they were still in charge. Jennie found herself dependent on a powerful father-in-law. Older husbands, such as John and Aden, did not wield authority as bluntly. Younger husbands who had not yet established their authority when they left for war may have attempted to do so by having their wives live with in-laws, who could act as surrogates for the husband. There are too few cases to know whether individual circumstances, age, or social class dictated the women's choice of residence, but it seems significant that the women often remained under the authority of the husband's family, even while the husband himself was absent.[88]

Notes

1. [Alice] to My Own husband, January 29, 1862, folder 1, box 1, Lucius Chapin Papers, William Henry Smith Memorial Library, Indiana Historical Society, Indianapolis; Daniel W. Layman Account Books, Manuscripts of the Indiana Division, Indiana State Library, Indianapolis, vol. 1850–56:183, 268. Vol. 1855–62: 98, details Lucius Chapin's medical bills.

2. J. W. Osborn to L. P. Chapin, July 20, 1862, folder 1, box 1, Chapin Papers.

3. L. P. C. to Wife, August 26, 1862, ibid.

4. Ibid.; Wifey to My Own Love, October 7, 1862, folder 3, ibid.

5. L. V. Chapin to Wife, August 12, 1862, folder 1, ibid.

6. Alice R. Chapin to Husband, September 17, 1862, folder 2, ibid.; [Alice to ?], September 21, 1862, ibid.; Alice to husband, September 27, 1863, folder 9, ibid.

7. [Alice to ?], September 21, 1862, folder 2, ibid.

8. Lu to Wife, April 25, 1864, folder 1, box 2, ibid. Rachel Filene Seidman argues

that women used their dependency both to emphasize the sacrifice they were making in sending their men to war and to demand support for themselves during the war, but they did not reject dependency or challenge their subservient role. "A Monstrous Doctrine? Northern Women on Dependency during the Civil War," in Paul A. Cimbala and Randall M. Miller, eds., *An Uncommon Time: The Civil War and the Northern Home Front* (New York: Fordham University Press, 2002), 170–88.

9. S. Chapin to Dearest Son, April 21, 1863, folder 7, box 1, Chapin Papers.

10. Alice to Husband, May 14, 1863, ibid.

11. J. E. Chapin to Lew, April 19, 1863, ibid.; Anna Chapin to Brother, May 20, 1863, ibid.; A. R. C. to Husband, [June 8, 1863], folder 8, ibid.

12. Nancy F. Cott, *Public Vows: A History of Marriage and the Nation* (Cambridge: Harvard University Press, 2000), 61–62; Chris Dixon, *Perfecting the Family: Antislavery Marriages in Nineteenth-Century America* (Amherst: University of Massachusetts Press, 1997); Carol Berkin, *Civil War Wives: The Lives and Times of Angelina Grimké Weld, Varina Howell Davis, and Julia Dent Grant* (New York: Knopf, 2009); Carol K. Bleser and Lesley J. Gordon, eds., *Intimate Strategies of the Civil War: Military Commanders and Their Wives* (New York: Oxford University Press, 2001); Amy Murrell Taylor, *The Divided Family in Civil War America* (Chapel Hill: University of North Carolina Press, 2005), 35–62; Stephen Berry, *House of Abraham: Lincoln and the Todds, a Family Divided by War* (Boston: Houghton Mifflin, 2007); Elizabeth D. Leonard, *Yankee Women: Gender Battles in the Civil War* (New York: Norton, 1994); Nina Silber, "Loosening the Ties That Bind: The Conflicting Moral Visions of Men and Women in the Civil War North," *North & South* 9, no. 1 (2009): 24–33; Carolyn J. Stefanco, "Poor Loving Prisoners of War: Nelly Kinzie Gordon and the Dilemma of Northern-Born Women in the Confederate South," in *Enemies of the Country: New Perspectives on Unionists in the Civil War South*, ed. John C. Inscoe and Robert C. Kenzer (Athens: University of Georgia Press, 2001), 148–71; Joan E. Cashin, *First Lady of the Confederacy: Varina Davis's Civil War* (Cambridge, MA: Belknap, 2006).

13. Tina Stewart Brakebill, *"Circumstances Are Destiny": An Antebellum Woman's Struggle to Define Sphere* (Kent, OH: Kent State University Press, 2006), 19–23, 31, 116–17, 200.

14. Marilyn Ferris Motz, *True Sisterhood: Michigan Women and Their Kin, 1820–1920* (Albany: State University of New York Press, 1983), 2, 6, 33–35, 46–49, 80. Tamara G. Miller argues for the same phenomenon on the Ohio frontier. "'Those with Whom I Feel Most Nearly Connected': Kinship and Gender in Early Ohio," in *Midwestern Women: Work, Community, and Leadership at the Crossroads*, ed. Lucy Eldersveld Murphy and Wendy Hamand Venet (Bloomington: Indiana University Press, 1997), 121–40. Naomi Tadmor's work indicates that such blurring of the lines between in-laws and birth family occurred in eighteenth-century England. *Family and Friends in Eighteenth-Century England* (Cambridge: Cambridge University Press, 2001), 153–54.

15. Donald C. Elder III, ed., *Love amid the Turmoil: The Civil War Letters of William and Mary Vermilion* (Iowa City: University of Iowa Press, 2003), 1–7, 32; Dollie to [William], May 19, 1863, ibid., 100; Dollie to [William], February 27, 1863, ibid., 64–65.

16. Dollie to [William], February 27, 1863, ibid.

17. Will Vermilion to My Dear Dollie, November 5, 1862, ibid., 13.

18. W. F. Vermilion to Dollie, December 7, 1862, ibid., 21, 23.

19. Dollie to [William], May 30, 1863, 116–17; Dollie to [William], June 4, 1863, 120–22; Dollie to [William], June 9, 1863, 126; Dollie to [William], September 13, 1863, 220, all in ibid.

20. W. F. Vermilion to My Dear Dollie, November 22, 1862, ibid., 17.

21. Mary to My Darling, December 9, 1862, ibid., 24–25.

22. W. F. Vermilion to Dollie, December 14, 1862, ibid., 26.

23. Dollie to [William], June 4, 1863, ibid., 120–22.

24. W. F. Vermilion to [Mary], December 1, 1862, ibid., 20.

25. W. F. Vermilion to Dollie, December 14, 1862, ibid., 26–27.

26. Dollie to [William], December 16, 1862, ibid., 27.

27. Dollie to [William], December 18, 1862, ibid., 29–30.

28. Ibid., 32; Will Vermilion to [Mary], December 19, 1862, ibid., 30.

29. Dollie to Darling, December 21, 1862, ibid., 33–34.

30. Will to Dollie, January 12, 1863, 44; Dollie to [William], January 18, 1863, 45; Dollie to Dearest Love, December 23, 1862, 35–37, all in ibid.

31. Dollie to [William], February 27, 1863, 64–65; Dollie to [William], April 28, 1863, 82; Dollie to [William], May 10, 1863, 92–93, all in ibid.

32. Gayle Thornbrough, Dorothy L. Riker, and Paula Corpuz, eds., *The Diary of Calvin Fletcher*, 9 vols. (Indianapolis: Indiana Historical Society, 1972–83), 4:xv, 6:21–22.

33. Ibid., 4:437n111, 6:xiii–xiv, 5:526, 7:10–11.

34. Ibid., 4:232.

35. Ibid., 4:229.

36. Miles to Father, June 1, 1852, folder 6, box 6, Calvin Fletcher Papers, William Henry Smith Memorial Library, Indiana Historical Society, Indianapolis.

37. Miles to Mother, September 25, 1852, folder 7, ibid.

38. Ibid.

39. Miles to Father, March 15, 1853, folder 1, box 7, ibid.

40. Miles J. Fletcher to Father, August 31, 1853, folder 3, ibid.

41. Miles J. Fletcher to Father, October 14, 1853, folder 4, ibid.

42. Miles to Father, September 20, 1852, folder 7, box 6, ibid.; Ann Douglas Wood, "The Fashionable Diseases: Women's Complaints and Their Treatment in Nineteenth-Century America," in *Clio's Consciousness Raised: New Perspectives on the History of Women*, ed. Mary S. Hartman and Lois Banner (New York: Harper and Row, 1974), 1–22; Carroll Smith-Rosenberg, "The Hysterical Woman: Sex Roles and Role Conflict in 19th-Century America," *Social Research* 39 (Winter 1972): 652–78.

43. Miles to Mother, September 25, 1852, folder 7, box 6, Fletcher Papers.

44. Miles to Father, October 5, 1852, ibid.

45. Miles J. Fletcher to Father, June 7, 1857, folder 7, box 8, ibid.

46. Jennie to Father, December 15, 1852, folder 7, box 6, Miles to Father, December 21, 1852, Miles to Father, October 5, 1852, all in ibid.

47. Thornbrough, Riker, and Corpuz, *Diary of Calvin Fletcher*, 5:513, 517, 526, 538.

48. Miles to Father, April 24, 1858, folder 10, box 8, Fletcher Papers.

49. Miles J. Fletcher to Father, May 17, 1858, ibid.; Thornbrough, Riker, and Corpuz, *Diary of Calvin Fletcher*, 6:427–28.

50. Miles to Father, January 20, 1854, folder 5, box 7, Miles to Father, January 23, 1854, Miles to Father, February 24, 1854, all in Fletcher Papers; Thornbrough, Riker, and Corpuz, *Diary of Calvin Fletcher*, 5:102n149.

51. Thornbrough, Riker, and Corpuz, *Diary of Calvin Fletcher*, 5:147.

52. Ibid., 5:562; Miles to Dear Friend, March 3, 1857, folder 7, box 8, Miles to father, April 27, 1857, both in Fletcher Papers.

53. Miles to Father, September 10, 1857, folder 8, Miles to Father, September 21, 1857, Miles J. Fletcher to Father, November 11, 1857, folder 9, Miles J. Fletcher to Father, November 24, 1857, all in Fletcher Papers; Thornbrough, Riker, and Corpuz, *Diary of Calvin Fletcher*, 5:526.

54. Miles J. Fletcher to Father, May 2, 1858, folder 10, box 8, Fletcher Papers.

55. Thornbrough, Riker, and Corpuz, *Diary of Calvin Fletcher*, 6:181–83, 7:422–25, 427n232, 428–29, 9:276, 7:423–25, 7:427–29, 437; Ingram to Father, June 23, 1862, folder 3, box 10, Elijah to Father, June 27, 1862, both in Fletcher Papers.

56. Thornbrough, Riker, and Corpuz, Diary of Calvin Fletcher, 9:276; Indianapolis (IN) Journal, December 23, 1876; Cooley to Father, May 12, 1862, folder 2, box 10, Fletcher Papers; Thornbrough, Riker, and Corpuz, Diary of Calvin Fletcher, 7:555, 570, 8:3, 35, 39.

57. Ibid., 7:31, 78, 579, 607; *Putnam Republican Banner* (Greencastle, Indiana), July 30, 1863. The 1880 census, when Jennie was widowed from her second husband, records her as having a lodger, a young lawyer. There is no indication that she did this after Miles's death. At thirty-four in 1863, Jennie may have been too young a widow to take in boarders without unsavory comment. "Jennie Fletcher Allen," *U.S. Federal Census*, 1880, ancestrylibrary.com (accessed July 2007).

58. Thornbrough, Riker, and Corpuz, *Diary of Calvin Fletcher*, 8:198, 263, 285, 299, 306.

59. Ibid., 8:263, 339, 342, 343, 12–13, 16, 149, 365, 433, 454, 500.

60. Ibid., 9:276; *Indianapolis (IN) Journal*, December 23, 1876; "Jennie Fletcher Allen."

61. Thornbrough, Riker, and Corpuz, *Diary of Calvin Fletcher*, 9:259–62.

62. Allen, 1-7-7, Cemetery Lots, book 1, p. 134, Forest Hill Cemetery, Greencastle, Indiana.

63. Folder of Biographical Information, Applegate Manuscripts, Lilly Library, Indiana University, Bloomington; Lauralee Baugh, Jinsie Bingham, Marilyn Clearwaters, and Rita W. Harlan, comps., *Putnam County, Indiana, Land Patents* (Evansville, IN: Evansville Bindery, 2003), 92–94; Jesse W. Weik, *History of Putnam County, Indiana* (Indianapolis: B. F. Bowen, 1910), 49–50; Record of Official Bonds, 1844–1911, 1, 4, 11, 14, 30, 38, 48, 476, Putnam County, Clerk's Office, Putnam County Courthouse, Greencastle, Indiana; Record of Official Bonds, no. 1, 310, ibid.; *Greencastle (IN) Banner*, April 5, 1877; *Indiana Press* (Greencastle), April 3, 1872.

64. *War Letters of Aden G. Cavins, Written to His Wife Matilda Livingston Cavins* (Evansville: Rosenthal-Kuebler, [1907?]), 37–38, in Alumni Files, Archives and Special Collections, DePauw University, Greencastle, Indiana; John J. Baughman to Nicole Etcheson, e-mail (in author's possession).

65. Wifey to Dearie, September 1, 1862, folder 2, box 1, Chapin Papers; Dollie to [William], February 19, 1863, in Elder, *Love amid the Turmoil*, 59; E. S. Applegate to husband, May 28, 1865, Applegate Manuscripts; Ever Your Wife Matilda to Aden, April 21, 1865, in *War Letters of Aden G. Cavins*.

66. [Alice] to Husband, September 28, 1862, folder 2, box 1, A. R. C. to Husband, [June 8, 1863], folder 8, Alice to My beloved, January 24, 1864, folder 1, box 2, all in Chapin Papers.

67. Dollie to My Dear Love, November 12, 1862, in Elder, *Love amid the Turmoil*, 15.

68. W. F. Vermilion to Dollie, December 29, 1862, ibid., 39.

69. [Aden to Matilda], March 23, April 5, 15, 26, May 31, and June 3, 1863, January 24 and February 8, 1864, in *War Letters of Aden G. Cavins*, 77–79.

70. Alice to Father, December 19, 1862, folder 4, box 1, L. P. Chapin to Wife, July 21, [1863], folder 8, A. R. Chapin to Husband, July 21, 1863, all in Chapin Papers.

71. Alice R. Chapin to Husband, August 4, 1863, folder 9, Lida to Brother, July 9, 1864, folder 2, box 2, S. Chapin to Lew, July 10, 1864, all in ibid.

72. L. P. Chapin to Wifey, February 2, 1865, folder 4, Alice R. Chapin to Husband, April 30, 1865, J. W. Osborn to Lucius, September 14, 1865, folder 5, all in ibid.

73. L. P. Chapin, May 18, 1865, Your Sister to Brother [Lucius], November 25, 1865, both in ibid.

74. W. F. Vermilion to Dollie, December 14, 1862, in Elder, *Love amid the Turmoil*, 26–27.

75. Dollie to [William], June 4, 1863, ibid., 120–22.

76. Dollie to [William], December 16, 1862, ibid., 27.

77. Dollie to [William], February 1, 1863, 52; Dollie to [William], January 29, 1863, 48–49, both in ibid.

78. Miles to Father, October 5, 1852, folder 7, box 6, Fletcher Papers.

79. Miles to Father, June 6, 1853, folder 2, box 7, Miles to Father, June 14, 1853, both in ibid.

80. John to Wife, November 10, 1862, Applegate Manuscripts.

81. John to Wife, August 4, 1863, ibid.; [Aden to Matilda], December 21, 1863, *War Letters of Aden G. Cavins*, n.p.

82. [Alice] to Husband, September 28, 1862, folder 2, box 1, Wifey to My Own Love, October 7, 1862, folder 3, [Alice] to My Dear Love, December 21, 1863, folder 10, [L. P. Chapin] to Wifey, October 2, 1862, folder 3, J. E. Chapin to Lew, April 19, 1863, folder 7, [Alice] to My Dear Husband, October 15, 1862, folder 3, L. P. Chapin to Wifey, December 21, 1862, folder 4, L. P. Chapin to Wifey, October 30, 1864, folder 3, box 2, all in Chapin Papers.

83. Miles J. Fletcher to Father, June 23, 1858, folder 11, box 8, Fletcher Papers.

84. James Marten, *The Children's Civil War* (Chapel Hill: University of North Carolina Press, 1998), 70, 89.

85. Matilda to Aden, December 25, 1863, 100–101, July 1, 1863, 53, December 2, 1862, 27, January 20, 1863, *War Letters of Aden G. Cavins*, 33–35.

86. John to Wife, June 6, 1863, and Folder of Biographical Information, Applegate Manuscripts.

87. Pa, J. S. Applegate, to Daughter, March 1, 1864, John to Wife, October 11, 1863, Pa, J. S. Applegate, to Daughter, March 1, 1864, John to Wife, May 22, 1863, Pa to Miss Alma Apple[gate], ca. 1862–64, John to Wife, July 26, 1864, John to Wife, October 11, 1863, John to Wife, August 1, 1863, Pa to Miss Alma Apple[gate], n.d., all in Applegate Manuscripts.

88. Thomas E. Rodgers, "Hoosier Women and the Civil War Home Front," *Indiana Magazine of History* 97 (June 2001): 105–28, esp. 111–13.

INESCAPABLE REALITIES

RURAL MIDWESTERN WOMEN AND
FAMILIES DURING THE CIVIL WAR

Ginette Aley

Come up from the fields father, here's a letter from our Pete,
And come to the front door mother, here's a letter from thy dear son. . . .
Lo, where the trees, deeper green, yellower and redder,
Cool and sweeten Ohio's villages with leaves fluttering in the moderate wind, . . .
(Smell you the buckwheat where the bees were lately buzzing?) . . .
Fast as she can she hurries, something ominous, her steps trembling. . . .
Ah now the single figure to me,
Amid all teeming and wealthy Ohio with all its cities and farms,
Sickly white in the face and dull in the head, very faint,
By the jamb of a door leans.

—Walt Whitman

The separation of families is one of the great evils of war.
—Alice Grierson to husband, Springfield, Illinois, July 22, 1861

Walt Whitman's poem "Come Up from the Fields Father" captures that desperate moment when the American Civil War crossed the domestic threshold and gripped the hearts of families in the reality of war's fatal consequences. A similar tragic scene is memorialized in a contemporary double-folio engraving "News from the War," by Winslow Homer that appeared in the June 14, 1862, *Harper's Weekly*. In it, the most arresting subject is a despondent woman (a wife, mother, lover, sister) who is placed near the center of the assortment of images. She is slumped forward in a chair, head down on her forearm on the table. Clutched in the other hand hanging at her side is a letter, one that has clearly just conveyed the kind of war news about a loved one that was all too familiar to this and other wartime generations.

The lives of individuals, families, and communities—representing a host of relationships—were forever altered by America's Civil War. What we know less about, even given the tremendous historiography of the war, is how Northern home-front women and families negotiated and managed the struggle to stabilize a relational and material world that was rapidly destabilizing, as is clear from the period's voluminous correspondence between family members, especially between husbands and wives. Whitman was speaking to this in the poem, as was Homer in his engraving, in that both of their observations turn to focus squarely on the soldier's female relatives to illustrate upon whose shoulders the heaviest combined emotional and situational burden fell, in terms of those who must carry on without their loved ones. This is not, in any way, to minimize the pain, depth of love, or loss felt by grieving fathers. However, when a solider enlisted and went off to war, he took his wife's, children's, and mother's futures with him, a sensibility made more clear when one considers that accepted nineteenth-century gender norms defined a woman's life almost entirely by her relationships and in terms of her family.[1]

Jennie Hall of Logan, Ohio, observed in 1863 how the war was leaving in its wake "many hearts and homes made desolate. As I look around me here and there I see a vacant place. A Mother's hope and a Father's pride taken away from their fond embrace no matter how dear." Women stood to lose even more than beloved son or husband; the very terms of their world as they knew and understood it as mothers and wives were at stake. That powerfully symbolic vacant chair at the family hearth held out the constant dark prospect of remaining empty and, thus, an uncertain future for women and families. Changes, some of them drastic, were inevitable. These inescapable realities and rural midwestern women's responses to them form the basis of inquiry and historiographic exploration in this chapter. Despite the fundamental significance of agriculture and farming to Civil War America, the wartime experiences of Union rural women and families have been overshadowed by the more high-profile home-front organizations, such as the U.S. Sanitary Commission (USSC).[2]

Another aspect of Whitman's poem that is striking is the context of the Midwest's home front. Along with the gendered implications of the poem and Homer's engraving, this convergence of event, time, and place represents a vital historiographic field to harvest. As noted in this volume's introductory essay, students of the Midwest's home front face a number of challenges in developing historical analyses, some of which are repeated here because they have a specific bearing on interpreting experiences of the region's women and families. There continues to be a great need to develop internal midwestern experiences and stories, with an eye towards analyzing and synthesizing a regional home-front perspective. Midwestern voices are clamoring to be heard on this momentous event, and their spirited perspectives leap from the pages of the growing number of published wartime correspondences. Overall, however, such historiography as there is relative to the Midwest's home front tends to be overshadowed by the loose application of the "Northern" label. To what extent was the midwestern experience also Northern? The answer turns less upon geography alone and more upon how geography and later settlement influenced the nature of the activities engaging the people. For example, in a regional area of the Union where agriculture dominated and where several of the states were less than two decades old, it is worth considering that the war's call for men, from where their labor was at a premium, would place a particularly heavy burden on agrarian women and families.[3]

Place and region matter as essential contexts for how women and families experienced the home front. The regional Midwest of the Civil War era is defined in the traditional sense as composed of the following Union states: Ohio, Michigan, Indiana, Illinois, Wisconsin, Minnesota, Iowa, and perhaps Kansas. With the possible exception of eastern Ohio, these states were generally not considered eastern, especially at the mid-nineteenth century, yet "Yankee" tended to be another word for easterner. In fact, the preceding states were often referred to as the Northwest or even vaguely as the West. These states were also overwhelmingly rural and agrarian in terms of description, livelihood, way of life, and more. Indeed, as agricultural historian Paul Gates points out, they were part of the boom in agricultural expansion typified by new farm creation and improved acreage that notably increased during the 1850s and continued, albeit much slower, during the war. Illinois, Indiana, and Wisconsin led the way in this regard.[4]

A region comprising widespread agrarianism and a number of new or lesser-developed states would pose a different range of wartime circumstances and hardships for women and families than in the more settled, developed, and urbanizing east. One Mount Carroll, Illinois, farm wife lamented her situation in the *Prairie Farmer* (a major farm paper published in Chicago) in February 1863: "I doubt if there were as many women and little boys hauling grain to the market, and chopping wood, and driving teams, as now." She believed the war's effects were especially hard on wives and mothers: "When the whole comes to fall on the woman's shoulders she staggers; and no wonder, for it is a burden to which she is unaccustomed." Farming was certainly not unique to the Midwest, but its pervasiveness as well as the frontier quality of large parts of the region during the war call to mind, for example, comparable situations of deprivation, even destitution, that many women and families experienced in the Confederacy. Backing away from the idea of a monolithic North to consider regional differentiations encourages these kinds of fertile comparisons.[5]

Similarly, the historical narrative of Union women needs to be expanded. We have gained tremendous insight on the perspectives of middle-class, white women's nursing, mobilization (USSC), and related efforts, such as teaching, and on the ways these led ultimately to gains in women's political activism, status, and labor opportunities. The same cannot be said about insight gained in other major areas. The literature on the experiences of rural and agrarian women of the Union, let alone the Midwest, is relatively quiet aside from a number of outstanding journal articles, published correspondences, and chapters in larger studies. Considering that the 1860 census data shows that nearly 75 percent of the Northern population lived either on farms or in villages smaller than twenty-five hundred people, clearly, we need to devote energy to cultivating monographic studies of the perspectives of agrarian women and families. Census data further reveal that the percentage of a region's rural population increased as one traveled west; New England's population was 63 percent rural, and the Midwest's population was nearly 90 percent rural, again suggestive of the prevalence of an underdeveloped or frontier quality of life in the emerging Midwest. Accordingly, for women, even the everyday routines were made more difficult and strenuous amidst the backdrop of rural life and agrarianism, a situation that caught the attention of the USDA's commissioner of agriculture and merited a section in the first annual report in 1862.[6]

Also, too little effort has been made in ascertaining how midwestern women saw themselves other than to accept the wartime designation as Northern (pro-Union) as opposed to Southern (pro-Confederate). An indication of the potential insight to gain from exploring meanings in regional differentiation is found in the self-identification of an Illinois teenager attending an Episcopalian girls' school in Tennessee in the antebellum period. To the relentless taunting of her Southern classmates, she retorted, "I am no Yankee, I am a Western girl, I am better than Yankee or Southern girls." *Western* apparently meant something distinct from eastern or Yankee to this Illinois girl.[7]

These factors ensured that rural midwestern women would face their own particular set of inescapable realities with the outbreak of war and the almost immediate loss of some or most of their male relatives as they enlisted. A cursory glance at earlier assessments of what home-front women encountered bears this out. They faced hard home-front conditions that, among other things, precluded their commitment to organized war work because their labor and time were needed in achieving their own survival. A 1910 Wisconsin study details the prevalent destitution and charitable efforts and includes interviews with surviving women or family members. It characterizes wartime Wisconsin as having to labor "under disadvantages due to the sparseness of her settlement. She was poor, compared with the Eastern states, and time given to such charitable purposes meant money; for if women attended aid societies, they could do less in their homes." Not uncommon was "Mrs. A.," whose eighth child was born after her husband enlisted, and she was left to manage their children and their four-hundred-acre farm. When her husband was killed fighting, a creditor took the farm, and the sheriff evicted her. It is unclear how common this may have been, but given the circumstances of the death of soldier-husbands, it may have frequently resulted in the loss of farms. Or, consider fourteen-year-old Anna Shaw, who, in 1861, watched all the men, including her brothers and later her father, enlist and depart their farms in their rugged northern Michigan settlement (which in her autobiography, she refers to as a western settlement). For the duration of the war, she recalled, "I was the principal support of our family, and life became a strenuous and tragic affair."[8]

These initial assessments appear to run counter to the current emphasis in the historiography on Northern home-front women. Not only have interpretations been cast broadly as Northern but also in terms of mobilization with the end result that organizations like the USSC figure prominently in the home-front literature. Undoubtedly, many midwestern women were motivated along these lines. However, as both contemporaries and scholars point out, these women were, by and large, urban women in an otherwise predominantly rural Midwest. "Northern women outside of the principal cities and towns did not often join" organized war-relief work, observes a current textbook on the war. J. Matthew Gallman in his important study of the Northern home front contends that with regards to volunteer war work, married women "remained far less involved but were ready to lend assistance" to the Union cause. In other words, the majority of rural women faced compelling yet no less significant circumstances that in reality prohibited their active participation in mobilization efforts. As one early historian of women during the war reasoned, they could "ill afford the time." Some, like Iowan Harriet Jane Thompson, apparently had the time but chose not to join a soldiers' aid society, "for they always end in a fuss." On the other hand, agrarian women were likely to contribute in an unorganized, situation-specific fashion. For example, when a sanitary commission committee's circular asked for contributions of "wheat, corn, oats, hay, potatoes, onions, dried fruit, canned fruits, wine, cider, vinegar—in fact every article of farm product, as well as that of the dairy," women responded affirmatively if they could plant and harvest it or if they could spare it. Nurse Dorothea Dix's appeals to women for dried fruits and vegetables for the Union's soldiers were reprinted in the *Prairie Farmer* (and in other papers). "If our ladies cannot go to war," Dix urged, "they can, at least, show their devotion to their country" by these contributions. That their contributions of foodstuffs and labor amounted to a patriotic act was not lost on these women.[9]

An important example of the situation-specific rural midwestern response to the Union's needs concerns the scurvy scare of 1863. In early March, the Chicago branch of the USSC sent out a succinctly worded circular to local chapters, aid societies, churches, and more: "General Grant's army in danger of scurvy. Rush forward anti-scorbutics." Put another way, gather and solicit all the fresh fruits and vegetables that can be had now and at harvest (since these combat the disease) and send them on to the Chicago branch, which will get them to Grant and the soldiers. This was a call tailored to the agrarian Midwest, and respond to it they did with whatever they could spare from their own use. Shortly thereafter, it was as if a "line of vegetables" linked Chicago and Vicksburg. The call went out again the next year, and farm women like Michiganite Lydia Watkins again did not hesitate. She wrote to her soldier son in July of 1864 that the family was "busy taking care of the cherries now . . . and we are drying all we can so we can have some to send to the soldiers." The next month, she was setting aside pickles and small melons "as thier is a call for one hundred thousand bushels for the Army and hospitals and I intend to have some to spare." Watkins's assertion of her intent to contribute but with the qualification that she has it to spare (presumably after meeting her family's needs) evinces women's desire to control their participation. Rural midwestern women's public efforts and motivations were not unlike those Northern women Jeanie Attie describes in her study of the USSC: "In voluntary acts women demonstrated a willingness to contribute labor for political purposes when those purposes were akin to their own, and the labor remained under their control."[10]

To go a little further, Attie's study of the USSC underscores the remarks of the editor of an Illinois farm woman's wartime letters that the writer made no references to participating in local or national aid societies, nor were remarks made concerning "local excitement" even shortly before the Northwest Sanitary Fair in nearby Chicago. Likewise, the editor of an extensive wartime correspondence between Catharine Peirce, a Des Moines, Iowa, wife and mother, and her soldier-husband found that the former mentioned the work of the Ladies Loyal League in one letter but gave no indication of attending meetings (although her sister-in-law made bandages for the army). Catharine did remark, however, on the number of soldiers' families suffering due to a lack of food and fuel. In the case of Helen Sharp, a poverty-stricken Iowa farm woman and mother ultimately of five, ambivalent noninvolvement was replaced by antipathy when she wrote to her husband: "we cant get any thing from the vollenteers aid society." Sharp's castigation of the aid societies (which was by no means rare) for not meeting—or being able to meet—the needs of soldiers' families presents an alternative image of them in terms of home-front effectiveness. Regular attendance to aid society meetings was elusive, as one Melrose, Wisconsin, woman related. In her comments, she also illustrated how rural people assisted on the home front. "We have not an average attendance of more than six," she lamented. "To raise funds to work with, we went around, and solicited donations of wheat from the farmers. We sent it eighteen miles to market, sold it, and bought materials."[11]

For these women, patriotism and patriotic acts were not necessarily associated with their involvement in the USSC's war work. Their hardships, endurance, and, especially for farm wives, the assumption of their absent husband's responsibilities served as proof enough of their national loyalty. "There was too much to be done by the most of us," said one Wisconsin woman, "to keep the wolf from the door, to give way to our feelings, and it was better so. It gave us the feeling that we, too, although not enlisted in the ranks South, had a battle to fight at home on more than one line." Others wrote in to the *Prairie Farmer* seeking advice on farm-related issues, such as the best way to prepare soil for planting wheat and oats. One woman said, "Please give us <u>inexperienced</u> farmers particular and minute instruction on this point. If we can save the labor of plowing for small grain in these times of scarcity of labor, it will be a great item. Will the same preparation do for barley? Where can spring wheat be obtained? Will not some of your numerous correspondents tell us, what will be the probable price of labor per month, for good hands. How are we ladies, who have to manage the farm, to find out these things." Given the fundamental relationship of agriculture to both the Midwest and the Union effort, these were undeniably important questions and undertakings. These women also demonstrated their loyalty in their "domestic economy" in making adjustments like adapting recipes to sweeten using sorghum: "We women of this country, in trying to practice patriotism and economy, have learned many lessons of profit." If, as at least one scholar argues, Northern society periodically questioned its women's patriotic fervor, it would have fallen on tired, deaf ears in the agrarian Midwest. Based upon their recent, extensive study of primarily wartime Ohio letters, Lucy E. Bailey and Nancy L. Rhoades realistically conclude, "For some women, survival during the war years may have been their ultimate contribution."[12]

Across the board, home-front women were constrained in becoming heavily involved in war work because the absence of men vastly increased responsibilities and also diminished resources. For married agrarian women, this often meant an assumption of farm and farm-management duties alongside the suddenly new single-parent role. In her study of rural and economically marginalized Mid-Atlantic home-front women, historian Judith Giesberg demonstrates how these women mainly "experienced the war as a withdrawal of labor from their farms and their rural communities." Filling that labor void, which very often meant the difference between survival and "mere" deprivation, trumped active participation in organized war work in the rural Midwest.[13]

The remainder of this chapter takes a step back from the historiographic analysis to explore rural midwestern women's writings for an overview of their responses to the war-imposed circumstances on their families and the home front. Among other things, their letters and diaries indicate a detachment from organized war relief work in the face of inescapable realities, those tremendous pressures in trying to meet the *new* needs of the day. Foremost in their thoughts was creating the means to stabilize their destabilizing world. If, as we know, nineteenth-century America defined women by their relationships, then to their thinking, those relationships must be preserved at all costs. This determination largely explains the tone of anxiety, growing weariness, and fear that coursed through their wartime writings. Not just their relationships but their very identity was at stake. To become a widow for the Union cause would certainly bestow respect; but a woman's identity as, for example, a farm wife and the life attached to it, would be gone.[14]

The writings of rural midwestern women reveal that preserving their world became their primary mission, and they quickly seized upon sustained letter writing with their husbands as the means to accomplish this. Their efforts can also be understood as an important facet of women's kinship work, a conscious strategy to maintain household and cross-household ties for emotional and pragmatic reasons. Certainly, contemporaries understood the great power and emotional energy that sprang from the writings of loved ones. One *Atlantic Monthly* columnist exhorted home-front women to envision the "great army of letters" they sent off each day as a "powerful engine of war." However, when the author urged women, "Be unwearying in details of the little interests of home. . . . Keep him posted in all the village-gossip, the lectures, the courtings, the sleigh-rides, and the singing-schools," the stated purpose was to bolster and embolden the soldier away from home to fight on. Midwestern women, on the other hand, wrote of these things in order to keep their world intact. The world they sought to safeguard was one of "unions," or those connections that made them whole and bespoke their identity and status in larger American society, the most important of which were marriage and family and the family farming enterprise, along with their ties to community and national identity. What they sought to preserve at home mirrored President Abraham Lincoln's oft-repeated objective at the national level, that of preserving the Union. One important conclusion that is immediately apparent is that despite the residual patriarchal structure of the family, midwestern wives and husbands seemed to operate more commonly as partners and companions. This is especially obvious as they consulted each other about their marriage, their family, and about how to manage the farm and/or property in the husband's or son's absence. Indeed, a common salutation was some version of "Dear Companion."[15]

For most rural midwestern women, the husband's departure for soldiering apparently brought the first significant break in their relationship,
and the reality of that separation could be dark and unnerving. On a
Sunday evening in May 1861, Emeline "Em" Ritner of Mount Pleasant,
Iowa, wrote to her husband Jacob, "Jake": "I received your letter yesterday
morning and almost cried when I got through reading because it was
so short. . . . Oh dear hasn't this been a long lonesome week! You have
been gone ever since last Tuesday. Oh how I did hate to come home that
day. I felt as if I had been to a funeral." Note how quickly letter writing
came to symbolize their relationship; in general, short or no letters were
often interpreted by the other as signs of weak affection and a failure
of marital obligation. Helen chided her husband, "You write so little
you will get out of practice and I shall feel as if I was neglected." Lydia
scolded her soldier son, Benton, for being a reluctant writer: "You say
you have nothing to write about [.] now I think if I was thier. I could
see something to write[.] you spoke of so many dying and some getting
shot[.] what is that for[?] give us a full account." Letter writing was a duty,
a pressing family obligation not to be shirked. And the letters became
treasured items. As Iowa transplant Mary "Dollie" Vermilion prepared
to travel, she placed all fifty-seven of her husband William's letters in
her hand box. "They are more precious than anything else I have," she
professed. "I may lose my trunk: I shall not lose them." To Jemima and
James Potts of La Grange County, Indiana, keeping track of letter writing was serious business. "[W]ell James," Jemima mildly informed him,
"you have made a mistake in the number of your letters. . . . [Y]ou have
wrote one more letter than you think you have so the one you number
15 was 16." Of course, throughout the war, letter writers were vexed by
the irregularity of mail delivery due to constant troop movements.[16]

The long-term separation affected women on a number of levels, including their mental health, an area that remains unexplored in the literature even though every collection consulted for this chapter and other
research includes references to the woman experiencing some degree
of anxiety or despair. "Lord, pity nervous, worried women this war has
made," one woman pleaded in the *Prairie Farmer*. Similar sentiments were
as likely to be expressed about their circumstances—usually followed by
an apology for their selfishness—as about that of their loved ones away
at war. Jemima, who frequently wrote about being "very lonely," also said
that things around her "look very lonely" without James. No doubt, the
implication that the loneliness ultimately could be a permanent state

was troubling to them. In October 1864, Catharine wondered aloud to husband Taylor if she was "one of the number that may have to mourn for thee at this very time if I knew it" and a few weeks later told of "being some what anxious all the time." Words to the effect of "if I only I could know how you are at this moment" appear over and over again in the letters from the home front. Typical were the words and complaints of Dollie to William: "If I could only see you for one hour tonight what would I not give? I <u>don't</u> get used to the separation or reconciled to it at all. It hurts me worse every day."[17]

Distraction about their loved one's condition could reach a debilitating level as when Sophronia Chipman explained to her husband, "If you were here my mind would be here and I could work so much better than I can when my mind is so distracted." Dollie described a female family friend as becoming "nearly crazy" after not hearing from her husband in over a month. Distraction and perhaps ensuing depression also caused some women to simply avoid going out or attending places where they used to go with their husbands as, for example, church meetings. To go alone was a reminder that their partner (or son and other male kin, as the case might have been) was somewhere else. Church also became uncomfortably synonymous with funerals, which now occurred so often. In August 1864, Jemima wrote James that she had finally gone to church, which she had not done since he left for the war, and attended the two funerals that were being held; "it is so lonely to go any where with out my dear companion that I do not feeal like going very often."[18]

With their letters, rural midwestern women endeavored to overcome the doleful separation and maintain their world by keeping their soldier-husbands connected to it. The "vacant chair" seemed less empty and permanent if the realities of the day could be exchanged on paper. Not surprising, patterns and conventions in their literary conversations emerged. Initially, as observed above, home-front letters convey the writer's disorientation at the disruption of what daily life used to be, and there is an obvious grappling with the terms of separation. Quickly, however, the routines and responsibilities associated with rural and agrarian families command their attention, and the letters take on the quality of a daily labor journal complete with accounts of the weather and, of course, news and gossip of every kind. Interesting, this gossip was delivered in the language of the agricultural world they knew, that is, the neighborhood was experiencing a "crop of babys coming on" or that the case of an older male neighbor marrying a teenage girl exemplified how "old hawks like young chickens." Catharine's soldier-husband, angry over Lincoln's assassination, suggested "a clean shucking of the South" as retribution. Women also employed the language of the military in describing their home-front activities, as when Lydia responds to her son's letter describing his new detail at Camp Nelson in Kentucky, "Now I will tell you of my department which consists of the garden kitchen celler and I have a very good garden[,] all kinds of vegetables plenty." Overall, rather than a simple recitation, the letters were what we would refer to today as "interactive," given the regular questioning of the other's health and the seeking of answers followed by the responses. Often, these questions took on an urgent tone: "oh how I wish I could hear you . . . if you are sik so you can not write[,] get some one to write for you & tell me just how you are for I will not worry half so much if you will tell me just how you are."[19]

Jemima was a young wife and mother of Dutch-German heritage during the Civil War. Her letters gave the usual accounting of the weather ("it has not rain[e]d any sins you left home") and life at home ("we have our garden bout all made & now we are making sope"). They also bore witness, as so many did, to the fear that soldiering and its negative influences would break the union of faith the couple shared before God. In this, we are reminded of the strength and pervasiveness of religion in nineteenth-century America even if many home-front women appear to have lapsed in their attendance. From the outset, Jemima promised to "trye to put my trus[t] in the Lord" and admonished James to do the same. Just as frequent were the concerns she expressed about him being "sorounnded with a grate many temptations but I hope you will not be led a way by any evils that there is in the army. . . . I hope when you com[e] home you will be the same good man that you always was." This last hope appeared frequently in home-front letters, Union and Confederate. In the same way, mothers had reservations and worries over their soldier sons' ongoing exposure to vices and the potential this had to weaken their faith and commitment to God. Lydia beseeched Benton to hold fast to his Christian faith and behavior: "I hope you will never allow yourself to be tempted to do wrong such as drinking swearing gambling or any of the vices so prevalent in the army." She went on to share with him that she retreated to a back bedroom daily "and thier Pray to God to keep and preserve you from harm." Of course, couples and families took no small comfort in believing that should death intervene and separate them from each other on Earth, their unions would be resurrected before God in heaven.[20]

Jemima's letters also illustrate very well how determined midwestern women were to not let the war break the family circle. Jemima and James were parents of an energetic and precocious young daughter named Ida, who was about three years old. Ida and her antics figured prominently in the recounting of events, but Jemima sought James's involvement: "[W]hen you write, you must write to Ida for she thought it was very nice for Pa to write to her. I could hardly read the letter often anough." In her rough English, Jemima relayed Ida's attempts to mimic her housework, how tall she was growing and how her appearance was changing, what she played with, her desire to learn how to read, as well as the times she became ill or, as she did one day, cut her foot while picking berries. Little Ida was being raised as an agrarian girl: "Ida has got lots of little chickens & she feads them meal every morning. She sayed I must make som[e] chickens on the paper so you could see them." She soon wanted to write her own letters to Pa, and Jemima would include these scratchings in her letters to James. The family, like many, also exchanged "likenesses," or photographs, poesies, and kisses on paper back and forth. Yet, the length of the war, and the weight of anxiety, increased responsibilities, and disruptions took their toll on women who had not counted on single parenthood and children acting out in their father's absence (as Ida began to do). In this, Jemima's despairing to James was rather common: "I hope & pray that your life may be spared so you can help ra[i]se our girl."[21]

While information, items, and expressions of affection could be exchanged, physically intimacy obviously could not without a furlough or discharge. This aspect became difficult for a relatively young and passionate generation separated from their lovers and mates. Detailed descriptions of sexual longing would have transgressed the period's social mores. Nevertheless, midwestern women and their husbands voiced their desires, usually coyly, for physical union, even if this was, in part, to keep their husband's attentions turned toward home. This seems quite apparent in Dollie's letter writing to William in her frequent references to having dreams about him, kissing and petting him, and the "happy days we spent together at Woodside? Do you think people were ever happier in the world?" Elsewhere, she told of "longing to see you, to hear your voice, to feel your kisses on my lips, to live with you again, all your own Dollie." Jemima was pleased with the photograph James sent to her, although she thought that he looked better when shaved: "[B]ut still if you should com[e] home I rather guess I could find a place in your face to kiss & I do not think I would [feel] very shye for I do not think shye would com[e] in[to] my mind"; elsewhere she expressed the wish that "I could kiss your lips this evening oh dear." Harriet frequently tantalized her husband with comments such as, "Do you not think of our bed at home when you lay down on your cot?" As one might expect, these attempts to preserve the marital bond through imagined sexual encounters provoked an enthusiastic response. Jake assured his wife, Em, that she could expect to see him come home "and get forty thousand kisses just as soon after my time is out as I can get there. And then you will see if I ever leave you again." At the end of the long war, Taylor wrote of his desire to "clasp" Catharine once more and of his hopes that they could "live so that our life may go down in one blissful dream of love and affection." Despite being "an old fellow," he wished he could send her a kiss and get one back; that not being feasible "Well send me some love any how."[22]

As the war dragged on, securing the marital and family relationship was superseded by the pressure to preserve farm or property ownership, the most visible sign of social status in nineteenth-century midwestern society. In all likelihood, the farm was in the husband's name, but one need only read these letters to recognize that wives and husbands understood this to be a joint endeavor, a partnership, and a family enterprise and that women were highly involved in the decision making. Certainly, under normal circumstances, household labor and farm labor were divided mainly but not exclusively along gender lines. However, the outbreak of war and the departure of large numbers of men from an agrarian home front for a long duration created an obvious deficiency in labor and laborers.

Rural, married women, in particular, felt this keenly. On top of new single parenthood, they faced additional labor burdens and the stress of now having to make important decisions while being hampered by the distance between them and their husbands. Although some scholars contend that the war did not really force married women into traditional male roles, this conclusion is hard to square with the multitude of references to specifically assuming many of the responsibilities—and chores—of the male head of household. Moreover, in large parts of the Midwest, such labor assistance that was provided by male kin and neighborhood networks could often only be categorized as "too little, too late." Helen was not alone in complaining after chopping wood herself on a frosty January morning: "I tell you if I should wait to have someone come and see if I wanted anything I would both freeze and starve for no one comes in the house unless I go beg for it and sometimes not then." On another occasion, someone did come by to chop wood but only thirty minutes' worth. Jemima's experiences also illustrate this too little, too late characterization. She relays that she and her mother "got old george to come up & moove that old garden fence[.] [H]e plowed the ground for us but on the west [s]ide he just put in rales for stakes & the wind blowed so hard it all blowed down [and] now we will hafto fix it ourselves." She was still voicing this frustration to her husband in February 1865: "I do hope this war will not last much longer[;] the times are geting harder all the while & no one [concerned?] to see wether we are alive or dead."[23]

Indeed, examples abound of women meeting the nontraditional, physical challenges that their husbands' absence posed—or being nearly defeated by them—as they struggled to hold on to their world. Em told her husband that his latest letter found her with "hands all greasy and salty. . . . We got the pig killed yesterday and they brought it home to-day so Lib and I went to work and cut it up ourselves. (don't you laugh). . . . We just had to do it. There was not a man on the hill that we could get." Sounding like a farmhand, Jemima relayed to her husband: "I tried to put a roof on our well but I did not get it cover[e]d very good. I na[i]led bo[a]rds on the cides so it is not quite so cold to get water." Midwestern women's letters reveal in numerous places that more reliably than neighborhood or male kin networks, women assisted women in completing farm chores, in the same way that Em was assisted by Lib in hog butchering. Jemima, for example, notes, "Mother sayes if I help to fat[ten] her hogs she will give me some [meat] for it"; elsewhere, she and her mother raked and put up the hay after finally finding some men to cut it. She and her mother then built a hog pen for the fattening hog. Jemima already had her hands full in being responsible for carrying wood into her house, all household chores, a cow, eight chickens, a pony, a runaway injured pig, an extensive kitchen garden, an orchard, and market crops (wheat and corn). Well before the war's end, she and other midwestern women were exhausted and discouraged, lamenting how "the time seems so long & there is no one to help me share a hevey burden." Jemima wanted James home with her and their lives and roles restored: "I am get[t]ing very tyred of having to be man & wife boath."[24]

Along with assuming responsibility for a daily round of chores that varied in intensity by season, rural midwestern women found that preserving the family farm required that they become highly involved in the decision-making process. One of the more interesting dynamics to emerge in these personal correspondences is how comfortable husbands appeared to be in sharing final authority with their wives and in numerous cases simply turning it over during their absence. Again, this challenges the rigid patriarchal or hierarchical mold often ascribed to nineteenth-century rural families when clearly more flexible gender roles were in play.

True, women still asked their husbands to make decisions via the mail, such as when Sophronia asked her husband to tell her whether to sell a colt in order to pay the interest on their railroad land, which he did. Women commonly solicited input and advice from their husbands as a "wish to know what you think about" an issue. The realization that some vital decisions had to be made immediately, without being able to consult their husbands, often provoked a lack of confidence in women and a fear of causing harm to "the business at home." "Now James," wrote Jemima, "if I do any thing that you had rather I would not do[,] I want you to tell me & also tell me what to do." But whereas Jemima was a young wife, Sophronia was older and more intimately familiar with all aspects of the farming enterprise. She thoroughly investigated the financial feasibility of selling their farm, rather than losing it, and after a month informed her husband: "I have come to the conclusion that we better try to keep the land a while longer." There also, clearly, was resistance to being told what to do, such as this response from Louisa Phifer: "Now George you wrote for me to get me a side saddle [to go visiting]. . . . I don't want you to think hard of me but I don't want to get a side saddle. . . . I want to learn to ride behind you." Research into published and unpublished correspondences shows that by and large, men trusted their wives, whom they viewed as partners, to "do just as you think best." More specifically, George reassured his family at home, "One great satisfaction to me is that I know mother will manage things and make them go all right"; and then to Louisa directly, "But you know best how to farm and what to do for you are there and I a[i]nt." Jemima's husband even pushed her to assert leadership in decision making; her concern, however, was that leadership meant an uncomfortable independence from her husband: "[Y]ou say I am my own free woman. I tell you James I will not be free[,] I do not wanto be[.] I want to please you as much as if you are hear." It may be that wives determined their own limitations when it came to decision making, which would indicate a significant shift in our understanding of rural patriarchy.[25]

Ultimately, the Civil War was a family drama, and so it seems paramount to assess the midwestern home front from the perspective of the hearth. With survival in mind, rural women tended to set aside gender norms as their wartime responsibility rather than fret about them; indeed, some took this on with an unabashed zeal and sense of personal accomplishment. By their letters, however, most home-front women appeared to long for the restoration of their prewar family relationships and roles. Their letters are remarkable windows onto many areas of mid-nineteenth-century life that await more and deeper analysis than is feasible here. For example, the war presented midwestern families with the opportunity to exchange ideas on paper about race and emancipation, the Union and Copperheadism, and references to considerations about the family's prospects after the war. Among other things, we hear women's voices emitting from the heart of the Heartland—their homes.

The war had interrupted and threatened to end their world as these women knew it; realizing this, their war objective became preserving unions. Louisa voiced these fears in urging her husband not to be taken prisoner: "Be careful on mine and your own account," fretting that if something would happen to him, she would not know how to "get along." The major fear was losing everything: "George you said there was twenty Widows made in Nashville a day. O may God grant that it may not be my lot to thus become a widow for if such a thing should happen I would go Crazy or die before an hour."[26]

Notes

Research supporting this chapter was originally presented at the Organization of American Historians (OAH) Regional, Lincoln, Nebraska, July 2006. Epigraphs are from Walt Whitman, "Come Up from the Fields Father," in Lisa Lipkin, ed., *Selected Poems by Walt Whitman* (Edison, NJ: Castle Books, 2000), 107, and Alice Grierson to Ben Grierson, July 22, 1861, quoted in Sean A. Scott, *A Visitation of God: Northern Civilians Interpret the Civil War* (New York: Oxford University Press, 2011), 72. As a hospital worker, Whitman was no stranger to seeing first-hand how the Civil War ruined individual and lives.

1. Drew Gilpin Faust illustrates how Southern women coped and worked to restructure their destabilized world in *Mothers of Invention: Women of the Slaveholding South in the American Civil War* (Chapel Hill: University of North Carolina Press, 1996). LeeAnn Whites presents the Civil War as a crisis in gender relations among Southerners. Similar to my point here, she notes that at the war's outbreak, Confederate women "were forced to contemplate the very real possibility that rather than being empowered, these men might well end up disabled or dead" and what this portended for themselves. LeeAnn Whites, *The Civil War as a Crisis in Gender: Augusta, Georgia, 1860–1890* (Athens: University of Georgia Press, 1995), 12. Catherine Clinton and Nina

Silber write that with the departure of male kin, women knew that their families "were threatened with permanent destruction." Catherine Clinton and Nina Silber, eds., *Divided Houses: Gender and the Civil War* (New York: Oxford University Press, 1992), 244. Of the studies on nineteenth-century women and gender, Glenda Riley's work on midwestern women is particularly relevant here, such as her *Female Frontier: A Comparative View of Women on the Prairie and the Plains* (Lawrence: University Press of Kansas, 1988).

2. Jennie E. Hall to Lieut. Ed Lybarger, Logan, Ohio, August 30, 1863, quoted in *Wanted—Correspondence: Women's Letters to a Union Soldier*, ed. Nancy L. Rhoades and Lucy E. Bailey (Athens: Ohio University Press, 2009), 172. My present analysis complements an examination of the Civil War's private side found in Randall C. Jimerson, *The Private Civil War: Popular Thought during the Sectional Conflict* (Baton Rouge: Louisiana State University Press, 1988). For an understanding of the powerful influence of family, community, and the home on the soldier, see Reid Mitchell, *The Vacant Chair: The Northern Soldier Leaves Home* (New York: Oxford University Press, 1993). A monographic study of agriculture during the war has not been done since Paul W. Gates, *Agriculture and the Civil War* (New York: Knopf, 1965). For a comparison of Confederate wartime home-front experiences and the role of agriculture, see Ginette Aley, "'We Are All Good Scavengers Now'; The Crisis in Virginia Agriculture during the Civil War," in William C. Davis and James I. Robertson Jr., eds., *Virginia at War: 1864* (Lexington: University Press of Kentucky, 2009), 81–98.

3. Andrew R. L. Cayton and Susan E. Gray, eds., *The American Midwest: Essays on Regional History* (Bloomington: Indiana University Press, 2001). Jimerson points to the limitations of using broad regional terms: "Use of the terms *northern* and *southern* is simply the historian's shorthand for the most common ideas in regions of remarkable diversity." *Private Civil War*, 7. In using the term *internal* as opposed to *local*, I am encouraging the development of broader local histories than the latter term usually implies, which will assist in understanding how larger, external processes (or events) played out internally but within a regional framework. I argue that the roots of regional identity lie within these internal histories in "'Dwelling within the Place Worth Seeking': The Midwest, Regional Identity, and Internal Histories," in Timothy Mahoney and Wendy Katz, eds., *Regionalism and the Humanities* (Lincoln: University of Nebraska Press, 2008), 95–109. While numerous important scholarly articles have appeared in state history journals across the Midwest, I am referring to the lack of interpretative regional perspectives that would bring cohesion, without denying the complexities, to understanding of this period of upheaval; an example of minimizing the significance of the regional Midwest is its omission from Edward L. Ayers, Patricia Nelson Limerick, Stephen Nissenbaum, and Peter S. Onuf, eds., *All Over the Map: Rethinking American Regions* (Baltimore: Johns Hopkins University Press, 1996). Iowa, Wisconsin, Minnesota, and Kansas gained statehood in 1846, 1848, 1858, and 1861, respectively. Essays by Nichol Etcheson and J. L. Anderson in the current volume speak to these issues.

4. Ginette Aley, "'Knotted Together like Roots in the Darkness': Rural Midwestern Women and Region," *Agricultural History* 77 (Summer 2003): 453–81; Gates, *Agriculture and the Civil War*, 222–23, 228–29. Because no studies have been done on the Midwest during the Civil War, I abstracted a regional definition for the era from a common twentieth- and twenty-first-centuries' interpretation as mapped in James H. Madison, *Heartland: Comparative Histories of the Midwestern States* (Bloomington: Indiana

University Press, 1988), 2. I dropped the Dakotas, Nebraska, and Missouri from the usual twelve-state definition because, in effect, they did not "fit the profile." That is, the Dakotas and Nebraska did not attain statehood until after the war, and Missouri was a Border State. Joan Cashin's recent collection of essays signifies an important shift in attention paid to the home front in reminding us, "Noncombatants constituted the majority of the nation's population." Interestingly, Cashin's collection of essays is divided into three parts: the South, the North, and the Border States, and one can easily envision how this could be adapted to include regional designations. Joan Cashin, ed., *The War Was You and Me: Civilians in the American Civil War* (Princeton: Princeton University Press, 2002), 1. A collection of soldiers' letters that makes a regional distinction within the North is Nina Silber and Mary Beth Sievens, eds., *Yankee Correspondence: Civil War Letters between New England Soldiers and the Home Front* (Charlottesville: University Press of Virginia, 1996). Tracy J. Revels offers a model for a differentiated perspective in her look at Florida women during the war in *Grander in Her Daughters: Florida's Women during the Civil War* (Columbia: University of South Carolina Press, 2004). R. Douglas Hurt's essay in the current volume focuses on the tremendous wartime agricultural activity of these states.

5. Interestingly, historian Allan Nevins, writing the foreword on behalf of the U.S. Civil War Centennial Commission in 1963, suggests that, in fact, the frontier experience, often going back generations, steeled these home-front women for what they would endure, even singling out the "rural girl of the Midwest." Sylvia G. L. Dannett and Katharine M. Jones, *Our Women of the Sixties* (Washington, DC: U.S. Civil War Centennial Commission, 1963), 3–4. Nineteenth-century farm papers are discussed in Albert Lowther Demaree, *The American Agricultural Press, 1819–1860* (New York: Columbia University Press, 1941), and *Prairie Farmer*, February 7, 1863.

6. Phillip Shaw Paludan, *A People's Contest: The Union & Civil War, 1861–1865*, 2nd ed. (Lawrence: University Press of Kansas, 1996), 151 (see chap. 7 for an informative overview of farming and agriculture at the time of the war). Since the late 1990s, historians of women have taken note of the predominant themes in the Civil War historiography. Drew Gilpin Faust observes that the historical literature on Northern women has devoted "considerable attention" to the upswing in political interest, if not activism, arising from antebellum reform impulses: "An emphasis on the mixed legacy of the Civil War experience for transformation or improvement in women's position has emerged as a central theme in recent historical writing." "'Ours as Well as That of the Men': Women and Gender in the Civil War," in James M. McPherson and William J. Cooper Jr., eds., *Writing the Civil War: The Quest to Understand* (Columbia: University of South Carolina Press, 1998), 234. A decade later in her excellent analysis of Northern (actually, eastern) women on the home front, Judith Giesberg acknowledges several times that the Civil War narrative "has favored the war stories of middle-class white women" (later saying, scholars of Northern women have maintained an "almost exclusive" focus on them). Her study includes a perceptive chapter on rural women, labor, gender relations, and the war in *Army at Home: Women and the Civil War on the Northern Home Front* (Chapel Hill: University of North Carolina Press, 2009), 6, 11. Examples of fine scholarship on Northern women include Elizabeth D. Leonard, *Yankee Women: Gender Battles in the Civil War* (New York: Norton, 1994), Judith Ann Giesberg, *Civil War Sisterhood: The U.S. Sanitary Commission and Women's Politics in Transition* (Boston: Northeastern University Press, 2000), Jane E. Schultz, *Women at the Front: Hospital*

Workers in Civil War America (Chapel Hill: University of North Carolina Press, 2004), and Nina Silber, *Daughters of the Union: Northern Women Fight the Civil War* (Cambridge: Harvard University Press, 2005); *Historical Statistics of the United States: Colonial Times to 1970, Part I* (Washington, DC: U.S. Department of Commerce, Bureau of the Census, 1975), 23–37; W. W. Hall, "Health of Farmers' Families," in U.S. Department of Agriculture, *Report of the Commissioner of Agriculture for the Year 1862* (Washington, DC: GPO, 1863), 453–70.

7. "Autobiography of Clarissa Emely Gear Hobbs," *Journal of the Illinois State Historical Society* 17 (1925): 651.

8. Ethel Alice Hurn, *Wisconsin Women in the War between the States* (Wisconsin History Commission, 1911), 42, 64–78; Anna Howard Shaw, *Anna Howard Shaw: The Story of a Pioneer* (New York: Harper, 1915; repr., Cleveland: Pilgrim Press, 1994), 51 (citations are to reprint edition).

9. Mississippi Valley Sanitary Fair, *Circular of the Select Committee on Produce* (St. Louis, MO, 1864); *Prairie Farmer*, August 22, 1861. The contemporary view that "country women" could not be as involved in the organized work of the soldiers' aid societies and U.S. Sanitary Commission, if at all, as compared to urban women is found throughout Hurn, *Wisconsin Women*; Michael Fellman, Lesley J. Gordon, and Daniel E. Sutherland, eds., *This Terrible War: The Civil War and Its Aftermath* (New York: Longman, 2003), 219; J. Matthew Gallman, *The North Fights the Civil War: The Home Front* (Chicago: Ivan R. Dee, 1994), 115; Hurn, *Wisconsin Women*, 43; Harriet Jane Thompson quoted in Riley, *Frontierswomen*, 127. Jeanie Attie finds that the "actual record of homefront participation" did not match enthusiastic, early historical assessments and that the USSC's "mobilization of the female homefront was far from complete." At least as of 1862, she points out, "many towns were still without any sort of war charity organization." See Attie, *Patriotic Toil: Northern Women and the American Civil War* (Ithaca, NY: Cornell University Press, 1998), 98, 103–4. On a general overview of women's war work, see the useful but older reprint Mary Elizabeth Massey, *Women in the Civil War* (Lincoln: University of Nebraska Press, 1994). The previous title was originally published as *Bonnet Brigades* by Alfred A. Knopf in 1966; clearly, I am not suggesting that rural women did not take part in the USSC or in soldiers' aid societies, although research in their home-front letters shows a lesser involvement in nonfoodstuffs contributions and even some criticism of such organizations.

10. Lydia Watkins to Son [Benton W. Lewis], July 17, 1864, and August 14, 1864, repr., Virginia Everham, ed., "Letters from Home," in Michigan Civil War Centennial Observance Commission, *Michigan Women in the Civil War* (Lansing, MI: Commission, 1963), 53, 55; Jeanie Attie, "Warwork and the Crisis of Domesticity in the North," in Clinton and Silber, *Divided Houses*, 254. On the scurvy campaign, see Hurn, *Wisconsin Women*, 42–46, as well as Sarah Edwards Henshaw, *Our Branch and Its Tributaries; Being a History of the Work of the Northwestern Sanitary Commission and Its Auxiliaries* (Chicago: Alfred L. Sewell, 1868), chap. 6.

11. "'Dear Husband': The Civil War Letters of Sophronia Joiner Chipman, Kankakee County, Illinois, 1863–1865," *Military History of the West* 29 (Fall 1999): 149; Catharine A[.] Peirce to Taylor, December 27, 1863, in Richard L. Kiper, *Dear Catharine, Dear Taylor: The Civil War Letters of a Union Soldier and His Wife* (Lawrence: University Press of Kansas, 2002), 165, 8; H[elen] M[aria] Sharp to John Sharp, December 19, 1861, "The Sharp Family Civil War Letters," *Annals of Iowa*, 3rd series, 34 (January 1959): 485;

[woman], Melrose, Wisconsin, to (?), in Hurn, *Wisconsin Women*, 42. In yet another example, Indianan Jemima Potts makes only one reference in her letters to women organizing to send things to soldiers, and she does so as if she herself is not involved. Jemima Potts to James M. Potts, July 26, 1864, folder 1, James Potts Collection (M481), Indiana Historical Society, Indianapolis (hereafter cited as Potts Collection).

12. Wisconsin woman quoted in Hurn, *Wisconsin Women*, 74; farm women, questions and comments, quoted in *Prairie Farmer*, February 28, 1863 (emphasis in original). Nina Silber pursues the theme that Northern women's patriotism was problematic to the point of being "at the center of a public debate" in *Daughters of the Union*, as well as in Silber, *Gender and the Sectional Conflict* (Chapel Hill: University of North Carolina Press, 2008). Yet, Giesberg's research on Mid-Atlantic women found that women (and those around them) understood their sacrifices to be evidence of their patriotism. *Army at Home*, introduction, chap. 1 and 2. Rhoades and Bailey have written a fine introductory essay about various Civil War era contexts in Rhoades and Bailey, *Wanted—Correspondence*, 1–116 (quote on page 41).

13. Giesberg, *Army at Home*, 19.

14. A perceptive work on agrarian women and families is Nancy Grey Osterud, *Bonds of Community: The Lives of Farm Women in Nineteenth-Century New York* (Ithaca: Cornell University Press, 1991). The Victorian "preoccupation with the family" is discussed in Anne C. Rose, *Victorian America and the Civil War* (Cambridge: Cambridge University Press, 1992), 146 and chap. 4. In asserting that midwestern women contended with a looming potential crisis in identity, I am underscoring the point that the mutuality associated with farm families as well as the partnership between the husband and wife would be destroyed upon the soldier-husband's death. In all likelihood, this would force the wife to have to leave the farm, perhaps for a different, unfamiliar life. For the argument that the war represented a crisis in gender among Southern women, see Whites, *Civil War as a Crisis in Gender*.

15. For more on the idea of kinship work, see Micaela di Leonardo, "The Female World of Cards and Holidays: Women, Families, and the Work of Kinship," *Signs* 12 (Spring 1987): 440–53; "Call to My Country-Women," *Atlantic Monthly*, March 1863, 347. My work on rural midwestern women and families is at times at odds with older (but still cited) characterizations John Mack Faragher made, such as "the regulation of the sexual division of labor was achieved through the perpetuation of a hierarchical and male-dominant family structure. . . . This relationship of the sexes was not only one of male domination but of female exploitation." "History from the Inside-Out: Writing the History of Women in Rural America," *American Quarterly* 33 (Winter 1981): 550. These gender dynamics are continued in *Sugar Creek: Life on the Illinois Prairie* (New Haven: Yale University Press, 1986) and are also prevalent in *Women and Men on the Overland Trail*, 2nd ed. (New Haven: Yale University Press, 2001). More recent scholarship on the family of the early republic and the Midwest in general tends to depart from such rigid casting of family relations and accepts the premise of the evolution of more *flexible* gender roles, which is certainly evident in Civil War–era letters.

16. Emeline Ritner to Jacob Ritner, May 12, 1861, in Charles F. Larimer, ed., *Love and Valor: Intimate Civil War Letters between Captain Jacob and Emeline Ritner* (Western Spring, IL: Sigourney, 2000), 18; H[elen] M[aria] Sharp to John Sharp, January 14, 1862, "Sharp Family," 488; Lydia Watkins to Son [Benton], February 12, 1865, in Michigan Civil War Centennial Observance Commission, *Michigan Women*, 60; Dollie to My

Dearest Love, April 19, 1863, in Donald C. Elder III, ed., *Love amid the Turmoil: The Civil War Letters of William and Mary Vermilion* (Iowa City: University of Iowa Press, 2003), 79; Jemima Potts to James Potts, August 14, 1864, folder 2, Potts Collection.

17. *Prairie Farmer*, February 7, 1863; Catharine to Taylor, October 1 and 22, 1864, in Kiper, *Dear Catharine, Dear Taylor*, 277, 285; Dollie to My Dear Love, November 12, 1862, and January 8, 1863, in Elder, *Love amid the Turmoil*, 15, 42. Jemima's references to being lonely run throughout the Potts Collection.

18. Sophronia Chipman to Albert Chipman, "Dear Husband," April 28, 1865, 197; Jemima Potts to James Potts, August 14, 1864, folder 2, Potts Collection.

19. H[elen] M[aria] Sharp to John Sharp, "Sharp Family," July 6, 1862, 503; Sophronia Chipman to Albert Chipman, "Dear Husband," January 25, 1865, 178; Kiper, *Dear Catharine, Dear Taylor*, 11; Lydia Watkins to Son Benton, August 14, 1864, in Michigan Civil War Centennial Observance Commission, *Michigan Women*, 55; Jemima Potts to James Potts, June 16, 1864, folder 1, Potts Collection.

20. Jemima Potts to James Potts, May 6, 1864, folder 1, Potts Collection (first three quotes); Jemima Potts to James Potts, January 26, 1865, folder 4, ibid.; Jemima Potts to James Potts, January 8, 1865, ibid.; L[ydia] W[atkins] to Benton, 26 [May 1863], in Michigan Civil War Centennial Observance Commission, *Michigan Women*, 37–38. In his study of their wartime writings, Sean Scott found, regarding Northern women, "Sincere religious devotion characterized the lives of numerous women, and this pietistic outlook was an integral component of daily life." *Visitation of God*, 72 (but see chap. 3).

21. Jemima Potts to James Potts, May 8, 1864, folder 1, Potts Collection; Jemima Potts to James Potts, May 28, 1864, ibid; Jemima Potts to James Potts, October 22, 1865, folder 6, ibid. Several scraps of paper with Ida's "scratchings" for her Pa appear in the collection including one with a letter dated July 24, 1864. A similar theme of women protecting their family circle in the Confederacy is explored in Ginette Aley, "'Uncertainties and Alarms': Women and Families on Virginia's Home Front," in William C. Davis and James I. Robertson Jr., eds., *Virginia at War: 1865* (Lexington: University Press of Kentucky, 2012), 15–38. An expanded discussion of the relationship between children and the Civil War is James Alan Marten, *The Children's Civil War* (Chapel Hill: University of North Carolina Press, 1998), but see also Marten, *Children for the Union: The War Spirit on the Northern Home Front* (Chicago: Ivan R. Dee, 2004), chap. 3.

22. Dollie to My Dearest Love, March 2 and April 7, 1863, in Kiper, *Dear Catharine, Dear Taylor*, 65, 75; Jemima Potts to James Potts, October 16, 1864, folder 2, and January 19, 1865, folder 4, Potts Collection; Harriet Jane Thompson to William G. Thompson, September 7, 1862, "Civil War Wife: The Letters of Harriet Jane Thompson," part 1, *Annals of Iowa* 44 (Winter 1978): 221; Jacob Ritner to Emeline Ritner, June 22, 1861, in Larimer, *Love and Valor*, 39; Taylor to Catharine, April 23, 1865, in Kiper, *Dear Catharine, Dear Taylor*, 388.

23. Helen Maria Sharp to John Sharp, January 14, 1862, "Sharp Family," 487, 488; Jemima Potts to James Potts, February 2, 1865, folder 4, and April 2, 1865, folder 5, Potts Collection. On the topic of midwestern women coping with absent husbands and the labor deficit, see also Anderson, "Vacant Chair on the Farm," and Rodgers, "Hoosier Women and the Civil War Home Front."

24. Emeline Ritner to Jacob Ritner, November 27, 1862, in Larimer, *Love and Valor*, 68–69; Jemima Potts to James Potts, November 21, 1864, folder 3, Jemima Potts to James Potts, September 12, 1864, folder 2, Jemima Potts to James Potts, July 2 and July 5, 1865,

folder 6, Jemima Potts to James Potts, December 18, 1864, folder 3, Jemima Potts to James Potts, September 12, 1865, folder 6, all in Potts Collection.

25. Sophronia Chipman to Albert Chipman, "Dear Husband," July 4, 1864, and August 16, 1864, 161, 169; Jemima Potts to James Potts, October 8, 1864, folder 2, Jemima Potts to James Potts, December 6, 1865, folder 7, Potts Collection; Louisa J. Phifer to George B. Phifer, December 17, 1864, and his letter to her dated January 22, 1865, "Letters from an Illinois Farm, 1864–1865," *Journal of the Illinois State Historical Society* 66 (1973): 392, 400n32; John Sharp to H[elen] M[aria] Sharp, August 31, 1862, "Sharp Family," 506. For similar findings on rural Mid-Atlantic women, see Giesberg, *Army at Home*, chap. 1.

26. Louisa J. Phifer to George B. Phifer, December 17, 1864, and March 8, 1865, "Letters from an Illinois Farm," 393, 396.

THE VACANT CHAIR ON THE FARM

―――・―――

SOLDIER HUSBANDS, FARM WIVES, AND THE IOWA HOME FRONT, 1861–65

J. L. Anderson

In late May 1865, Ann Larimer wrote to her absent husband, Union soldier John Larimer, about the state of their family farm in Adams County, Iowa. She reported that the two sheep she had purchased the previous fall had increased to four. It was important news; keeping twin lambs alive can be demanding work. The prospect of raising more lambs meant more fleeces, which promised more income. During the war years, there was high demand for wool for military uniforms, and it commanded a premium price. Any doubt about Larimer's satisfaction with her accomplishment vanished with the next line: "Don't you think I would make quite a farmer providing I had a husband to do the work?" Larimer's comment simultaneously reveals pride in accomplishment and recognition of the limits imposed by wartime separation of spouses.[1]

Ann and thousands of other women lived with a "vacant chair" on their farms that transformed their lives for the duration of the war. "The Vacant Chair" was the title of a popular song George F. Root composed in 1862 that describes the loss of a loved one killed in action. But the song's reference to the vacant chair was also a daily symbol of wartime separation and the unresolved issue of whether men would return to occupy their chairs in parlors or at family tables. Even more than a symbol, it was a reality that shaped the wartime experiences of Iowa farm men and women in significant ways.

Women had always been partners and, to varying degrees, decision makers in the farm enterprise. But confronted with the absence of husbands, they often made significant decisions about farm affairs on their own, sometimes in consultation by correspondence with husbands or other male kin. Some women performed new tasks in fields and farmyards, although relatively few women conducted the kinds of physical farm labor that their husbands had performed before the war. Farm women were busy with other farmwork and childrearing and, in what appears to be a common occurrence, left the farms they operated in partnership with their husbands and moved in with the husband's or wife's parents. For many women, then, the war was a retreat from the farm to a more secure position within the homes of kin. Suffering and sacrifice were widespread on the home front, just as they were on the battlefront. In the absence of their husbands, women confronted many hardships and in many cases performed unfamiliar tasks, although they confronted those challenges with a high degree of cooperation or mutuality with husbands via correspondence. The provoking lines from Ann to her husband suggest that the war brought limited but important change for farm women whose husbands were in the military.[2]

Traditional interpretations of wartime agriculture and rural life in the North emphasize the role of mechanization and the labor of women, children, the elderly, and immigrants in meeting the surging domestic and foreign demand for commodities. In the only book-length study of agriculture during the war, now over forty years old, Paul W. Gates concludes, based on reports from the farm press, that women played a critical role in work in the fields and farmyards across the North.[3] Evidence from the farm press, however, needs to be supplemented by correspondence between spouses, the most intimate evidence we have, to discover actual conditions on the farm. Understanding the ways farm families coped with the problem of keeping farms intact while enduring the separation of military service requires a fresh look through the lens of the couples who endured the war.

The correspondence between soldiers and their wives is central to understanding the wartime experience on Iowa's farms.[4] Of the extant collections of letters, those from men are more common than those of their wives since it was easier for someone at home to keep letters than it was for soldiers to keep all of the letters they received. But even in collections with one-sided correspondence from the husband and few or no letters from the wife, it is still possible to understand at least some of the expectations and hopes that men had for their spouses and to learn what they reported that their wives did on the farm. What emerges from these exchanges is the extent to which managing the farm, at least during wartime, was characterized by a high degree of mutuality, or a shared sense of responsibility for the success of the farm. Mutuality did not necessarily mean equality, although it sometimes did, but it is better understood as a form of reciprocity, in which the lines between "men's" and "women's" work were blurred by the demands of family agriculture.

When newly enlisted men left their homes for training camps or for the front, they upset the fundamental unit of social organization in the countryside—the family. Men and women were concerned about how the family would survive without a man at home. Productive activity and socialization began at home, with each member of the family playing a different role, depending on age, gender, and position within the family hierarchy.[5] Some of the most extensive discussions of farm affairs that women and men exchanged in their correspondence occurred during the period shortly after the men left home and things were newly unsettled. Such exchanges demonstrate varying degrees of cooperation between men and women and show the importance that the recently departed men and their wives attached to kin and community on the home front.

When the American Civil War began, Iowa was an overwhelmingly rural place, even as its urban areas experienced striking growth in the 1850s. In 1860, approximately 62 percent of Iowa's workforce of 188,011 consisted of farmers or farm laborers. Since attaining statehood in 1846, Iowa had emerged as a significant force in America's agricultural production. The states of the Old Northwest and their neighbors to the west, Iowa and Minnesota, were part of the new wheat belt of the 1850s and were becoming the nation's leading livestock producers thanks to ample corn crops that resulted from exceptionally fertile soil, adequate rainfall, and optimal day lengths and growing season. In 1860, Iowa ranked seventh in the nation in corn production and eighth in wheat production.[6]

The war brought tremendous changes for all Iowans, but those in rural areas experienced the war in distinctive ways. A farm was simultaneously an economic enterprise and a family residence. Men and women cooperated as husbands and wives to raise children, crops, and livestock with human and animal power. Almost all farm families relied on the labor of children and others, including adults who worked as long-term hired men or girls and occasional or itinerant laborers who were often the sons and daughters of neighboring farmers or even townspeople.

The war and the recruitment of thousands of mostly young men created a labor shortage in Iowa. In 1861, the first fourteen of a total of forty-eight infantry regiments mustered, along with four regiments of cavalry and three artillery batteries. The next year marked a significant increase, with twenty-five infantry regiments and one cavalry regiment mustered for service along with the Northern Border Brigade recruited to defend Iowa's frontier from a perceived threat from the Sioux, who attacked Indian agents and settlers in Minnesota in 1862. The next year, only one regiment of infantry formed, the 1st Colored Regiment of Iowa, later renamed the 60th U.S. Colored Infantry, although four regiments of cavalry and one artillery battery also entered service. In 1864, the state formed five infantry regiments for one-hundred-days' service. Estimates of the total number of men who served in Iowa military units range from seventy-two thousand to seventy-six thousand, figures that include many men who served as replacements in existing regiments.[7]

The nature of military recruitment and organization meant that the labor shortage compounded with each passing year. With the exception of the 1st Iowa Infantry, which was a ninety-day regiment, men who enlisted in 1861 served three years or until discharged, killed, or captured. A portion of the men in those 1861 regiments reenlisted in 1864, earning the designation "Veteran Volunteer"; they continued to serve until the summer of 1865. Most of the regiments formed in 1862 served until July or August 1865 and, therefore, missed most of that year's growing season; the 1863 and 1864 enlistees were absent until midsummer 1865. More than thirteen thousand Iowans died in military service, and another eighty-five hundred men were wounded. The farm labor shortage that was significant in 1862 and 1863 became acute in 1864 and 1865 as a growing percentage of Iowa's men was in the military or killed, disabled, or captured because of their service.[8]

Letters from the home front indicate the concern over the labor situation. When the war began, widow Emeline Guernsey of Wright County had two adult sons at home to handle most of the farming. One son, William, enlisted in 1861, which left the family shorthanded. Emeline reported to William in November 1861 that her younger son, Henry, was not able to finish the fall plowing because of frost. Guernsey and other neighbors were "nearly all disappointed about getting their plowing done," a situation that might have been mitigated had more young men been home. Conditions became more severe in 1863 after Henry enlisted. In a letter to William written during the small grain harvest of that summer, Emeline observed that it was difficult to get men to bind the crop after it was cut by men with mechanical reapers: "Mrs. Mark Loring was in this week, and she said Mark was going to have a machine cut his [grain] down, and bind [it] himself afterwards. Others speak of having only four men when they harvest." An agent for the McCormick Company, the noted Chicago manufacturer of mechanical reapers, wrote from Oskaloosa in November 1864 to his employers and commented on the labor shortage in his area. Instead of hiring neighbors' sons, local laborers, or itinerant workers, the Guernsey and Loring families made do with less by doing for themselves.[9]

Even after the war ended in the spring of 1865, it was a struggle to get hired help since most regiments did not muster out until midsummer 1865, and some did so late that fall and into 1866. In the summer of 1865, John Sharp urged his wife to have some hay made in preparation for his return. Helen replied that "to get a man to do anything is out of the question." It might have been possible to purchase hay and corn, but to get hired help was nearly impossible. Not long after that exchange, John reiterated his desire to have as much as fifteen tons of hay made, and Helen stated that she would "see what I can do," a vague but honest appraisal of a difficult situation.[10]

When Mary Livermore traveled throughout the Midwest as part of her service with the U.S. Sanitary Commission, she observed, from her vantage point in rail cars and carriages, that women were busy in the fields, planting, cultivating, and harvesting to a much greater extent than they had before the war. According to a hard-working farm woman she spoke with in either Wisconsin or Iowa during the summer of 1863, "the men have all gone to the war, so that my man can't hire any help at any price, and I told my girls that we must turn out and give him a lift in the harvesting," which they willingly did.[11]

Livermore's account is instructive, but what follows in her narrative has escaped the attention of most historians. One of the young women Livermore met in that harvest field was a daughter-in-law whose husband was in the army. The young woman's three-year-old son was in the field that day "tumbling among the sheaves, and getting into mischief every five minutes," according to Livermore. The young wife considered herself "as good a binder as a man, and could keep up with the best of 'em," but her primary attention was on her son, not the harvest. Most of the young, married women left at home were busy in similar positions: raising children, preparing food, tending gardens, cleaning, and washing. Even if soldiers' wives wanted to do fieldwork, they would have had a difficult time balancing that with their other responsibilities.

The experiences of soldiers' wives were more complicated and often more difficult than a simple story of wives serving as proxies for their departed husbands. The complexity of the story requires attention to both parties to the marriage. Charles Ackley of the 7th Iowa Infantry balanced his advice with the recognition that his wife was in a position to know best about farm affairs. In August 1864, he inquired about the availability of harvest labor. "I knew you could drive the reaper if it was not for the children," he explained, emphasizing the importance of the family life cycle in shaping the ways women worked at midcentury. Ackley recognized that his wife's ability to drive horses and operate an expensive machine was not the limiting factor in determining what she did on the farm. Instead, it was her duties as a mother of young children that prevented her from conducting the harvest.[12]

Young and unmarried women were most likely to work in the fields. Just as the sunburned woman put her daughters to work, so did other mothers and fathers. A farmer named Joseph Miller was proud enough of his daughter's abilities as a binder of sheaves that he was willing to wager on her. In a notice in the *North Iowa Times*, Miller offered a ten-dollar bet that his daughter Sarah Jane "can beat any one binding wheat who will enter the field with her as a contestant." By way of qualifications, he stated that "she weighs 205 pounds, and carries no extra flesh." Machinery manufacturers occasionally emphasized the ease of handling their products by advertising those machines with an illustration of a young woman driving the team and operating the machine. Tellingly, the woman depicted in one 1865 advertisement claims, "My brother has gone to the war," not her husband. A much more likely scenario than the advertiser's vision would have been a young woman following a mechanical reaper or men with cradle scythes, gathering the stalks of cut grain and tying sheaves, as Sarah Jane did.[13]

Many soldiers' wives did not work in the fields because at some point during the war, they moved in with their parents or in-laws, where they were subsumed under the hierarchy of existing families. For women who returned to parental homes, fieldwork was already taken care of by older men and sons who were too young to enlist. After Matilda Peterson held an auction at her farm, she moved to Fairfield, Iowa. Cyrus Wyatt urged his wife to stay with the "Wyatt tribe" until she could "lay up enough" from her county allotment to return to Iowa, while William James of the

3rd Iowa Cavalry told his wife, "I am happy to hear of your staying at fathers if you can get along on good terms." William Sudduth composed a letter to his wife, Martha, about life at home that indicates the division of labor that he anticipated at his in-laws' farm. "Well, My Dear," he began, "How are you all getting along in Old Monona? I suppose your Pa has commenced planting corn, got his wheat and oats in, early potatoes + sorghum planted, wound up his sugar camp and felt business and settled himself once more to steady farming while you and Ruth and Nett are gardening, cooking, washing, milking &tc." Part of the sustaining power of this idyllic domestic image came from the knowledge that Martha was in the care of kin. As far as William knew, his wife was not exposed to fieldwork. She enjoyed the protection of loved ones, performed what people considered typical women's tasks, such as cooking and washing, and also attended to livestock chores, such as milking, much as she would have if William's chair at their home been occupied rather than vacant.[14]

The importance of kinship networks is underscored by the large number of soldiers' wives who moved in with relatives. Of the twenty-nine farm women represented in this study, at least seventeen left the farm for residences elsewhere in Iowa or other states, including Indiana, Kansas, and Pennsylvania.[15] Both husbands and wives recognized that women faced tremendous difficulties in living apart from their husbands. Thomas Ball of Story County confessed to his wife, Serilda, that "to move out on your place to stay this winter is a dark picture to me." Ball preferred that she remain with his brother, James. "I understand James and his plan like a Book," he explained, "and that is he wants you to stay with him and I am not afraid to trust him with the whole affairs of my interest at home."[16]

When Robert Stitt enlisted in the summer of 1861, his wife, Hannah, and daughter, Hilde, moved to Kansas to live with his brother. Like so many other husbands, Robert rented out the farm and arranged to have a trusted friend care for the livestock. He was, however, ambivalent about his wife's status as a dependent in his brother's home. For her part, Hannah wanted to move back home to rural Winterset. She was unhappy in Kansas and wanted to "go to keeping house a gain," although she assured her husband that she was getting along with his people and that there was plenty to eat. Robert confessed that he did not know what to advise her about living at home again but was willing to accommodate her wishes so that she would be content. Hannah allowed that she could continue the arrangement with a friend to conduct the livestock "trading" and, underscoring the importance of kin, suggested that Robert's sister could move to Iowa with her as a help.[17]

Kin networks also shaped the ways women who remained on the farm experienced the war. The first priority for husbands and wives was how to provide for the family. Husbands often approached a trusted friend, neighbor, or relative to manage the farm in their absence. Elisha Leaming was relieved that "father" had found a good renter for their farm. Jasper and Mary Rice parted in August 1862, when Jasper responded to President Abraham Lincoln's call for three hundred thousand men. Rice told his wife that a Mr. Boyce would attend to the farm and see to her needs. Adam Schaefer of the 17th Iowa corresponded with his Jefferson County neighbor William Whisler about managing the farm on his wife's behalf after he departed in spring 1862. In March of the following year, Schaefer expressed his wish to Whisler that he would "see to renting my farm to the best advantage, and see that my family are not suffering." C. J. Peterson of the settlement at New Sweden urged his wife to ask her brother Anders for assistance. William Donnan of Buchanan County advised his brother to take care of taxes on his family farm. Husbands and wives understood that there were many decisions to make and tasks to perform and that it was an added burden for women to bear alone. Furthermore, most land was in the husband's name, reinforcing traditional male roles as the head of the household. Securing help, while in part an exercise of patriarchal authority, was also a caring gesture.[18]

It made sense to most families with absent husbands for kin to help run the farm and for wives and children to move in with parents or in-laws, but for a male who was not a family member to move in with a wife whose husband was away challenged conventional morality. The rarity of such an event is the exception that proves the rule of reliance on kin for live-in support. John and Ann Wright, farmers from the Pacific Junction area, faced this kind of scrutiny late in the war. Wright enlisted in the summer of 1863 and immediately counseled Ann that someone known as Ap, possibly a relative, would provide advice and assistance. In the summer of 1864, however, a man named Peter moved in with Ann to take care of livestock and cut wood. Ann stated her concern that "staying alone with Peter" would be a source of gossip among the neighbors; however, John assured her that she was "doing perfectly right." "For my part," John explained, "it would look more suspicious to see a woman liveing alone than to have a man about the house," implying that a single woman would be suspected of being a prostitute. John believed that Peter was a good man and that Ann had nothing to fear as long as she would "carry yourself strait which I am satisfied you will do. . . . Let the scalawags of the country talk." The arrangement of an unmarried man and an unmarried woman living together who were not kin was a violation of social norms of the time and was unique among separated couples. The pressure of gossiping neighbors was an acknowledged fact. That a brother-in-law moved in with his sister-in-law would have been unlikely to raise questions about the woman's morality. The Wrights breached the unspoken rule of moving off the farm to live with kin or inviting a brother or brother-in-law to move in to conduct farmwork and preserve the household during soldiers' absences.[19]

In many cases, relatives took over the day-to-day work in addition to the management. When Samuel Glasgow of Page County enlisted in 1862, he asked his father to harvest the corn crop that fall and to sell one of their three horses. Agnes and Amasa Allen counted on Amasa's father and a man named Charles, who appears to have been a brother, to run the farm. Agnes wrote to her husband shortly after he left home in the summer of 1862, hoping that his father would see to harvesting and processing the sorghum crop. Later that fall, Amasa's father marketed their hogs and promised to send Agnes some of the proceeds from the sale and to keep some money for the purchase of hay to winter the rest of the livestock.[20]

During the long separation of Rachel and William Coffin, William relied on a man named Anderson to manage affairs at home. William regularly reported to his wife whether he had heard from Anderson and provided her with details about farm affairs. In the summer of 1863, William told Rachel about what was happening back home based on correspondence from a neighbor, who reported that the grain crop on the Coffin farm was excellent, with oats "the heaviest he ever raked off of the platform [of a reaper]." After the harvest, William, not Rachel, arranged to have the wheat ground and hauled.[21]

Many women left the farm or relied on the assistance of male kin and neighbors because the challenges of staying on the farm without a husband were immense. Husbands and wives plotted and planned about fuel procurement, payment and collection of debts, disposal of unneeded chattels, management of farm tenants, care of livestock, and numerous other tasks. These were the subjects of countless exchanges between spouses.

Some couples made careful arrangements to provide security for the family before the husband left. As soon as Samuel Rogers joined the 30th Iowa Infantry as assistant surgeon, he and his wife rented out their farm and sold most of their cattle, horses, chickens, and turkeys, retaining one cow and some poultry to meet family needs. Machinery and wagons, assets that required less care, remained on the farm until the family returned.[22]

Not all families were able to put all their affairs in order. Some husbands recognized early in their military service that women were the managers whose opinions mattered since they were the ones who had to make decisions and implement plans. Just two weeks after John Sharp enlisted in November 1861, he wrote to his wife, Helen, and advised her to have the deed, presumably to the farm near Fort Des Moines, made out in her name. In her reply, Helen chided her husband for not recording the deed before he left: "Now if you want me to have a deed, write to the one that has the deeds to make and then maybe they will do it." Helen, in effect, redelegated a task to her husband that he had hoped she would do.[23]

Women often acted on their own in making decisions about the farm. Helen is one of the best examples of an assertive farm woman, although she seldom appeared to be happy about it. She often asked her husband for advice, but in many cases, she relied on her own counsel either because she wanted to do so or felt she had no choice. In April 1862, she reported to her husband all the work she had done to move the family to a new farm that spring. She was unable to move all of her flock of chickens because of a lack of cages, so she sold the balance to a neighbor and used the proceeds to purchase cornmeal and molasses for her family and hay for her cow. She made these decisions and presented them to her husband after the fact with no mention of any guidance by outsiders.[24]

Financial decisions were among the most common management issues women confronted. Less than a month after Jasper Rice departed, he urged Mary to use her discretion to dispose of things on the farm that would not be needed until he returned. That next spring, she did so with some success. In a letter dated April 1863, Jasper conceded, "I must give you credit for your good management. I think when I get home I will let you do the financiering." He reckoned that she was "making some prety good trades" for farm implements. Similarly, C. J. Peterson praised his wife, Matilda, for her success in liquidating assets on their farm: "I see that you have had an auction." He assured her that she had made a good decision to do so. Two weeks later, he noted that the family had earned seventy-two dollars from the sale, which, among the many items sold, included eighty shocks of corn in the field, a move that not only generated income but also saved a great deal of labor or expense for Matilda or some other family member who would have had to haul it to a barn or livestock pen for feeding.[25]

Collecting and paying debts often fell to women, although men regularly provided reminders and advice. Amanda Barnes's husband, William, urged her to "sell pork enough to pay George Shurman and our taxes if you can." William Donnan of rural Independence reminded his wife, Mary, to notify him "if Fs pay us what little they owe us before they go away," which served as an indirect reminder for her to collect the debt. Little more than a week later, he wrote that the paymaster had arrived, and he would be sending money home, which meant that Mary needed to visit creditors to reconcile accounts: "I want that Butler matter paid. Then [pay] our taxes and Jim then if you have any more than you want for your own use apply it to that 400 still due for that land." Joseph Coffman urged his wife, Maggie, to sell forty to fifty bushels of wheat in December 1864 to "try to get money enough to pay of[f] the Reaper [note]." Admonitions to pay or collect debts were most frequent toward the beginning of the soldier's enlistment when the family's future seemed most unsure to the newly separated. As husbands' directives about debts suggest, women and men collaborated to manage the farm. It is unclear whether the reminders and advice were always welcome, but absent husbands continued to advise wives and exercise a limited degree of control over the financial management of the farm.[26]

In addition to providing guidance on farm finances, men offered practical suggestions about livestock husbandry and crops. Not surprising, women often sought counsel on such farm issues since men were generally responsible for that knowledge. Helen asked her husband's opinion about selling a cow that was a good milk producer but continued to lactate and, therefore, did not come into estrus, or heat. "Had I better sell her to a drover if I can?" she inquired. "I do not think she will pay to keep though I think she is a first best young cow." In the fall of 1862, Harriet Thompson of Linn County informed her husband that a man wanted to purchase the family cow for thirteen dollars. "I wish you would tell me what to do," she pleaded. Harriet had just returned to Iowa from Pennsylvania and was possibly unfamiliar with the cow's current condition and value.[27]

Husbands regularly responded to pleas like these throughout their enlistments, offering financial advice and practical guidance about maintaining the farm. Emma and Samuel Glasgow often discussed the farm in their letters, and Samuel retained a high degree of control. He continued to make financial arrangements long after his departure, informing Emma of his dealings mostly after the fact. In early 1863, he told his wife that he owed twenty-four dollars to a man in his company for a wagon, which he planned to repay as soon as the paymaster arrived to pay off the regiment. Charles Ackley of rural Marble Rock pressed his wife in the spring of 1865 to hire a breaking outfit to plow up more prairie acres that spring in preparation for an expansion of operations. As the summer peaked in August 1865, Silas Shearer provided his wife with specific instructions about tasks to be accomplished before his return home, including directions to hire someone to cut hay and stack it near the stable for feeding calves that winter, since he would not be home in time to make hay. Similarly, C. J. Peterson offered extensive instructions about plowing and planting for his wife to relay to her brother and a man named Lind.[28]

Women sometimes increased the size of their families' herds or added new livestock. In an exceptional case, Sarah Lacey acquired nine milk cows during her husband's absence and sold large quantities of butter that provided income for her family. More often, women made modest changes in family herds. Like Ann Larimer, Elizabeth Jane Shearer purchased two sheep in 1864. Her husband, Silas, then on campaign in Arkansas, applauded the move and urged her: "If you can get two or three more I want you to do it. They will not be very much bother to you until I get home if I am so lucky as to get home." Even as he encouraged her in the sheep business, Silas assured his wife that he understood that it was likely difficult to obtain more sheep, given the premium on wool. Maria Kimberly innovated and purchased geese in 1864. Although her letters are not extant, Uriah wrote that he was "quite well pleased with your experiment with geese." He commented that he would not have wanted to tend geese because they were "a dirty set of things," but she must have done well when she sold them, based on his positive response to the experiment.[29]

In spite of some successes with livestock husbandry, women often sold off livestock to reduce the management task they faced. Farm animals were portable assets, but they also required a lot of work. Sometimes, the work was defensive, such as building fences around the house in the fall to keep animals away from the home in the winter. Chores required exposure in severe weather, which was a burden for women with small children. A reasonable solution was to cull the herd, often keeping only a milk cow, some poultry, and a hog or two to meet family needs. Elisha Leaming urged his wife, Louisa, to have her father "sell off all the [live]Stalk that you cant git along with." C. J. Peterson was so pleased that his wife had sold the family's steers that he subsequently requested that she ask her brother to board their horses to minimize her extra work. In the summer of 1865, John Larimer counseled Ann to sell the cattle if she had a chance. Although she was unsure why he wanted her to do so, Ann responded that she would if she could "sell them for a good price . . . & if not, why, I will keep them until fall & see if you are not home to attend to them."[30]

One of the most vexing wartime issues for couples was how to provide firewood for women who lived without an adult male in the household. Such women relied on others to meet that basic need. It is impossible to know the extent to which the firewood supply was a source of marital tension when husbands and wives lived together, but it is apparent that both parties were dissatisfied with the way the men on the home front did the job. Sometimes, the comments were comparatively benign, such as Uriah's suggestion that his wife invite neighbors to "make a wood hauling" and get it chopped on her behalf. Most couples were disgusted or angry with those who were appointed or agreed to assist. Helen complained to her husband on several occasions that she had "something of a hard time about wood," although on at least two occasions, a neighbor came to provide her with some. In early June 1864, Joseph Coffman wrote to his wife, "I see you are somewhat neglected by the so called friend in not keeping you in plenty of wood." The renter who was supposed to operate the farm had left before completing his term, forcing Coffman to find another solution. He advised that it was not safe for Maggie to stay on the farm alone "and be without wood half the time." In another June letter, he expressed the hope that "you will not have to do all the chores, and chop your own wood."[31]

Managing tenants was a time-consuming task that usually fell to men. The Coffins' relations with their neighbor Anderson were cordial, at least as far as can be discerned from the letters between Rachel and William. Amasa and Agnes Allen also appear to have successfully rented out their farm with absentee management by Amasa. Allen told his wife in early 1863 that if his brother Charles had not yet sold the farm, "I can rent the land to the Bigalow boys and Father next season." He apparently did, as that March, Amasa wrote to his wife that his father and the neighbors "will sow our land to wheat if they can get the seed[,] if not they will sow it to Oats so it will not lay waist."[32]

Landlord-tenant relations were often strained, and men and women sometimes found themselves powerless due to their separation. Maria reported to Uriah that a local man who had agreed to rent a portion of their farm had backed out. "I was sorry to hear how Frank Longwell had served you," he said. Uriah complained that Longwell had "rented 20 acres of that land fare and square and then back out when it was to[o] late to let it out to any body else." Later in that letter, he told his wife to extend thanks to a woman named Vina who served as a proxy by exchanging strong words with Longwell: "I thank her very much for takeing my place whilst I am in the army and I don't care how she talked to Frank for I think that he has treated you very mean indeed." Uriah could only dream about settling scores with the person who wronged his family.[33]

Numerous other problems dogged farm families—problems that were and are not unique to wartime conditions but, like the Kimberlys' dispute with Frank Longwell, were complicated by the absence of men folk. When Emma Glasgow informed her husband, Samuel, that some hogs had ventured into their cornfield and damaged the crop, he lamented that he was not there to help: "I ought to be there with the old shot Gun." Samuel inquired if his wife could find out who owned the hogs "and tell them for me that any man that will let his hogs distroy a soldier's corn is worse than a Secesh and no man atal." Glasgow's sense of manhood was threatened when he could not be present to solve a problem that would have been easier had he been at home. Maria Kimberly struggled with a new and faulty pump, but Uriah was the one who had purchased it and possessed knowledge of the terms of sale. In a long and rambling section of a letter, Uriah insisted that the agent could not make her pay for the pump if it did not work properly. His sense of outrage was matched by a sense of powerlessness and a recognition that his wife was doing the best she could. He concluded that if he was at home, they "would talk some any how but I don't know as it would do any good any how."[34]

For most Iowa farm couples, farming during the war was a true partnership, regardless of whether couples used affectionate prose and pet names or businesslike language. William Vermilion, a physician and farmer, often inquired of his wife, Mary, about the farm and tenants. In

May 1863, he wrote, "I want you to write me everything. . . . All about how Teater [the tenant] is getting along. If you think he is doing all right tell me so Dollie, and if he is doing wrong tell me." William's letters indicate that he assumed that Mary was knowledgeable about the farm but did not expect that she would take an active role in managing it. The few times he asked her to engage in farm affairs were in regards to livestock. In June 1863, he urged her to sell a heifer, oxen, mules, and corn "if you think best." He followed up with an explanation that the corn was likely to go to waste where it was. Later that summer, he urged her to "sell cattle to the best advantage as soon as you can," and he wanted greenbacks rather than promissory notes. This is a typical pattern in many couples' correspondence—respectfully offered advice qualified by a statement of recognition of the limitations of advice from afar.[35]

Even husbands who gave direct orders recognized that their authority had limits and that their wives would be the ones living with the immediate consequences of any management decisions. Most soldiers, like Vermilion, almost always extended the benefit of the doubt to their wives and understood that wives were more knowledgeable about current farm affairs than they could be from afar. In a letter in February 1865, Silas Shearer wrote, "Well Jane I wrote to you to traid that place off [but] I am not very particular whether you do it or not. It is a nice little place and it will make us a good home. Make a good traid if you traid it, if you can't keep it." If absent husbands did not have a high level of confidence in their wives' abilities to preserve the farm when they enlisted, they must have gained it during their service.[36]

Couples shared management duties while separated, but they still had to contend with the absence of the husband as a farmworker who milked the cows, mended fences, plowed the fields, and planted, cultivated, and harvested the crops. The absent husband rendered judgment and provided advice, but the chair remained vacant; someone needed to provide the skilled and unskilled labor to keep the family together. Mary Vermilion protested to her husband that "when I can do nothing else, I am willing to work to raise corn, to pay taxes, to help sustain the government, and carry on the war." Mary was willing to take hoe in hand, but she was not driven to fieldwork. She resided in town and later with her parents in Indiana. Meanwhile, renters carried on the work at the farm they called Woodside.[37]

Some women did take on a heavy load of the physical labor required to operate a farm. Under the headline, "VALUABLE WOMAN," a newspaper report from Guthrie County in the fall of 1865 noted an instance of a woman who tended a nine-acre cornfield that yielded 550 bushels. The editor of the Des Moines paper that ran the piece commented that women were not only responsible for operating farms but also for performing the physical labor. Helen assisted in stripping sorghum cane in preparation for making molasses in 1862, but her notation of that kind of fieldwork was rare among the correspondence of soldiers and wives.[38]

For many native-born citizens, there was a stigma associated with women working in the fields. Supposedly, only immigrant women, perceived by the native-born as ignorant, muscular, and dirty, stooped to such work, a view shared by Mary Livermore until her conversations in the fields of the Midwest in 1863 changed her mind. Many foreign-born women who were accustomed to field work did it without complaint. Some immigrants who settled in Iowa actually looked down on American women who refused to work in the field. According to a Dutch immigrant, American farm women were more interested in new dresses and horseback riding than in farm production. But for the majority population, only the most desperate circumstances could compel a woman to take up a hoe or plow.[39]

The editor of another Des Moines newspaper combined nativist sentiment with Democratic suspicions about abolition as a war aim when he printed a notice from a Wisconsin newspaper describing the farm-labor shortage. The notice highlighted the role of "German, Norwegian, and Bohemian servant girls" in conducting the summer grain harvest. It was not necessary, he stated, to go to Wisconsin to observe "female labor in the corn fields. Such instances can be found all over this state." In his view, that development was the lamentable product of a war for abolition, and he blamed those who had precipitated war and would continue it until the South was subjugated "in order that the Negro may be freed." A writer for the *Dubuque Herald* disagreed, contending that women would benefit from abandoning "corsets, belts, and cosmetics" and, by working in the fields, "strengthen their frames . . . grow robust instead of slender, rosy instead of pallid, brown rather than delicate." Most Iowans, regardless of party affiliation, hoped to avoid being driven to such extremes as women with suntans, strong backs, and muscular arms. They were spared the discomfort of witnessing many soldiers' wives doing men's work although many young women were hard at work in the fields.[40]

Wartime correspondence indicates that wives who went to the fields to plow, plant, cultivate, or harvest were the exception, not the rule. Larimer's comment to her husband about the sheep is suggestive of the physical work women did in addition to traditional gendered labor, such as gardening, food preparation and preservation, cleaning, and child care. Unlike field crops, the animals, or "stock," as husbands and wives stated, were property that retained value or even appreciated in value from year to year and, therefore, represented a larger share of family resources than any single field crop or combination of crops. William Barnes offered only the most general advice to his wife about livestock, urging her to tend to the animals "as well as you can." Ann and many other women often took over livestock chores, even if they rented their farms to others.[41]

Women who remained on farms sometimes performed livestock chores and confronted extreme weather, which was a source of complaint by their husbands. In the fall of 1862, Thomas Lewis inquired what his wife, Lucinda, had done with their livestock. His concern was less about financial security and more about Lucinda's health. He did not want her to "expose" herself to severe weather by doing demanding livestock chores. He cautioned her that "you had Better Sell it [livestock] rather than weary youre Self to take care of it." Jasper Rice told his wife that he did not want her to do too much work outdoors. Similarly, Charles Ackley was concerned about his wife's health. She was also a schoolteacher, and he urged her to obtain a teaching position and even to seek appointment as postmaster to avoid the exposure of feeding and watering animals in all kinds of weather. An observer from Floyd County captured the prevailing mood of Iowa's menfolk when he stated that women should be encouraged to do light work outdoors "that tends without degradations to improve women's physical condition, to make her fairer, and less dependent on the man." Heavy work, he advised, was to be avoided.[42]

The most important role women assumed during the separation from their husbands was as farm managers. Historians dispute the extent to which women were involved in farm decision making before the war. During the war, however, farm women made important decisions, often in consultation with their husbands or male kin, about raising crops, tending livestock, acquiring land, and making rental arrangements. But even as the war brought new roles and new labor for farm women who lived with vacant chairs at their tables and in their parlors, it also reinforced traditional roles and positions within family hierarchies. The majority of soldiers returned from the war to resume their work on the farm. Some, including Uriah and Adam, did not come home. Their wives confronted the continuing reality of dealing with farm affairs in addition to their suffering.

The Civil War was a great test for rural Iowans, just as it was for the nation. Farm women with absent husbands became managers and diplomats who negotiated relationships with kin and neighbors to provision and shelter their families and to preserve their farms. They confronted tenants, creditors, and debtors and sometimes marketed livestock and crops. They asked kin and husbands for advice, received it, and, it appears, generally followed it. Husbands almost always recognized the limits of their counsel, however. Even when husbands provided copious advice, they reminded themselves and their wives that the women were in a position to know best. Few soldiers' wives were compelled to work in the fields, but many of them shouldered a greater share of livestock chores than they had before the war. A significant percentage, perhaps even a majority, of women with husbands in the military left their farms, taking refuge with kin for periods of varying length until their husbands returned. Surviving letters of farm couples separated by the war indicate that farm women, whether they remained on their farms or departed, were successful in doing what they and their husbands desired, providing for their families to best advantage.

Notes

Reprinted from J. L. Anderson, "The Vacant Chair on the Farm: Soldier Husbands, Farm Wives, and the Iowa Home Front, 1861–1865," *Annals of Iowa* 66 (Summer–Fall 2007): 241–65. Copyright 2007 State Historical Society of Iowa. Used with permission of the publisher. The following acknowledgment appeared in the original: I am grateful to the State Historical Society of Iowa (SHSI) for a research grant as well as to Marvin Bergman and the anonymous reviewers for the *Annals of Iowa* for their critiques. Historians and archivists gave valuable assistance at different stages of this project. They include Ginette Aley, Sharon Avery (SHSI, Des Moines), Tom Colbert, Mary Bennett (SHSI, Iowa City), Kathy Hodson (University of Iowa Libraries), Alexandra Kin, Kären Mason (Iowa Women's Archives), and John Zeller.

1. Ann Larimer to John W. Larimer, May 28, 1865, Ann Larimer Collection, Iowa Women's Archives, University of Iowa Libraries, Iowa City.

2. Reid Mitchell, *The Vacant Chair: The Northern Soldier Leaves Home* (New York: Oxford University Press, 1993). Only a handful of historians have paid attention to Northern farm women during the Civil War, in spite of a recent flowering of Northern home-front studies and a long-established subfield of the history of Southern women during wartime. Glenda Riley emphasizes the hardships and painful adjustments endured by Iowa farm women. *Frontierswomen, the Iowa Experience* (Ames, IA: Iowa State Press, 1981). Nancy Grey Osterud contends that while most women and men cooperated to maintain the family, the most successful women enlarged their scope of activities to include work that traditionally had been performed by men. "Rural Women during the Civil War: New York's Nanticoke Valley, 1861–1865," *New York History* 71 (1990), 357–85. More recently, Thomas E. Rodgers concludes that the war was not a watershed

for most Indiana women in terms of gendered work on the farm. "Hoosier Women and the Civil War Home Front," *Indiana Magazine of History* 97 (2001): 105–28. Judith Ann Giesberg concludes that when husbands of rural Pennsylvania women left for war, "women's work on the farm expanded to fill the void." "From Harvest Field to Battlefield: Rural Pennsylvania Women and the U.S. Civil War," *Pennsylvania History* 72 (2005): 158–91. For the most part, however, Northern home-front studies have focused on urban women and those involved in public affairs or organizations. Recent home-front studies that offer little on rural women include Paul A. Cimbala and Randall M. Miller, eds., *Union Soldiers and the Northern Home Front* (New York: Fordham University Press, 2002); Jeanie Attie, *Patriotic Toil: Northern Women and the American Civil War* (Ithaca, NY: Cornell University Press, 1998); Elizabeth D. Leonard, *Yankee Women: Gender Battles in the Civil War* (New York: Norton, 1994); J. Matthew Gallman, *The North Fights the Civil War: The Home Front* (Chicago: Ivan R. Dee, 1994); and Phillip Shaw Paludan, *"A People's Contest": The Union and the Civil War, 1861–1865* (New York, Harper and Row, 1988).

3. Earle D. Ross, *Iowa Agriculture* (Iowa City: State Historical Society of Iowa Press, 1951), 54; Edwin J. Gilford, "The Agricultural Labor Shortage in the Northwest during the Civil War and How It Was Met, 1860–1865" (master's thesis, Miami University, 1956), 100; Paul W. Gates, *Agriculture and the Civil War* (New York: Knopf, 1965), 242–43.

4. The major research effort for this project was to locate manuscript collections and published letters of married farm men and women. That task required reading many collections to determine if the letter writers actually discussed farm affairs and consulting the *Roster and Record of Iowa Soldiers in the War of Rebellion* to assess if the men listed their occupations as farmer.

5. For an examination of these family roles, see John Mack Faragher, *Sugar Creek: Life on the Illinois Prairie* (New Haven, CT: Yale University Press, 1986); and Susan Sessions Rugh, *Our Common Country: Family Farming, Community, and Culture in the Nineteenth-Century Midwest* (Bloomington: Indiana University Press, 2001), 20–21.

6. *U.S. Census of Population, 1860* (Washington, DC: GPO, 1864), 662, 680; Ross, *Iowa Agriculture*, 56; *U.S. Census of Agriculture, 1860* (Washington, DC: GPO, 1864), 185.

7. Marshall McKusick, *The Iowa Northern Border Brigade* (Iowa City: University of Iowa, 1975); Leland L. Sage, *A History of Iowa* (Ames: Iowa State University Press, 1974), 153–54. Muster dates for Iowa regiments can be found in S. H. M. Byers, *Iowa in War Times* (Des Moines, IA: W. D. Condit, 1888).

8. Sage, *History of Iowa*, 153–54.

9. Emeline Guernsey to William Guernsey, November 26, 1861, July 31, 1863, Emeline D. Guernsey Collection, Huntington Library, San Marino, California.

10. George Mills, ed., "The Sharp Family Civil War Letters," *Annals of Iowa* 34 (1959): 527, 531.

11. Mary A. Livermore, *My Story of the War* (1887; repr., Williamstown, MA: Corner House, 1978), 145–49.

12. Charles T. Ackley to Elizabeth Ackley, undated letter (probably August 9, 1864), Charles T. Ackley Collection, Special Collections, University of Iowa Libraries, Iowa City.

13. *Iowa State Register*, August 16, 1865. For examples of such advertisements, see *Prairie Farmer*, May 27, 1865, and June 10, 1865.

14. Earl D. Check and Emeroy Johnson, eds., "Civil War Letters to New Sweden, Iowa," *Swedish-American Historical Quarterly* 36 (1982): 13; Cyrus Wyatt to Catherine

Wyatt, November 9, 1863, Cyrus Wyatt Letters, SHSI, Des Moines,; William F. James to Marcia James, October 1864, William Francis James Letters, SHSI, Des Moines; William J. Sudduth to Martha Sudduth, May 4, 1863, William James Sudduth Collection, SHSI, Des Moines.

15. Six women appeared to remain on the farm for the duration of the war; it was impossible to determine the location of another six women.

16. David B. Danbom, "'Dear Companion': Civil War Letters of a Story County Farmer," *Annals of Iowa* 47 (1984): 539.

17. Hannah Stitt to Robert Stitt, July 4, 1864; Robert Stitt to Hannah Stitt, July 2, 1863; James G. Craine to Robert Stitt, August 21, 1863, all in Robert A. Stitt Collection, SHSI, Des Moines. It is unknown if Hannah was able to begin housekeeping again in Iowa, since the correspondence between her and Robert ended in August 1863 after a letter from one of the Kansas relatives to Robert informed him about his wife's itinerary for the trip home to Iowa.

18. Elisha Leaming to Louisa Leaming, April 1, 1865, Elisha Leaming Collection, SHSI, Des Moines; Jasper Hazen Rice to Mary Rice, September 12, 1862, Special Collections, University of Iowa Libraries; Adam Schaefer to William Whisler, March 6, 1863, Whisler-Reppert Family Papers, SHSI, Iowa City; Check and Johnson, "Civil War Letters to New Sweden," 8–9, 12–14; William Donnan to Mary Donnan, November 20, 1862, William G. Donnan Collection, SHSI, Des Moines.

19. John D. Wright to Ann Wright, August 18–19, 1864, John D. Wright Collection, SHSI, Iowa City.

20. Samuel Glasgow to Emma Glasgow, December 22, 1862, Samuel H. Glasgow Collection, SHSI, Des Moines; Agnes Allen to Amasa Allen, undated letter (probably September 1862), and Amasa Allen to Agnes Allen, November 25, 1862, Amasa Orlando Allen Collection, SHSI, Des Moines.

21. John B. Chapman and Donna L. Chapman, eds., *Love Letters from the Civil War* (Ames, IA: Sigler, 2000), 53, 55.

22. M. A. Rogers, "An Iowa Woman in War Time," *Annals of Iowa* 35 (1961): 541.

23. Mills, "Sharp Family Civil War Letters," 483, 486.

24. Ibid., 494.

25. Jasper Rice to Mary Rice, September 12, 1862, April 13, 1863, Special Collections, University of Iowa Libraries; Check and Johnson, "Civil War Letters to New Sweden," 12–13.

26. William Barnes to Amanda Barnes, August 29, 1864, William R. Barnes Collection, SHSI, Des Moines; William Donnan to Mary Donnan, April 3, 1863, April 16, 1863, Donnan Collection; Joseph Coffman to Maggie Coffman, December 13, 1864, Joseph A. Coffman Collection, SHSI, Des Moines.

27. Mills, "Sharp Family Civil War Letters," 499; Glenda Riley, ed., "Civil War Wife: The Letters of Harriet Jane Thompson," *Annals of Iowa* 44 (1978): 311.

28. Samuel Glasgow to Emma Glasgow, February 5, 1863, Glasgow Collection; Charles Ackley to "Dear Wife," May 2, 1865, May 26, 1865, Ackley Collection; Check and Johnson, "Civil War Letters to New Sweden," 14.

29. E. May Lacey Crowder, "Pioneer Life in Palo Alto County," *Iowa Journal of History and Politics* 46 (1948): 160; Harold D. Brinkman, ed., *Dear Companion: The Civil War Letters of Silas I. Shearer* (Ames, IA: Harold Brinkman, 1995), 111; Uriah M. Kimberly to Maria P. Kimberly, June 10, 1864, Uriah Kimberly Collection, SHSI, Des Moines.

30. Elisha Leaming to Louisa Leaming, April 1, 1865, Leaming Collection; Check and Johnson, "Civil War Letters to New Sweden," 8–9; Ann Larimer to John Larimer, July 13, 1865, Larimer Collection.

31. Uriah Kimberly to Maria Kimberly, August 13, 1864, Kimberly Collection; Mills, "Sharp Family Letters," 487, 495, 497, 513; Joseph Coffman to Maggie Coffman, June 3, 1864, June 13, 1864, Coffman Collection.

32. Amasa Allen to Agnes Allen, January 26, 1863, March 12, 1863, Allen Collection.

33. Uriah Kimberly to Maria Kimberly, June 14, 1864, Kimberly Collection.

34. Samuel Glasgow to Emma Glasgow, September 14, 1862, Glasgow Collection; Uriah Kimberly to Maria Kimberly, August 30, 1864, Kimberly Collection.

35. Donald C. Elder III, ed., *Love amid the Turmoil: The Civil War Letters of William and Mary Vermilion* (Iowa City: University of Iowa Press, 2003), 90, 125, 180.

36. Brinkman, *Dear Companion*, 127.

37. Elder, *Love amid the Turmoil*, 85.

38. *Iowa State Register* (Des Moines), November 26, 1865; Mills, "Sharp Family Civil War Letters," 513.

39. Jon Gjerde, *The Minds of the West: Ethnocultural Evolution in the Rural Middle West, 1830–1917* (Chapel Hill: University of North Carolina Press, 1997), 151, 171–73. For a description of how one immigrant described native-born women, see Robert P. Swierenga, "A Dutch Immigrant's View of Frontier Iowa," in Dorothy Schwieder, ed., *Patterns and Perspectives in Iowa History* (Ames: Iowa State University Press, 1973), 58–59.

40. *Des Moines (IA) Daily Statesman*, August 13, 1864; *Dubuque (IA) Herald*, cited in Dorothy Schwieder, *Iowa: The Middle Land* (Ames: Iowa State University Press, 1996), 80.

41. William R. Barnes to Amanda M. Barnes, November 6, 1863, Barnes Collection. Economic historians Lee A. Craig and Thomas Weiss argue that much of the productivity gain on Northern farms during the 1860s resulted less from mechanization and more from "an increase in the time and effort men, women, and children devoted to the production of marketable farm products. The fact that much of this increase came from women is of particular interest." The authors suggest that the Civil War's counterpart to Rosie the Riveter could be "Hilda the Hog Herder." At least in Iowa, productivity gains from women's work must have come from women whose husbands were not in the military. "Agricultural Productivity Growth during the Decade of the Civil War," *Journal of Economic History* 53 (1993): 527–48.

42. Thomas J. Lewis to Lucinda J. Lewis, October 10, 1862, Thomas Jefferson Lewis Collection, SHSI, Des Moines; Jasper Rice to Mary Rice, September 12, 1863, Special Collections, University of Iowa Libraries; Charles T. Ackley to Elizabeth Ackley, October 23, 1864, Ackley Collection; *Iowa State Agricultural Society Report*, 1863, 355, cited in Gilford, "Agricultural Labor Shortage," 35.

LIMITING DISSENT IN THE MIDWEST

OHIO REPUBLICANS' ATTACKS
ON THE DEMOCRATIC PRESS

Brett Barker

In the early months of 1863, the Union war effort teetered near collapse—
or so many Northern Republicans feared. For the first time since the
conflict erupted, it had become unclear whether a majority of civilians
on the Northern home front supported the war. As the struggle entered
its third year, Democrats had begun to openly and consistently con-
demn the Republican conduct of the war. Some dared publicly question
whether continuation of the war under the Republicans would lead
to victory or would instead lead to further deaths, the erosion of civil
liberties, and a transformation of the federal government and even the
Union itself. This chapter explores the Ohio Republicans' responses at
the community level. By looking at the experience of three counties
in southeastern Ohio, patterns emerge that are lost when viewing the
North as a whole. While these counties may not be fully representative
or offer an all-inclusive picture of the midwestern home front, these
cases are suggestive of local patterns not fully appreciated by larger
studies, such as Mark Neely's *Fate of Liberty: Abraham Lincoln and Civil
Liberties*.[1] As this local study reveals, attacks on Democratic opponents
of the war did not always consist of military arrest or press censorship.
In southeastern Ohio, Republicans used boycotts, intimidation, vigi-
lantism, and violence to silence critics of the war effort. One of their
central targets was Democratic newspapers, where Republican actions
proved chillingly effective.

The last six months of 1862 had been tumultuous ones in the North, as Republicans continued, enacted, or proclaimed several controversial wartime measures: emancipation, the draft, an income tax, and suspension of the writ of habeas corpus. The unpopularity of these new policies, along with military reversals, helped the Democrats score impressive gains in the fall 1862 elections, winning several key governorships and making gains in Congress and in many state legislatures.[2] Emboldened by their electoral success, Democrats continued their attacks into 1863. In January, a leader of the Northern Peace Democrats, Clement L. Vallandigham of Ohio, rose in the House of Representatives and gave a speech titled "The Great Civil War in America." In it, he attacked Republican policies and linked the administration's failures with soldiers' deaths.[3] Democratic newspapers throughout the North reprinted the speech and joined the chorus of voices attacking the Republicans' conduct of the war.[4]

Republicans on the local level realized the importance of Democratic newspapers in the newfound Democratic assertiveness of 1863 and the press's role in transmitting the ideas of Vallandigham and others to Northern readers. One of the most influential studies of civil liberties during the Civil War, Neely's *Fate of Liberty*, chronicles the arrest of Vallandigham in the spring of 1863 and suspension of the writ of habeas corpus, but Neely's work emphasizes how unusual such overt actions were within a national context.[5] If one only considers military arrests and formal suppression of the *Chicago Times* in 1863, then this conclusion is sound.[6] Yet, even looking at just one part of the Midwest, the surviving evidence suggests that, if more broadly conceived, attacks on the Democratic opposition were not rare at all.

In the first six months of 1863, Republicans in southeastern Ohio set out to silence the Democratic press in Muskingum, Morgan, and Washington Counties. Together, they constitute the Muskingum River Valley. Then, the Muskingum Valley had three Democratic newspapers: the Zanesville *Citizens' Press* (Muskingum County), the McConnelsville *Enquirer* (Morgan County), and the Marietta *Republican* (Washington County). In late winter and early spring of that year, each paper and its editor would be boycotted, threatened, or mobbed.[7]

In critical ways, the history and settlement patterns of the Muskingum River Valley reflected the distinct character of the mid-nineteenth-century Midwest.[8] In the previous three generations, white Americans from New England, the Mid-Atlantic, and the Upper South had moved into the valley, bringing their lifeways, beliefs, and cultural preconceptions with them. Often, they had mingled with settlers from other parts of the east, but in many cases, they created villages and rural districts with the flavor of their communities of origin. While this usually produced little more than good-natured rivalry, sectionalizing events on the national level could occasionally erupt into local conflict. The most striking example occurred in Muskingum County. Zanesville, the county seat, on the east side of the river, was filled with migrants from the Upper South, especially Virginia. Across the river lay the smaller community of Putnam, settled by New Englanders, proud of their heritage and vocal in their hostility to slavery.[9] While community studies of the early Midwest often note this settler mix, they are less inclined to trace this community dynamic as they do political affiliation, ethnicity, and socioeconomic divisions.[10] In the cauldron of the war years, this became one more distinctive regional variation woven into the complex social web across the Northern home front.

The residents of the Muskingum River Valley in 1861 held the range of political views typical of the Midwest. Politically, Muskingum County was the most evenly split between Republican and Democratic voters; Washington County also remained competitive, with Republicans enjoying a slight edge. In Morgan County, the Republicans polled a significant majority. In the fall 1862 elections, Republicans suffered significant electoral setbacks in each of these counties, in a pattern found throughout most of the North. In Muskingum County, this outcome was more the result of Republicans staying home rather than switching to the Democratic camp, as the Republican total dropped by 617 votes while the Democrats' tally rose by only 106. Either through Republicans defecting or staying home, the Republican percentage of the vote in each of these counties fell between 5.1 and 6.6 percent.[11]

Muskingum River Valley election results, 1861 and 1862								
	1861				1862			
	Union*		Democrat		Union		Democrat		Union change (%)
County	Votes	%	Votes	%	Votes	%	Votes	%	
Morgan	2,106	58.2	1,512	41.8	1,932	51.6	1,812	48.4	-6.6
Muskingum	3,813	50.8	3,693	49.2	3,196	45.7	3,799	54.3	-5.1
Washington	2,879	52.0	2,655	48.0	2,613	46.2	3,038	53.8	-5.8

*In the 1864 election, Republicans adopted the name Union.

The actions of Republicans in the spring and summer of 1863 can best be understood within this local political context. As they thought their opponents were gaining adherents and feared that they might lose the support of a majority of Northerners, Republicans attacked Democrats and, most especially, the Democratic press in the Democrats' own communities.[12]

This assault on the voice of the Democratic Party in McConnelsville began in late February 1863 when Republicans took economic action against Cyrus McGlashan and the *Enquirer*. The editor warned readers "to be cautious with whom you spend your money when you come to town. All the Abolition and Republican Merchants have withdrawn their patronage from the ENQUIRER." Since local merchants called for proscription because the *Enquirer* was "A DEMOCRATIC PAPER AND ADVOCATES DEMOCRATIC PRINCIPLES," McGlashan made a case for economic retaliation by Democrats: "Do you feel like supporting such merchants?"[13] Two weeks later, the *Enquirer* published the actual document drawn up by these Republicans under the heading "Proscription List."[14] Its first resolution summarized their criticism of the paper: "Whereas, The McConnelsville *Enquirer* has been conducted in such a manner, since the outbreak of the present rebellion, as to prevent enlistments and discourage our soldiers in the field, and of late, is absolutely opposed to the war now waged to suppress rebellion and preserve the Union." The writer calculated the wording of this resolution very carefully, using phrasing that conformed to the War Department's definition of "treasonable practices"—namely, discouraging enlistments. Presenting the preservation of the Union as the main goal of the war, it offered an appeal more unifying and less controversial than emancipation. Finally, the resolution's phrase "and of late" also points to the increased aggressiveness of Democrats like McGlashan since the fall 1862 election.

The Republicans' second resolution explained why they had chosen this tactic: "Whereas, we are in favor of remedying all evils by peaceable and civil methods, when it can be done." They would try this tactic first but already offered a threat of more serious action if this did not subdue or silence the *Enquirer*. The last resolution promised to "withdraw all patronage, support, and influence" from the paper "so long as it shall be conducted as it has been." The writers had allowed McGlashan to copy down the resolutions but not the names of the merchants who had signed, so he had to repeat them from memory. Twenty-seven influential merchants in town appeared on the list, and it is unlikely that a Democrat could shop in McConnelsville without doing business with some of them. It appears McGlashan approached at least one of the signers and asked him about his actions, as the article ended by noting that "by virtue of a satisfactory arrangement and explanation, Joseph Black's name, which appears on the original paper, is omitted in the above list."[15]

Soon, McGlashan faced much more than a boycott. Directly under the proscription list appeared another item titled "Fifteen Day's Grace." "On Tuesday evening of last week, we received through the Post Office here the following letter," wrote McGlashan. "We give it here just as we received it. Comment is unnecessary." Bearing the date of March 2, the poorly spelled letter was addressed to McGlashan personally. "The good of our caus and country, the protecttion of the union for which we freely shed our blood require that we take all in hand that in anny way simpathise with the south, they are considdered the worst kind of traitors, and you are one of that kind and must be dealt with accordingly," it began. "We have considered it and think it only fair to give you warning, if you are found here 15 days from this date you will be shot certain as a traitor deserves to be." Warning that it was no "idle threat," it cautioned "not only you but all that is found hereafter in any way [to] simpathise with the rebels." The writer "was once a great friend of yours and thought I would warn you so you can get out of the way." Claiming that the deed would be done by "desperate carricters" who had been in the army and knew how to use weapons, the writer's foreboding conclusion reinforced how small Civil War communities were and how closely an individual could be watched. "Your steps are doged you cant escap even as you go to the church one of our number is there to hear all you say in your office, on the street so beware beware." The writer signed the letter "once your friend."[16]

McGlashan did not cave to the threat and boldly proclaimed that "a certain time has been given us to leave, or be shot. We have considered the matter and concluded, that if shooting is the alternative, to play our part. Democrats, when the time expires we will be here." He would not flee or go into hiding and with a bit of bravado concluded, "All of you who wish to see us on that day (next Tuesday), will find us as usual at our office." Would-be assassins could find him, but so presumably could his supporters. The threats also failed to soften his editorial tone. Next to the proscription list and the death threat, McGlashan published a scathing critique of "stay-at-home" Republicans under the banner "Patriotic Cowards."[17]

No one shot the editor of the *Enquirer*, and no new threats appeared through March and April. McGlashan claimed subscriptions increased after the boycott and death threat, yet his continual pleas for new subscribers and for delinquent subscribers to pay indicate that he was feeling the effects of proscription. He also continued to publish the proscription list weekly and told readers that he needed support against this attack.[18]

A new threat on McGlashan's life appeared in a broadside in early May posted on a bulletin board at a busy corner in McConnelsville: "PROCLAMATION.—Whereas C. McGlashen a determined and malicious Butternut has refused to take the oath of Allegiance to the Government or enrole himself in the service. This is to give notice that I will pay a reward of $250 to shot him. HANS VAN KEMPER."[19] Again, McGlashan refused to back down: "We advise the poor cowardly villain to hide his face in shame. His action is a disgrace not only to himself, but to all connected with him. He dare not say publicly that he wrote the above." The last sentence might be a challenge to Van Kemper to come forward, but it also may reveal the power of the threat. The discussion of the broadside in the McConnelsville press and other extant sources leaves the identity of the threat's author shrouded in mystery. McGlashan himself never said anything more specific about the alleged author of the note. The editor of the Republican *Morgan County Herald* never commented on the incident. Indeed, it is unclear whether Hans Van Kemper even existed—no one by that or a similar name appeared in the 1860 census for McConnelsville, Morgan County, or the entire state of Ohio. Since newspapers and even the federal census are at best imperfect records of nineteenth-century communities and individuals, it is possible, though far from certain, that Van Kemper was real. Yet, in some ways, the exact identity of the person who made the death threat is not nearly as important as the threat itself.

The verbal attacks continued. Another letter in June suggested that McGlashan should be handed over to Union soldiers "and let them take your hide to make whip lashes or to lash your sole to that dark Reegons of dispare." The editor called the anonymous writer a "base, cowardly, insolent scamp," but despite his brave tone, McGlashan must have been circumspect in his movements about town that spring.[20] Remarkably, McGlashan fared the best of the three Democratic editors, since the threats of violence never materialized, and the paper limped along despite the burden of proscription.

If Robert Rhoads, editor of the Democratic Marietta *Republican*, received threats against himself or his paper, he did not publish them.[21] Yet, action against his newspaper came in March in the form of a mob. This vigilante action was not unique in the experience of the Muskingum Valley or wartime Ohio. Mob action had been a constant, if often decried, feature of antebellum northern society.[22] In the Muskingum Valley, Zanesville had been the scene of several mob actions, usually resulting from the tension between southern-born citizens of Zanesville, with a tolerant attitude toward slavery, and residents of the small community of Putnam on the west bank of the Muskingum River opposite Zanesville. As mentioned earlier, Putnam had been settled by New Englanders and became a center of abolition in Ohio; in fact, it was one of the few outside the Western Reserve. In 1835 and 1839, mobs from Zanesville crossed the river and attacked abolition meetings, even holding noted abolitionist Theodore Dwight Weld hostage briefly during the earlier incident.[23] The mobbing of the *Enquirer* also came on the heels of a similar incident against Samuel Medary's stridently antiwar and anti-Republican *Crisis*, published in Columbus and destroyed in early March 1863 by a group of soldiers from nearby Camp Chase.[24]

Only two weeks later, a mob in Marietta broke into the offices of the *Republican* late on a Saturday night and wreaked havoc. The perpetrators destroyed much of the paper's type, throwing it into piles, melting some in a stove, and throwing the rest out of the window. They also damaged the press itself. Rhoads only discovered the act the next morning and did not know the identity of the attackers. The mob must have made considerable noise, and yet no one had intervened, and no authorities had tried to stop it. This troubled Rhoads, and he asked for the help of "the officers of the law for the maintenance of our rights of free speech, of person, and of property." He warned what would happen in Marietta if community leaders failed to act and promised that while Democrats decried mob action, they would resort to it "if the law does not and will not intervene to put down such outrages."[25] He attacked both those who condoned the mob's actions and those in town who claimed the destruction resulted from personal animosity rather than political motives.

While the press was not a complete loss, the mob was effective. Not only had damages totaled several hundred dollars but also the loss of type and equipment forced the *Republican*'s editor to reduce the paper's size from four large pages to a "half-sheet," one smaller page printed on both sides. During the critical period from March 23 to May 7, the *Republican* could print only a small amount of news, clippings, and editorials. Rhoads bristled when the editor of the Republican Marietta *Register* first boasted that his paper was now the only one in town to print a full four pages and then accused Rhoads of engineering the attack to gain support and sympathy, an unlikely scenario given the extent of the damage.[26]

Washington County Democrats responded to the mobbing of the *Republican* by holding a mass meeting on March 30.[27] Many well-known Democrats, including Vallandigham, had been invited to attend but declined because they could not reach Marietta on such short notice. Interestingly, Vallandigham and others planned to use the steamship *Jonas Powell* to reach Marietta, but at the last moment, it was impressed by military authorities to transport troops and no replacement could be found. Though at first glance, this appears to have been more than mere coincidence, no one at the meeting made any accusations about this last-minute action that deprived the meeting of many of its speakers. Nonetheless, local Democrats gave speeches and endorsed the resolutions Columbus Democrats passed after the *Crisis* had been mobbed weeks earlier. These resolutions argued the importance of a free press, the right to debate, publicly declare and vote one's political convictions, and the existence of these rights in wartime. They ended with a promise not to surrender these rights no matter what the outcome. A final resolution read: "Resolved. That the Marietta *Republican* is our county organ, the exponent of our principles, and shall and will be maintained by the people of this County, and that the suppression of Newspapers and Public Meetings by mobs and violence comes with a bad grace from a party who so recently declared for Free Speech and Free Press." Democrats in Washington County understood the importance of their newspaper in spreading their political thoughts and beliefs and how its mobbing produced a chilling effect on their freedoms and public discussions of the war effort.

Yet, they could not save their paper. Throughout the spring and summer of 1863, Rhoads reported that many local Republicans cancelled their subscriptions. Before the war, many northerners purchased both their local Republican and Democratic newspapers, thereby seeking to monitor the activities and political positions of friend and foe alike. But within the heightened partisanship and suspicions of the wartime North, many Republicans decided that it was either wrong or disloyal or unnecessary to read and financially support the Democratic press. Complaining of an atmosphere of hostility and declining subscriptions, the *Republican* published its final issue on November 5, 1863. Democrats in Washington County were without their own newspaper for almost eleven months until the *Marietta Times* started in September 1864.

The experience of the final Democratic editor, Samuel Chapman of the Zanesville *Citizens' Press*, reveals most clearly the links between suspension of the writ of habeas corpus, community enforcement of loyalty, and the chilling effect on freedom of speech and of the press. As early as April 1861, Chapman had received threats from a "Vigilance Committee" to leave town or "abide the consequences."[28] In June, Chapman reported that "the highly civilized and christianized no-party editor of the *Courier*, is again at his old trade, trying to get this office mobbed again."[29] From the fall of 1862 through early 1863, Chapman reported no more such threats, claiming it as evidence that a majority of Zanesville's citizens agreed with him on war matters.

The threats resumed and reached their height in the late spring of 1863. Chapman claimed that "the infamous shallow-brained low bred editor of the Zanesville *Courier* has not succeeded . . . in having any of its [Zanesville's] citizens murdered," despite the *Courier*'s constant refrain in every issue for "the necessity of stopping the *Citizens' Press*."[30] Apparently emboldened, Chapman lashed out at Republicans in the next issue on May 7. In an editorial titled "Why Don't They Go?" Chapman argued that while Republicans refused to join the army and applauded the conscription of Democrats, Republican mobs were all too eager to enforce conformity at home through threats and violence. Given Republican actions and the unfair and unconstitutional nature of conscription, Democrats should avoid enlistment and encourage others to do the same.[31]

Republicans saw their chance. Not only did the *Courier* denounce the editorial as treason but it also then called on the community to quiet this dissident voice: "All the Union-loving men, without any distinction of party, will know how to appreciate such an effort."[32] A crowd soon formed outside the *Citizens' Press* office, and it only disbanded after the sheriff arrested Chapman for his own protection.[33]

Chapman's opponents did not stop there. Because his editorial discouraged enlistments, the federal authorities became interested in the case. A few days later, Chapman received the following letter from Assistant Adjutant General D. A. Larned:

> Saml. Chapman, Editor Zanesville
> *Citizen Press*, Zanesville, Ohio
> Sir,
> I am directed by Maj Genl Burnside to call your attention to
> "General Order No 38" of this Department with which you do
> not seem to be familiar. That order prohibits the Expression of

disloyal Statements, and of sympathy with those engaged in rebellion against the Government.

The issue of your paper of May 7th inst in its whole tone and spirit, and especially in the Article headed "Why Don't they go" is in direct violation of that Order. Under a thin disguise of devotion to the Constitution you exhibit feelings and opinions utterly traitorous and disloyal, and publish matter calculated to discourage patriotism, to weaken the Government in its efforts to put down the rebellion, and incite the ignorant to resistance of the laws.

The General Com'dg warns you against persistence in such a course and will consider the further publication of such matter in your paper as sufficient cause for its suppression.[34]

Given the timing and specifics of this letter, it appears likely that someone had forwarded a copy of the May 7 issue of the *Citizens' Press* to Ambrose Everett Burnside, the commander of the military district encompassing Ohio. Samuel Chapman gave up. Now under pressure from both his community and the federal military, he stopped publication in early June and left Zanesville a few days later. No Democratic newspaper was published in Zanesville again until early 1864.[35]

Knowledge of life at the community level on the Northern home front places similar but more famous events of that spring and summer into context. Inviting political martyrdom, Vallandigham challenged Burnside's Order Number 38 by giving public speeches throughout Ohio condemning the Lincoln administration and its policies. After sending subordinates to hear several of these speeches to confirm that Vallandigham had violated the order, Burnside had him arrested at his home in Dayton on May 5.[36] The trial by a military court ended with Vallandigham's conviction, exile to the Confederacy, and subsequent passage to Canada, an odyssey that made Vallandigham a hero to the war's opponents. Democrats nominated him for the governorship of Ohio that fall. On June 1, Burnside ordered that the *Chicago Times* be suppressed, and the paper ceased publication until Lincoln rescinded the order a week later.

Many accounts of the war claim these two actions created a furor because they were so ill considered and represented isolated cases of officials overstepping their authority. The specific experiences of Chapman and the *Citizens' Press* and the fate of Democratic newspapers, more generally, offer an alternative perspective on these events. Though Vallandigham and the *Times* became symbols, they represented a phenomenon on the

Northern home front that was neither isolated nor unusual. Union authorities arrested thousands of civilians, threatened to suppress scores of Northern newspapers, and relied on local war supporters to limit dissent within their communities through intimidation and violence. In this context, the fears of the war's opponents did not constitute paranoia but a reasonable calculation of the chilling effect on freedom of speech and freedom of the press throughout the North. Only the details of this debate and partisan actions at the community level place events that garnered national attention into proper context.[37]

Did these attacks have their desired effect? Did the closing of the Zanesville *Citizens' Press* and the Marietta *Republican* have a discernible influence on their communities' support for the Union war effort? The elections in Ohio in 1863 offer a partial answer. The Republican actions against the Democratic press in the spring were in part a response to the electoral setbacks the party of Lincoln suffered in fall 1862. Many Republicans feared that if that trend toward the Democrats continued into 1863 and 1864, the war effort might be difficult or impossible to sustain. Silencing Democratic voices was a strategy calculated to make certain that the election results of 1862 were an aberration, not a trend. In the Muskingum Valley, that proved to be the case—Vallandigham's arrest and exile did not translate into his victory in the governor's race that fall.[38]

Muskingum River Valley election results, 1862 and 1863								
	1862				1863			
	Union		Democrat		Union		Democrat		Union change (%)
County	Votes	%	Votes	%	Votes	%	Votes	%	
Morgan	1,932	51.6	1,812	48.4	2,387	58.6	1,688	41.4	7.0
Muskingum	3,196	45.7	3,799	54.3	4,244	54.6	3,526	45.4	8.9
Washington	2,613	46.2	3,038	53.8	3,650	56.7	2,785	43.3	10.5

Republicans scored impressive gains over 1862, reversing the trend. While the explanations behind this shift involve a complex amalgam of local, state, and national events and were influenced by much more than local Republicans' attempts to stifle Democratic critiques of the Union war effort, these actions were an important factor. Indeed, it is noteworthy that the smallest Republican gains occurred in Morgan County, the only county of the three that had a Democratic newspaper in continuous publication throughout the war.

Victory at the polls in the autumn of 1863 bolstered the flagging spirits of Ohio Republicans, but they soon realized that another major challenge awaited them in the coming year. Abraham Lincoln faced an uncertain reelection, and his supporters began to worry as the war went badly during the spring and summer of 1864. With armies bogged down near Atlanta and Richmond, and Democrats decrying the losses suffered by Ulysses S. "Butcher" Grant, Ohio Republicans adopted the same tactics in the presidential campaign that had proven so effective in 1863. Though the violence and even the tone of the rhetoric proved a bit more muted in 1864, Lincoln's supporters in the Muskingum Valley (and beyond) again proved willing to engage in intimidation and violence in order to hold on to the presidency and control of the Union war effort.

Republicans had good reason to worry. The Democratic press continued its attacks and argued that the upcoming election would decide the future of the nation. In McConnelsville, the *Valley Democrat*, taking up the fallen standard of the now-closed *Enquirer*, warned its readers that "the Democratic masses do not fully realize the necessity of defeating Lincoln at the coming November election."[39] Its words might just have easily been penned in 1862 or 1863: "A reign of terror is being exercised over the people, in which the iron hand of tyranny is seeking to destroy popular rights and popular liberty; and to establish a despotism." After providing a long list of examples, the editor concluded, "There is but one remedy for all these evils, and that is peace;—that the only way by which any thing can be saved from the general wreck of war, is to stop." This editorial, in content and tone, was entirely consistent with Vallandigham's argument in "The Great Civil War in America," but now the stakes were higher. Democrats must "elect a man to the Presidency, who is in favor of stopping the war and restoring the country to peace and tranquility." Such editorials created a familiar response: Local critics threatened to have the editor arrested and the press destroyed by a mob.[40]

Supporters of the war effort also continued to disrupt meetings and attack the individual Democrats who attended them. In Marietta, the Democratic *Republican* had ceased publication in late 1863, and the *Times* took its place. Its report of the large outdoor Democratic rally in Marietta on September 29 made clear the difficulties and dangers Democrats faced.[41] The response may have been particularly strong because the main speaker would be Vallandigham, returned from exile in Canada and stumping for the Democratic ticket. On the way to the meeting, bystanders shouted insults and then began to throw stones at a wagon carrying a George Brinton McClellan banner. When Vallandigham rose to speak, a crowd of young men caused a disturbance near the stand. A hundred Democrats attempted to block the young men's movements toward Vallandigham and push them away from the meeting. The Democrats' efforts failed, and though Vallandigham asserted bravely "that he had made speeches for twenty-four years, without allowing himself to be overmastered in this way, and he did not begin in Marietta," a fight broke out between the two groups of young men below him and threatened to spill over onto the stage. A brickbat narrowly missed Vallandigham, and though he continued to speak, it is hard to imagine that the attendees could have heard and contemplated his points in such an environment.[42]

Personal threats and intimidation against individual Democrats continued right up to the election. Just days before the vote, a Marietta Democrat named Lewis Anderson was on his way home from a trip to Illinois. Most of the passengers in the railroad car he occupied were soldiers, and they decided to hold a straw poll. When they noticed that Anderson remained silent and did not raise his hand for Lincoln, "a scene of threatening and bitter abuse ensued." Soldiers shouted, "See the damned old traitor!" "The damned old rebel!" and "Put him off the cars!" before Anderson had even been allowed to say whom he intended to vote for or if he even intended to vote. After rebuking Anderson and declaring that "McClellan was 'a damned traitor'" and that "any man who should vote for him was a traitor," the soldiers returned to their seats. Anderson shared the story with his local newspaper and said the incident would not keep him from the polls. The soldiers were strangers to him, he was wealthy, and he had "unwavering faith in the Democracy." Yet, such incidents happened to many Democrats, and since not all the others had these same advantages, such tactics doubtless discouraged some voters. Anderson's story also revealed to Marietta residents that the tactics they had seen employed by local Republicans were being practiced on a much-wider scale.[43]

The editor's commentary on the incident reveals his recognition of one last Republican tactic, branding Democrats with "epithets such as nobody who respects himself should ever use:—'copperheads,' 'butternuts,' 'sympathizers with treason,' and 'traitors'"—a partisan ploy to discredit them and their ideas.[44] Democrats had learned what a powerful progression of words that was and the ways Republicans used them to press their advantage. Calling "copperheads" a "slang term" used to stigmatize "neighbors and fellow-citizens," the writer thought he understood the real purpose: "Criminal epithets, if they demonstrate anything, demonstrate the unsoundness of the party that employs them. They show that it is afraid of the truth, and wanting the arguments to convince, is compelled to resort to the means to defame and intimidate."[45]

In Muskingum County, the new Democratic paper, the *Signal*, offered a milder tone and critique of the war effort when it began in April 1864. Not until the last days of the election did editor James Milholland show his true feelings. Given the events of the previous four years and with victory yet to be secured, Milholland could not comprehend the possibility of a Lincoln victory. In an acrostic, he offered his indictment against Lincoln:

> **A** rouse ye freemen of the land
> **B** e no longer cowards, or servile slaves!
> **R** epulse this Abolition, Traitor, band,
> **A** nd stop this wholesale work of filling graves.
> **H** oist high your banner, for Union and Peace!
> **A** nd no longer give the tyrant lease,
> **M** en to slaughter, widows and orphans increase!
> **L** et your voices resound, throughout the land,
> **I** n Abe Lincoln, will [*sic*] no longer place our trust,
> **N** or allow him, with ruthless, and tyrannic hand,
> **CO** nstitution to trample in the dust!
> **L** et the millions living, and e'en the dead,
> **N** o longer have an usurper at their head![46]

In "A Few Words with a Voter," Milholland made his strongest statement: "We assume that you regard Abraham Lincoln as unfit to be President. We have a right to assume it. There is not an intelligent man in America today who thinks him fit for office."[47]

In the end, a majority of Northern voters went to the polls and cast their votes for Abraham Lincoln. He won the popular vote by 400,000 votes out of 4,000,000 cast and received 212 electoral votes to McClellan's 21.[48] In the Muskingum Valley, turnouts declined, but overall there were no clear dramatic trends such as had occurred in the previous two general elections.[49]

Muskingum River Valley election results, 1863 and 1864								
	1863				1864			
	Union		Democrat		Union		Democrat		Union change (%)
County	Votes	%	Votes	%	Votes	%	Votes	%	
Morgan	2,387	58.6	1,688	41.4	2,606	60.1	1,727	39.9	1.6
Muskingum	4,244	54.6	3,526	45.4	3,406	49.7	3,444	50.3	-4.9
Washington	3,650	56.7	2,785	43.3	3,068	53.8	2,638	46.2	-3.0

The experience of these three counties suggests that the existing historiography, including Neely's *Fate of Liberty*, should contemplate more carefully the actions of Republicans on the local level. Although correct in asserting that most political arrests occurred in the loyal Border States and that the arrest of civilians in the rest of the Union was relatively rare, the existing literature underestimates the impact of the actions of Republicans, especially on the local level, in two ways. First, as the examples of the Ohio Democratic newspapers and their editors show, it was not only actual arrest or suppression but the *threat* of such action that opponents of the war faced. Further, the true power of intimidation and violence can only be understood by recognizing the ways Republicans at the local level reinforced military and civil authorities. It proved a powerful and coercive combination and suggests that Neely's view of the "fate of liberty" in the North during the war may be overly optimistic.[50] The experience of the Muskingum Valley suggests some fine-grained patterns that a national-level analysis can miss but that a local study can reveal. Though it would take further research to confirm these findings for the entire region, the record of one small corner of the Midwest is clear. During the critical period between early 1863 and the election of 1864, when many Northerners were contemplating their continued support for the war amidst a string of military defeats and a growing death toll, local Democratic voices in that debate were muted, with disturbing effectiveness, by the calculated actions of their Republican opponents.

Notes

1. Mark E. Neely Jr., *The Fate of Liberty: Abraham Lincoln and Civil Liberties* (New York: Oxford University Press, 1992). Although Neely does not focus on attacks on the Democratic press as a way of measuring "the fate of liberty" in the wartime North, his study suggests that more attention could be paid to this aspect of Northern wartime society and political culture.

2. The results are described in James McPherson, *Battle Cry of Freedom: The Civil War Era* (New York: Oxford University Press, 1988), 560–62. My argument differs from McPherson's on the meaning of the Democratic victories—while he is technically correct in pointing out the limits of Democratic gains, I give greater weight to the Republicans' *perception* of the size of Democratic victory. In this, my interpretation is closer to that made in Jennifer L. Weber, *Copperheads: The Rise and Fall of Lincoln's Opponents in the North* (New York: Oxford University Press, 2006), 81–83, which argues that Republican fears of disloyalty in the Northwest motivated Republicans to act in spring 1863.

3. Frank L. Klement, *The Limits of Dissent: Clement L. Vallandigham and the Civil War* (Lexington: University of Kentucky Press, 1970), 102–15. The full text of the speech appears in *The Record of Hon. C. L. Vallandigham* (Columbus, Ohio, 1863), 168–204.

4. One of the best studies of the wartime Democracy remains Joel H. Silbey, *A Respectable Minority: The Democratic Party in the Civil War Era, 1860–1868* (New York: Norton, 1977). It should be supplemented with Melinda Lawson, *Patriot Fires: Forging a New American Nationalism in the Civil War North* (Lawrence: University of Kansas, 2002); Phillip Shaw Paludan, *A People's Contest: The Union and Civil War, 1861–1865* (New York: Harper and Row, 1988), esp. 85–102, 231–59; and Mark E. Neely Jr., *The Union Divided: Party Conflict in the Civil War North* (Cambridge, MA: Harvard University Press, 2002). Although Neely, at times, underestimates the value of a robust political culture in a democracy during wartime, he captures the heightened tone of wartime political rhetoric well.

5. See Neely, *Fate of Liberty*, 65–68, for Vallandigham. Neely points out, correctly, that Union military arrests occurred much more frequently in the Border States.

6. In *The Fate of Liberty*, Neely does not examine the suppression of the *Chicago Times* in June 1863; ironically, his only mention of this paper was its 1861 *defense* of Lincoln's arrest of members of the Maryland legislature. He did, however, include the *Chicago Times'* suppression in *Union Divided*, 98–100, 110. See also Silbey, *Respectable Minority*, 72–73.

7. While a study of three counties cannot make definitive conclusions about the entire region, the experiences chronicled here were not unique. Another better-known Ohio example involves the mobbing and destruction of the *Columbus (OH) Crisis* in March 1863, which is discussed later in the chapter. What is clear, both in southeastern Ohio and the Midwest, more generally, is that the intimidation and violence were obvious tactics used by Republicans against Democrats.

8. For a fuller discussion of defining the Midwest, see Andrew R. L. Cayton and Peter S. Onuf, *The Midwest and the Nation: Rethinking the History of an American Region* (Bloomington: Indiana University Press, 1990), as well as James Shortridge, *The Middle West: Its Meaning in American Culture* (Lawrence: University of Kansas Press, 1989).

9. The details of this rivalry can be traced in Norris Schneider, *Y Bridge City: The Story of Zanesville and Muskingum County, Ohio* (Cleveland: World, 1950).

10. Three fine examples that mention settler mix but do not explore its implications in the way suggested here are Kenneth J. Winkle, *The Politics of Community: Migration and Politics in Antebellum Ohio* (New York: Cambridge University Press, 1988), Don H. Doyle, *The Social Order of a Frontier Community: Jacksonville, Illinois, 1825–70* (Urbana: University of Illinois Press, 1978), and John Mack Faragher, *Sugar Creek: Life on the Illinois Prairie* (New Haven: Yale University Press, 1988); an important one that does

do this as fully is Nicole Etcheson, *The Emerging Midwest: Upland Southerners and the Political Character of the Old Northwest: 1787–1861* (Bloomington: Indiana University Press, 1996).

11. For full election returns broken down by township and ward, see *Zanesville (OH) City Times*, October 19, 1861, October 25, 1862 (Muskingum County); *Morgan County (OH) Herald*, October 17, 1861, *McConnelsville (OH) Enquirer*, October 23, 1862 (Morgan County); *Marietta (OH) Intelligencer*, October 30, 1861, *Marietta (OH) Republican*, October 15, 1862 (Washington County).

12. Weber, *Copperheads*, 14–17, makes the same point about local studies, arguing that only there can opposition to the war, present in some areas since April 1861, be clearly discerned. She is also right to point out there that often this opposition failed to enter the national press and the national consciousness before late 1862.

13. *McConnelsville (OH) Enquirer*, February 25, 1863.

14. Ibid., March 11, 1863. This issue of the *Enquirer* is central to understanding the relationship between McGlashan and McConnelsville and is, thus, quoted from extensively. Republican newspapers, in this case and the others examined here, acknowledged all of these attacks and threats on the Democratic press, downplayed their significance, and quickly jumped on anything they saw as an error. Since the intent here is to gauge the impact of these attacks on both the viability of the Democratic press and the possibility of these attacks cowing Democratic opponents of the Republican prosecution of the war, Democratic editors' words seem most relevant and are more extensively quoted.

15. Ibid., March 11, 1863 (emphasis added).

16. Ibid.

17. Ibid.

18. Appeals for subscription and the proscription list appear in every issue of the paper from March 11 through May 6, 1863.

19. *McConnelsville (OH) Enquirer*, May 6, 1863.

20. Ibid., June 3, 1863.

21. None of Marietta's editors ever commented on the possible confusion (or unintended irony) of the Democratic newspaper in Marietta being named the *Republican*. This newspaper began publication in 1849, before the formation of the Republican Party. Presumably, the editor saw the name as an endorsement of republican principles, not the Republican Party.

22. For a fuller discussion of the phenomenon of antebellum mobs, which often formed in communities as local echoes of the national debates on slavery, abolitionism, and sectionalism, see David Grimsted, *American Mobbing, 1828–1861: Toward Civil War* (New York: Oxford University Press, 1998).

23. For the conflicts between Zanesville and Putnam in the 1830s, see Schneider, *Y Bridge City*, 200–210, and Thomas J. Sheppard, "An Abolition Center," *Ohio State Archaeological and Historical Quarterly* 19, no. 3 (1910): 266–69. For a wider context, see Leonard L. Richards, *Gentlemen of Property and Standing: Anti-Abolition Mobs in Jacksonian America* (New York: Oxford University Press, 1974).

24. Eugene H. Roseboom, "The Mobbing of the *Crisis*," *Ohio State Archaeological and Historical Quarterly* 59, no. 2 (1950): 150–53. This incident also plays a central role in Reed W. Smith, *Samuel Medary and the* Crisis: *Testing the Limits of Press Freedom* (Columbus: Ohio State University Press, 1995).

25. *Marietta (OH) Republican*, March 26, 1863. The attack occurred during the night of March 21.

26. Ibid., April 9, 1863; *Marietta (OH) Register*, April 7, 1863.

27. *Marietta (OH) Republican*, April 2, 1863. Because of its reduced size, nearly the entire issue of the paper was devoted to an account of the meeting.

28. *Zanesville (OH) Citizens' Press*, April 18, 1861.

29. Ibid., June 20, 1861. The editor of the *Courier* occasionally claimed to be nonpartisan, but his editorial tone and endorsements during elections remained unflinchingly Republican.

30. Ibid., April 30, 1863.

31. Ibid., May 7, 1863.

32. Ibid., May 8, 1863.

33. Ibid., May 14, 1863.

34. Letters Sent Regarding Censorship, entry 3484, part 1, record group 393, Department of Ohio, 19, National Archives, Washington, D.C.

35. In the weeks after Chapman's departure in May, there appears to have been an attempt to continue the *Citizens' Press*, although no issues were actually printed. By July, the attempt failed, and the *Zanesville (OH) Aurora* bought the equipment of the *Citizens' Press*. See *Zanesville (OH) City Times*, July 11, 1863.

36. The standard account remains Klement, *Limits of Dissent*, 138–89, and is preferable to Neely, *Fate of Liberty*, which contains errors in its chronology. Vallandigham's arrest also occasioned the uncommon spectacle of Democrats attacking a Republican newspaper in Dayton, Ohio, a newspaper that had attacked Vallandigham as a traitor and had called for his arrest. See Paludan, *People's Contest*, 240–45.

37. On the motivations, realism, and earnestness of opponents of the war on these issues, my interpretation differs sharply from Weber, *Copperheads*. In several places, that work claims that opponents were blind to the true threat to the Union posed by secession and the Confederacy. They were far from blind to that threat; rather, they believed Republican prosecution of an unwinnable war posed the greater threat. See Weber, *Copperheads*, 73, 89, for the sharpest of these critiques of antiwar Democrats.

38. For full election returns broken down by township and ward, see *Zanesville (OH) City Times*, October 25, 1862, *Zanesville (OH) Courier*, October 19, 1863 (Muskingum County); *McConnelsville (OH) Enquirer*, October 23, 1862, *Morgan County (OH) Herald*, October 23, 1863 (Morgan County); *Marietta (OH) Republican*, October 15, 1862, *Marietta (OH) Register*, October 23, 1863 (Washington County).

39. *McConnelsville (OH) Valley Democrat*, July 22, 1864.

40. Ibid., August 5, 1864.

41. *Marietta (OH) Times*, October 1, 1864.

42. For a less-violent incident, in which "Loyal Leaguers" disrupted a Democratic meeting by continually interrupting the speakers to ask questions, see *McConnelsville (OH) Valley Democrat*, September 30, 1864.

43. *Marietta (OH) Times*, November 10, 1864.

44. This phenomenon occurred throughout the North and is well analyzed in Lawson, *Patriot Fires*, esp. 82–88.

45. *Marietta (OH) Times*, October 6, 1864, and September 24, 1864. At times, Weber comes very close to accepting this Republican rhetorical strategy as factual while also splitting opponents of the war in ways that seem artificial. The Democrat editors of the

Muskingum Valley were undeniably antiwar in the spring of 1863, whether labeled as "Copperhead" or not. Yet, in her interpretation, Weber often splits off editors as "elite" who have different arguments and tactics than "hardcore" Copperheads. In these communities, such differences seemed irrelevant to those on both sides of the debate in the spring of 1863. For the clearest statement of this alleged split, see Weber, *Copperheads*, 17. Though speaking there about the early days of the war, this interpretation informs much of the rest of the work.

46. *Zanesville (OH) Signal*, October 20, 1864.

47. Ibid., October 27, 1864.

48. David E. Long, *The Jewel of Liberty: Abraham Lincoln's Re-Election and the End of Slavery* (Mechanicsburg, PA: Stackpole Books, 1994), 285. McClellan lost all states except Kentucky, Delaware, and New Jersey.

49. For full election returns broken down by township and ward, see *Zanesville* (OH) *Courier*, October 19, 1863, October 17, 1864 (Muskingum County); *Morgan County (OH) Herald*, October 23, 1863, December 16, 1864 (Morgan County); *Marietta (OH) Register*, October 23, 1863, *Marietta (OH) Times*, October 20, 1864 (Washington County).

50. It is worth noting that in his more recent work *The Union Divided*, Neely does give more weight to the role of local newspapers in public debate (see esp. 89–117). Yet, the *Fate of Liberty* is the much better known of the two and the one for which he received the Pulitzer Prize.

CONTRIBUTORS
INDEX

CONTRIBUTORS

Ginette Aley is an author, editor, and visiting assistant professor of history at Kansas State University. Her numerous publications include those in the Civil War series Virginia at War, edited by William C. Davis and James I. Robertson Jr. She recently served as associate managing editor of *Kansas History* and research director at the Chapman Center for Rural Studies. In 2019, she gave the 21st Annual Lincoln Lecture at the University of Saint Mary.

J. L. Anderson is professor of history at Mount Royal University in Calgary, Alberta. His most recent book is *Capitalist Pigs: Pigs, Pork, and Power in America*. He is a past president of the Agricultural History Society.

Brett Barker is professor of history and chair of history and international studies at the University of Wisconsin–Stevens Point. His research focuses on the Midwest during the Civil War. He received the UW Colleges' Chancellor's Excellence in Teaching Award.

William C. Davis, retired director of the Virginia Center for Civil War Studies and professor of history at Virginia Tech, is the author or editor of more than fifty books on the Civil War era and was chief on-camera consultant for the History Channel series *Civil War Journal*.

Nicole Etcheson is the Alexander M. Bracken professor of history at Ball State University. She is the author of *A Generation at War: The Civil War Era in a Northern Community*, *Bleeding Kansas: Contested Liberty in the Civil War Era*, and *The Emerging Midwest: Upland Southerners and the Political Culture of the Old Northwest, 1787–1861*.

Michael P. Gray is professor of history at East Stroudsburg University and the editor of the Voices of the Civil War for the University of Tennessee Press. He wrote the new introduction to *History of Andersonville Prison* by Ovid Futch (2011), *The Business of Captivity: Elmira and Its Civil War Prison* (honorable mention for the Seaborg Award, 2001) and *Crossing the*

Deadlines: Civil War Prisons Reconsidered (2018). He is also the cofounder of HistoryFit, which blends history tours with group fitness.

R. Douglas Hurt is a professor of history at Purdue University and a fellow of the Agricultural History Society. He is a past president of the Agricultural History Society and has served as the editor of *Agricultural History*, the *Missouri Historical Review*, and *Ohio History*. He is the author of *Agriculture in the Midwest, 1815–1900*.

Julie Mujic is a visiting assistant professor of global commerce and coordinator of faculty partnerships for the Knowlton Center for Career Exploration at Denison University. In this role, she blends her background in business and history to teach classes such as Commerce and Society and to help faculty implement strategies in the classroom that connect academic learning objectives and career exploration. She has published in both academic and mainstream presses on the midwestern home front during the Civil War and particularly considers the intersection between the region's economic and intellectual history.

INDEX

abolitionism, 2, 3, 36, 41, 50, 52, 53, 61n4, 99, 103, 163, 172, 175, 182

African Americans, xiii, 2, 9, 29, 30

agriculture (midwestern) during the Civil War, 3–4, 12; breeding, calls for improved, 69–70; butter, dairying, and eggs, 74–75, 87, 130, 159, 162; and Chicago market, 3, 71, 72, 73–74, 76, 78, 88, 89; chickens and poultry, 75, 87, 137, 139, 157, 160; and children (*see* children, experiences of); and Cincinnati market, 69–71, 72–73, 91; contractors, 68–71, 77–78; cotton, 88–90, 91; crop production (wheat, corn, oats), 3–4, 71–92, 128, 130–32, 139, 150–58, 161–63; draft animals (horses, mules), 68–70, 74, 81–86, 92, 153, 156, 157, 160, 162; and family farming, 10, 13, 78, 84, 86, 87, 89, 133, 138–40, 148–65; and farm machinery (including advances in), 76–77, 79–87, 90, 151–53; and farm woman, 10, 12–13, 80, 81, 82, 84–87, 92, 127–41, 148–65; greenbacks, money issues, and farmers, 69, 75–78, 81, 84, 88, 89, 90, 91, 162; hemp and flax, 90; hogs (and pork packing), 70–75, 77–79, 87, 139, 156, 158, 161, 168n41; in Illinois, 68, 71–73, 75, 76, 78, 80, 81, 83, 85–92, 127–28; in Indiana, 70–73, 75, 77, 78, 80, 81, 84–85, 87, 88–91, 127; and Indianapolis market, 72–73; in Iowa, 71–74, 78, 79, 82, 84–87, 148–65; and labor problems, 10, 79–82, 94n28, 127, 129–32, 135, 138, 149–54, 158, 162–64; livestock (cattle and beef packing), 73–79, 87, 88, 91, 93n13, 139, 150, 154–65; markets, 69, 72–74, 77, 78, 83, 88, 128, 131, 139, 156, 165, 168n41; markets (Southern), 71, 79, 90, 92 (*see also* individual major midwestern city markets); in Michigan, 73, 78, 78, 130; and Milwaukee market, 71, 72, 73, 78; in Minnesota, 3, 72, 78, 87, 150; in Ohio, 69–70, 71–72, 76–83, 85–89, 91, 92; *Prairie Farmer* (including farm women's connection to), 74, 77, 80, 81, 92, 127, 130, 132, 134; prices, 12, 70–80, 83, 84, 90–92; and railroads (and transportation), 70–74, 76, 77, 83, 87, 89; sugar and sorghum, 87–88, 91, 132, 154, 156, 163; tobacco, 89–91; in Wisconsin, 71, 72, 73, 78, 79–80, 82–83, 86, 87

Sherman, General William Tecumseh, 51, 100
Shiloh, Battle of, 110
Sioux Uprising, or Dakota War (1862), 8, 151
slaves and slavery, 2, 3, 9, 14n5, 171, 175, 182, 185n22; opinions about, among college students, 44, 47, 50, 51, 52, 53, 61n4
Stowe, Harriet Beecher, 2 passim

Tappan, Henry P. (president of University of Michigan, 1852–63), 35, 37, 39, 42, 45, 47

Uncle Tom's Cabin, 2 passim
underground railroad, 2 passim
University of Michigan, 12, 33–59. *See also* college students during the Civil War; Tappan, Henry P.
U.S. Colored Infantry (Iowa Colored Regiment), 151
U.S. Department of Agriculture (USDA), 128
U.S. Sanitary Commission (USSC), 126, 127, 128–31, 144n9, 152; Chicago branch, 130

Vallandigham, Clement L., 14 passim, 43, 45, 63n15
Vermilion, Mary, 100–105, 114–16, 120, 134, 161–62
Vicksburg campaign, 75, 130

Weld, Theodore Dwight, 175
Whitman, Walt, 125–26

Wisconsin, 2, 3, 4, 37, 127, 129, 131, 152, 163. *See also under* agriculture
women, Northern (midwestern): and families, 6, 7, 12–13, 86–87, 97–120, 125–41 (*see also* children, experiences of); farm and agrarian (including rural), 6, 10, 12–13, 125–41, 148–65 (*see also under* agriculture); and gender dynamics, 10–11, 48, 58, 86–87, 126, 138, 140–41, 142n1, 143n6, 145n15, 150, 164, 166n2; historiographic depiction of, 5, 8, 9–10, 12, 99–101, 126–33, 143n6, 149–50; and home front activities (including ladies aid societies), 1, 129–32, 144n9, 145n11 (*see also* U.S. Sanitary Commission); and in-law relations (including kin networks), 12, 13, 97–120, 131, 138–39, 152–56; and Johnson's Island (OH), 21–22, 28; and labor problems (*see under* agriculture); and letter writing, 125–26, 127–28, 132–41, 149–50, 151; as nurses (and nursing), 5, 10, 128, 130; and patriotism (*see under* patriotism); and political dissent in the home, 5, 100–105
women, Southern (Confederate), 10, 30, 68, 86, 141n1

Zanesville, Ohio, 170, 171, 175, 177–79, 185n23